Asian American Women's Popular Literature

D1559573

ASIAN AMERICAN WOMEN'S POPULAR LITERATURE

Feminizing Genres and Neoliberal Belonging

PAMELA THOMA

Temple University Press

PHILADELPHIA

Temple University Press
Philadelphia, Pennsylvania 19122
www.temple.edu/tempress

Chapter 3 appeared as "Romancing the Self and Negotiating Consumer Citizenship in Asian American Labor Lit" in *Contemporary Women's Writing* 2013; doi: 10.1093/cww/vps036.

Published 2014

LIBRARY OF CONGRESS CATALOGING-IN-PUBLICATION DATA

Thoma, Pamela S. (Pamela Sue), 1961–
    Asian American women's popular literature : feminizing genres and neoliberal belonging / Pamela Thoma.
        pages cm
    Includes bibliographical references and index.
    ISBN 978-1-4399-1018-4 (cloth : alk. paper)
    ISBN 978-1-4399-1019-1 (pbk. : alk. paper)
    ISBN 978-1-4399-1020-7 (e-book)
    1. American literature—Asian American authors—History and criticism. 2. American literature—Women authors—History and criticism. 3. Asian American women—Intellectual life. 4. Women and literature—United States. 5. Asian American women in literature. I. Title.
PS153.A84T48 2013
810.9'895—dc23

                                                          2013016619

⊗ The paper used in this publication meets the requirements of the American National Standard for Information Sciences—Permanence of Paper for Printed Library Materials, ANSI Z39.48–1992

Printed in the United States of America

2 4 6 8 9 7 5 3 1

THE
AMERICAN
LITERATURES
INITIATIVE

A book in the American Literatures Initiative (ALI), a collaborative publishing project of NYU Press, Fordham University Press, Rutgers University Press, Temple University Press, and the University of Virginia Press. The Initiative is supported by The Andrew W. Mellon Foundation. For more information, please visit www.americanliteratures.org.

CONTENTS

ACKNOWLEDGMENTS

I have many to thank for their support while I worked on this project. I owe Andy Dephtereos a great debt of gratitude for being involved in nearly every aspect of this book and for always believing in my work. You have journeyed with me, Andy, to all the places I wanted to go and to those places I needed to go. Thank you. I also thank Randy and Maisie, who have been exemplars of the best companion species *ever*. They have been beside me in the still snows of the Maine woods and the roaring winds of the Palouse hills, always reminding me of the world beyond human knowledge. I owe them many more walks and hope they will wait for me to catch up.

I want to thank mentors who were especially attentive and caring, including Katherine Burkman at The Ohio State University; Carol Cantrell and Paola Malpezzi-Price at Colorado State University; and Janet Jacobs, Alison Jaggar, Suzanne Juhasz, Ann Kibbey, Beth Robertson, Marcia Westkott, and especially Katheryn Rios at the University of Colorado at Boulder. My graduate school mates also made that time a terrifically rewarding experience, and include Joan Gabriele, Kayann Short, Damian Doyle, and DeLinda Wunder. Several colleagues from my years at Colby College have contributed to this work, supporting me through their friendship and in other ways that cannot be fully acknowledged here: Betty Sasaki, Lyn Mikel Brown, Jorge Olivares, David Suchoff, Hannah Roisman, Yossi Roisman, Tarja Raag, Maritza Straughn-Williams, and Mark Tappan. At Washington State University I thank colleagues in the former Department of Women's Studies: Luz

María Gordillo, Linda Heidenreich, Judy Meuth, Marian Sciachitano, Nishant Shahani, and Noël Sturgeon; colleagues in English: Kristen Arola, Joan Burbick, and TV Reed; the creative minds in Fine Arts, especially Io Palmer, Reza Safavi, Kevin Haas, Michelle Forsythe, and Maria DePrano; and colleagues in Critical Culture, Gender, and Race Studies, with special thanks to fellow Asian Americanists Rory Ong and John Streamas and to Rose Smetana. I also thank Gabriella Reznowski at WSU for fabulous research assistance (at lightning speed). And what would any of this work be without the hope and inspiration of students? I want to acknowledge my former and my current students for their enthusiasm and insight, with special thanks to Mary Jo Klinker, who helped me maintain perspective as I completed this project.

I'd like to thank the many colleagues in American studies, Asian American studies, and women's, gender, and sexuality studies at various institutions for their abiding commitment to interdisciplinary research, teaching, and dialogue, often of the feminist sort, especially Tamara Bhalla, Leslie Bow, Noelle Brada-Williams, Chris Breu, Yoonmee Chang, John Cheng, Floyd Cheung, Marilyn Chin, Monica Chiu, Karen Chow, Shilpa Davé, Patti Duncan, Karen Leong, Cynthia Franklin, Lynn Fujiwara, Ruth Hsu, Paul Lai, Rachel Lee, Rich Lee, Suzanne Leonard, Anita Mannur, Katarzyna Marciniak, Elizabeth Nathanson, Diane Negra, Crystal Parikh, Viet Nguyen, Art Sakamoto, Gayle Sato, Yvonne Tasker, Linda Trinh Võ, and Judy Tzu-Chun Wu. In the process of writing and completing this project, I was also fortunate to have had the wise counsel of people who kindly gave advice and/or read proposals, chapters, or even the entire manuscript. Thank you to Marc Stein, Gina Herrmann, Christine Hughes, Jane Iwamura, Daniel Kim, and Min Hyoung Song for helping me complete this book. I especially want to thank Jigna Desai for being a wonderful mentor and friend, for extending her dazzling mind and generous heart. Finally, I thank Janet Francendese and the professional editorial team at Temple University Press for their fine work on this project.

1 / Asian American Women's Popular Literature, Neoliberalism, and Cultural Citizenship

In *American Woman: A Novel* (2003), Susan Choi fictionalizes the "missing year" of unknown events following the 1974 kidnapping of Patty Hearst by the Symbionese Liberation Army, a radical political group loosely connected to the Weather Underground Organization.[1] Choi's version features Japanese American protagonist Jenny Shimada as an antiwar activist of the militant New Left variety who has bombed a government draft office in California and gone underground in upstate New York as Iris Wong. Soon, Jenny summons inspiration to follow her political conscience from the history of her father's internment, draft resistance, and incarceration during World War II, and returns to the West Coast. While Jenny is arrested in California, she continues to explore politics in feminist separatist and cultural nationalist communities and joins her father in a pilgrimage to Manzanar.

A finalist for the Pulitzer Prize in fiction, Choi's second novel is a bracing indictment of US imperialism, capitalism, and Orientalism that draws connections between World War II and the American war in Viet Nam, not only through an unequivocal challenge to US foreign policy and militarization in Asia but also through a condemning representation of the racialization of Jenny as immutably foreign in the United States. *American Woman* thematizes, in fact, the orthodoxy in Asian Americanist critique that Asian Americans and especially Asian American women are invisible in the United States as citizens or understood only as racial Other, alien, or even enemy.[2] As the title implies, the novel undertakes a corrective, which it accomplishes through an excavation of the historical struggle for Japanese American citizenship. Moreover, *American Woman* details how national belonging may also be claimed outside of liberal citizenship, through radical political movements and even armed struggle for international justice, especially because the book is based on what Choi calls the "odd footnote" of Wendy Yoshimura's actual involvement in the SLA (Hong 2). Yoshimura, an artist who was born in the Manzanar War Relocation Center in 1943 while her family was interned, was arrested with Patty Hearst in 1975 but quickly disappeared from headlines. Although she denied involvement in key activities, a garage rented by Yoshimura under an assumed name contained a pipe bomb and a machine gun and led to a conviction on explosives and weapons charges. She served about a year in prison.

Through the use of the underground as a literal space and time outside the nation, as a vantage point from which to survey discourses of belonging, and as a metaphor for a citizenry invisible to a larger public sphere but sharing at least some of its terrain, *American Woman* interrogates the dominant terms of political participation and affiliation. It provides a trenchant assessment. It is also quite critical of radical and underground organizations. The racism and sexism of Jenny's comrades painfully grate against her sense of social justice, and she concludes that "bombing a building that 'ought' to be empty was not so different in type, if very different in scale, from bombing a village that 'ought' to house only enemies and not any civilians" (Choi 351). *American Woman* represents Jenny as deeply engaged but clearly constrained both by a narrowly delimited mainstream political culture and by a counterculture that is not all that alternative. When she begins to write her own version of the politics of the late 1960s and 1970s, Jenny redefines citizenship for herself, and *American Woman* highlights redefinition as an important practice, indeed the most salient, of her belonging.[3] Recasting citizenship as both cultural practice and expression, and far from being a footnote to a more famous political figure, Jenny, with her deeply political imagination, is centralized. Indeed, *American Woman* artfully attests to how "the subject becomes, acts, and speaks of itself as 'American'" through culture (Lowe 3). Choi's novel may well be placed among Asian American bildungsromane that function as "strategic interventions in American literary constructions of race, ethnicity, and gender" (P. Chu 11). "Because it has been accorded a place of honor in literary curricula that are, in turn, used to socialize pupils in approved American values," Patricia Chu contends, "the literary genre of the *bildungsroman* is a central site for Asian American re-visions of American subject formation," with gendered stories of authorship conspicuously replacing the well-married hero plot (11).[4]

In many ways *American Woman* addresses the contemporary reformulation of US citizenship or belonging that *Asian American Women's Popular Literature: Feminizing Genres and Neoliberal Belonging* takes as a primary concern, especially since the novel seems to challenge the invisibility of Asian American women to the larger body politic. But Choi's rendition of the development of cultural citizenship ultimately revives what I would call "the citizenship of the past," a nostalgic and deeply seated liberal conception of American political culture that purportedly existed outside commercial culture. Further, although *American Woman* fits the pattern of generic revision for bildungsromane that Chu identifies, it remains firmly attached to a highbrow literary culture that largely disavows the market forces that also created the contemporary shift toward cultural citizenship. As refreshing as the direct treatment of Asian American women's political subjectivity is, in the end *American Woman* is a conventional text that tells readers little about social belonging within contemporary neoliberal capitalism, relying on the allegory of growth in the bildungsroman for its form, preapproved literary craft for its technique, and familiar scripts of citizenship for its content.

This opening discussion of Choi's novel is intended to briefly highlight the limitations of writing and reading practices that remain tethered to canonical genres and aesthetic theories of value. But what becomes of Asian American literature when canonicity and the hallmarks of quality in individual character development, figurative language, and psychological interiority are no longer the exclusive currencies of value in the symbolic economy of cultural production? In what ways does Asian American literature contribute to or intervene in the notions of political subjectivity and contemporary belonging that are practiced and produced in popular culture, which functions, Mimi Nguyen and Thuy Tu write, as the daily "battleground for fantasies of desire and identification, as well as anxieties about alienation and incursion" (6)? Finally, what role does gender play and what can we say of the textual effects—subjective, political, or aesthetic—of contemporary Asian American women's writing when it participates in a literary culture with overt popular and commercial functions?

Motivated to more fully chart Asian American women's political subjectivity and to understand the "changing form and ethics of citizenship" in the United States, where the political rationality of neoliberalism has been reshaping governance, economic policy, and subjectivity for forty years, this study reframes several of the concerns that *American Woman* narrates in the fine-grain textures of realist literary fiction (Ong, *Neoliberalism* 14).[5] Its underlying premise is that definitions of citizenship and citizenship practices are displayed, communicated, and revised through a vast array of commercial media that speak the lingua franca of the marketplace, and through the particular idiom of neoliberal consumer culture. More specifically, the book examines cultural citizenship, which has become increasingly important in the neoliberal era (1970–present), to pursue questions about the legibility of Asian American women's belonging, the gendered racial constraints of contemporary discourses of citizenship for Asian American women, and especially the ways in which Asian American women writers negotiate the reformulation of belonging within popular narrative genres. Building on recent citizenship studies, I define cultural citizenship as "the imperative to prove and claim Americanness" through the consumption or production of mainstream cultural narratives that circulate in the neoliberal marketplace in popular or commercial media (S. J. Lim 10).

Asian American Women's Popular Literature focuses on innovative genre fiction written by Asian American women—mother-daughter narrative, chick lit, detective fiction, and food writing—works that are intended to reach an Asian American and a broader audience and that engage public dialogue about belonging. Because these are crossover texts, both in the sense that they extend themselves to multiple reading publics and in the sense that they are self-conscious of connections between contemporary popular media culture and literary culture, I refer to them as "popular literature," although they have not all enjoyed critical and commercial success in equal measure.[6] Troubling the false opposition between the popular and the literary and recognizing the imperatives of neoliberal belonging through the mobilization of popular genres, the eight Asian American women writers whose novels I consider participate in the fashioning of new literary cultures and contribute to the reformulation of cultural citizenship within neoliberalism. But even as the works demonstrate their authors' cultural citizenship, they are not uniformly or unequivocally affirmations of Americanness.

My readings show how these texts negotiate discourses of neoliberal belonging under the limelight of popular culture, illuminating the limitations of cultural citizenship and other highly recognizable dimensions of belonging that also operate within neoliberalism, including biological, consumer, cosmopolitan, and transnational citizenship. In chapter 2, I situate the mother-daughter novels of Patti Kim and Lan Cao in relation to Asian American women's cultural citizenship practices and consider how *A Cab Called Reliable* (1997) and *Monkey Bridge* (1997) contend with aspiring, white, middle-class motherhood and participation in consumer culture. Chapter 3 explores how Michelle Yu and Blossom Kan's *China Dolls* (2007) and Sonia Singh's *Goddess for Hire* (2004) recombine the fantasy and reality of neoliberal consumer culture in an innovative form of chick lit to reveal the fluidity of identification within the cultural fantasies of postfeminism, as well as the substantial labor required in the model of the citizen as romantic consumer. Examination in chapter 4 of Sujata Massey's *Girl in a Box* (2006) and Suki Kim's *The Interpreter* (2003) contends that detective fiction effectively addresses the ethical claims of neoliberal cosmopolitanism, which purports to transcend boundaries of nation, gender, and culture but more accurately appropriates the gendered racial subject by denying her status outside the global market. The explosion of culinary narrative in contemporary culture is considered in chapter 5 through analysis of Ruth Ozeki's *My Year of Meats* (1998), which both acknowledges food writing as a complex site of social belonging and comments upon its circulation within a global media capitalism that produces subjects as transnational citizens with taste distinctions that hew toward the United States.

Taken together, the novels analyzed in this study disclose neoliberalism's rearticulation of gendered racial citizenship and demonstrate various ways in which social belonging is an object of contest for Asian American women. They impart the specific implications for Asian American women of citizenship models that demand that "good citizens" conform to mainstream cultural narratives of Americanness and normative femininity while simultaneously calling on the female subject to balance and regulate a revised combination of marketplace activities: managing family and fertility, gaining qualifications and expertise for employment, working in the global economy, and participating in consumer culture (McRobbie, *Aftermath of Feminism* 54).

Although debates about citizenship's waning or waxing relevance continue, there is near consensus that neoliberal globalization has inaugurated an especially dynamic and generative period of reformulation, one in which citizenship has been destabilized, with elements of citizenship shifting and multiplying. Instead of being static, definitions of citizenship are understood as historically contingent, continually organizing and reorganizing categories of difference and inequality.[7] Citizenship not only determines who is legally included and excluded from membership, it is also a normative ideology that dictates "how members of a given nation-state should behave depending upon particular social markers including race and gender" (L. Park 5). To be sure, formal, legal citizenship retains importance for social belonging, but contemporary formations and frameworks have enabled a more complex recognition of citizenship as culturally inflected. Since the emergence of cultural citizenship studies in the 1990s, citizenship has become widely accepted, Lok C. D. Siu explains, "as a set of cultural and social processes rather than simply a political status or juridical contract—a set of rights, entitlements, and obligations. Feminists and critical race theorists have long understood that citizenship is not universal and that one's gender, race, class, and sexuality, among other categories of difference, all shape experiences of citizenship" (7). But this understanding is certainly not limited to progressive ethical projects, and forms of cultural citizenship have been articulated consistently through neoliberalism as well. As Lisa Duggan observes, "During every phase, the construction of neoliberal politics and policy in the U.S. has relied on identity and cultural politics. The politics of race, both overt and covert, have been particularly central to the entire project. But the politics of gender and sexuality have intersected with race and class at each stage as well" (xii). Indeed, the recent reconfiguration of citizenship has created new exclusions in the United States, exclusions that have placed additional constraints on Asian American women's belonging. At the same time, changes and particularly the ascendance of cultural citizenship within neoliberalism have simultaneously encouraged its heightened visibility. Although this may seem paradoxical, the genealogy of cultural citizenship I present later in this chapter shows how cultural citizenship, now with attendant mandates for publicity, has become a primary component of neoliberal belonging in the United States as an additional constraint. For the moment, I emphasize that the development of cultural citizenship undergirds my theorization of the proliferation of popular novelistic genres and generic transformations in the category of Asian American women's literature.

Popular Literature

The novel is perhaps not the first form that comes to mind with the mention of popular culture, and in Asian American studies film, fashion, and music have attracted considerably more attention from scholars than has contemporary popular literature, with the exception of the most celebrated works, such as those by Henry David Hwang, Maxine Hong Kingston, Jhumpa Lahiri, Chang-rae Lee, Amy Tan, and Gene

Luen Yang.[8] *Asian American Women's Popular Literature* addresses this imbalance not simply because it is a gap in the scholarship but instead because the book is now more socially influential than it has been for some time, as evidenced by such phenomena as Oprah Winfrey's Book Club and Hollywood's current dependence on the adaptation of best-selling books and canonical classics for a ready and willing fan base. And as my reference to famous Asian American authors and their popular works above indicates, Asian American women are a significant part of the renewal of the book, as author-producers and reader-consumers. Moreover, I tend to agree with the feminist cultural studies dictum that "the genres of literature and popular entertainment we take least seriously are precisely those that best chronicle how we think about ourselves," as Linda Mizejewski puts it in her recent study of the woman detective in popular culture (15).

Rather than diminishing in popularity or social significance, as some observers feared when new information technologies threatened a "digital revolution," in the late twentieth and early twenty-first centuries the book, and specifically the novel, has adapted to a multimodal age (J. Collins 13) to become an important component of a "synergistic media environment" (Negra 9). Arguably, the novel is centrally located in the complex media landscape that has emerged within neoliberalism. Recent concerns about the novel's demise are part of a historical pattern of cultural anxiety in which any new technology threatens the literary establishment and the privileged subjects who inhabit it (Fitzpatrick 4–10). Such concerns are always specious, even in the very recent context of economic crises and budget cuts that target the arts and cultural projects as "luxuries," but this was particularly the case in the late 1990s and early 2000s, when Borders and Barnes & Noble outlets polka-dotted the United States in a manner resembling Verizon and AT&T service provider maps. The confusion should now be clarified as the e-reader phenomenon shrinks superstore bookstores, and Amazon.com blasts past competitors with its bestselling Kindle and the capacity to deliver downloadable electronic books in less than a minute: "Old media are not being displaced. Rather their functions and status are shifted by the introduction of new technologies" (Jenkins 14).

Recognizing the relationship between the novel and electronic technology is crucial because it highlights the mechanisms of media convergence, in which media collide and coexist, and the dynamics of re-mediation, in which new media arise when each medium "responds to, re-deploys, competes with and reforms other media" (Bolter and Grusin

35). It also acknowledges how global media conglomerates have savvily placed booksellers physically and especially virtually in the center of a sophisticated, media-driven consumer culture, creating new modes of access, delivery, and circulation for rapidly cycling markets. As Kathleen Fitzpatrick reminds us, "These merchants are not striving ... in some altruistic fashion to promote the Arnoldian cultural uplift of literacy against a debasing mass culture but are responding to existing markets and creating new ones" for a ten-billion-dollar-a-year industry (4). Merchants are especially interested in devoted female book buyers, who predominate in every category of fiction and who purchase more books than men in the United States, across race/ethnicity, by a margin of 3 to 2.[9] Booksellers and publishers (and authors) are keenly aware of the novel's reliance on female readers, historically and especially in our own time, for, as Ian McEwan observes, "Reading groups, readings, breakdowns of book sales all tell the same story: when women stop reading, the novel will be dead" ("Hello"). In the context of women's overall increased participation in the workforce and the rapid emergence of new media, publishers have internalized this story and deployed a variety of mechanisms to ensure that women do not stop reading, with marketers both horizontally segmenting female readerships into niches by ethnoracial group, life cycle, religion, and a host of other categories, and "developing" these consumer markets to cross categories and to purchase adjacent media products and technology. According to *Romance Writers of America*, in 2010, US women surpassed men as e-book readers, fueling popular literary culture in significant ways. Sales drivers that also help to produce popular literature (and can be read as measurements of popularity) include a broad variety of phenomena: online book clubs such as those of *RealSimple*, *Jezebel*, and *Martha Stewart Living*; Amazon's "Best Books of the Month" selections and NPR's "First Read" selections; reader-generated reviews and fan fiction; as well as the more traditional accolades of literary awards, well-placed or positive reviews in major newspapers and magazines, and appearance on bestseller lists.

While contemporary convergence culture cultivates relationships among old media forms such as the novel and new media technology such as the electronic book for the dynamic production of popular media texts, it also revises forms of sociality, the function of culture, and older and more recent ideological constructions of the gendered, raced, and classed subject. In *Bring on the Books for Everybody: How Literary Culture Became Popular Culture*, Jim Collins asserts that the contemporary novel has been "shaped by the increasing convergence of literary, visual, and material cultures" to such an extent that it is now integrated into popular visual media, so reading literature has become, far more than it previously was, an "exuberantly social activity" (8, 4). Further, "whether experienced on the page, or on the screen, or on the laptop," the contemporary novel may be used for a variety of social purposes (10). Perhaps most germane to this examination of Asian American women's literature and neoliberal citizenship is how the narratives in current popular literary culture complexly combine models of subjectivity inherited from the past and those that have emerged more recently to produce the figure of the empowered reader, a subject whose novel reading is a therapeutic "self-cultivation" project (10):

> This culture may indeed rely on twenty-first-century technologies of scanning, storage, and downloadability, but it also draws on early nineteenth-century notions of reading as self-transformation, filtered through late twentieth-century discourses of self-actualization, all jet-propelled by state-of-the-art forms of marketing "aesthetic experience." (23)

Crucially, such work on the self is necessary for other forms of labor and consumption in contemporary models of subjecthood. The recent popular novel and popular literary culture are linked in function then to individual subject formation and the interpellation of ideal American citizens, processes that were commonly performed through canonical literature and modern national education in the industrial era.

In the postindustrial United States, popular literature is connected specifically to neoliberal political rationalities, which scholars suggest enlist commercial media as socializing agents to instruct citizen-subjects in appropriate conduct.[10] In her study of the televisual production of consumer citizenship, Sarah Banet-Weiser asserts that "commercial media play a pivotal role in creating cultural definitions about what it means to be a citizen—indeed, our sense of ourselves as national citizens emerges *from* (not in spite of) our engagement with the popular media" (2, emphasis in original).[11] It may be that the media is now the most important storyteller in and about society, but without a doubt commercial popular culture is a primary site of US citizen-subject formation.[12]

One important lesson communicated in popular media, Collins recognizes, is the necessity of self-governance or disciplined work on the self. But, as others have pointed out, the primary target of contemporary makeover culture in the United States, from self-help manuals to reality TV to inspirational novels, is women.[13] Micki McGee argues that "changes in the nature of the labor market have made efforts at self-making and self-invention increasingly urgent," and she frames the contemporary preoccupation with the self in the United States as illustrated in makeover culture through an analysis of the production of the "belabored self," a phenomenon in which workers, and especially female workers clustered at the low end of the wage scale, are required to continually work on themselves in an effort to remain employable (16, 12). Feminist media studies scholars who draw on Michel Foucault's ideas about governmentality and modern technologies of power, especially his notions of "biopower" and the "care of the self," have rigorously interrogated the aggressive address of female audiences in commercial popular culture.[14] In analyses of the advice-driven forms of women's magazines, talks shows, and reality TV, but also of fictional forms, such as Hollywood romantic comedies and dramedies, scholars pay particular attention to how texts position women and girls as newly empowered workers and consumers, and how they communicate neoliberal modes of female citizenship that carry with them normative gender, racial, and sexual ideologies.

Although the understanding of the media as a tool of social pedagogy that tacitly and with varying degrees of subtly instructs female audiences in individual conduct, extensive marketplace knowledge, and neoliberal values may simply update for some the long-standing view of popular art forms or mass culture primarily as reflections of dominant beliefs, my analysis of a selection of Asian American women's popular literature is more nuanced and intends to show how popular literary culture may simultaneously illustrate, chronicle, and provide commentary on the blurring of cultural, commercial, and political practices under neoliberalism. Still, within this context, and since I do not presume an epistemic homogeneity among Asian American women writers or the oppositionality of racial, ethnic, and gender identity, I consider how novels may participate in the discursive production of preferred citizen-subjects. The phrase "feminizing genres" of this book's subtitle refers to how popular genres participate in the gendered and racialized processes that comprise belonging and to how Asian American authors use popular genres to engage discourses of citizenship.

As will become clear, the popular literature I discuss is in dialogue with public discourse that frequently positions Asian American women as ideal neoliberal female citizens. This is part of a new round of racialization, one that extends the model minority or honorary white racial stereotype that has been firmly established in the United States and combines with the normative femininity and domesticity with which Asian American women have been required to conform for entry and belonging. In a recent controversial instance, the June 2012 Pew Center report titled "The Rise of Asian Americans" includes Chinese, Filipina, Indian, Vietnamese, Korean, Japanese American, and "Other Asian" women in aggregate statistics that praise Asian Americans as "the highest-income, best-educated and fastest-growing racial group in the United States." The first chapter of the 215-page report features a "portrait of Asian Americans" celebrating the fact that in 2009 Asian immigrants overtook "Hispanic immigrants" in number and highlighting the fact that most Asian adults come to the United States with college degrees. Add to this the citation of documented or papered entry and formal permanent resident (green card) acquisition, the report pits Asians against Latinos in a "good immigrant" versus "bad immigrant" hierarchy of foreigner racialization. In certain ways, the report constructs Asian Americans as better or more successful neoliberal citizen-subjects than everyone else in the United States since it emphasizes that, compared to other racial groups and the general population of US adults, they are more likely to have college degrees and higher median household incomes. The report claims that Asian Americans "place more value than other Americans do on marriage, parenthood, hard work and career success" (Taylor 3). A response from the Association for Asian American Studies points out that this kind of rhetoric implies "an Asian Invasion," perpetuating another stereotype that pulls in a different, less welcoming direction but one that is equally destructive with regard to the potential for backlash.[15]

While Asian American women are included in the Pew Center report in aggregate statistics for education and income and some attention is paid to the exclusion era and family reunification, when they are identified by gender Asian American women are praised for high rates of outmarriage: "When newly minted medical school graduate Priscilla Chan married Facebook founder Mark Zuckerberg last month, she joined the 37 percent of all recent Asian American brides who wed a non-Asian groom."[16] Further broadcasting a heteronormative bias, the report also praises Asian American women for their regulation of fertility, particularly for their higher rates of childbirth within marriage, as compared to the general population, and for valuing family and parenting. Crucially, all of the positive traits attributed to Asian American women also somehow include their value as workers or productive contributors to society. Early in the report, just after a bar graph quantifying "The Asian-American Work Ethic," a section asks "Who's a Tiger Mom?" referring to Amy Chua's 2011 memoir, *Battle Hymn of the Tiger Mother,* in which the author writes that Chinese parents are better than Western parents because they assume strength and expect their children to achieve success (Taylor 4). Of course, such positioning disregards differences among Asian ethnic groups and obscures the struggles of many Asian American women and children, particularly impoverished women without higher education or employment skills that would help them secure a livelihood, education for their children, and neoliberal belonging. In this decidedly public light, however, "the Asian American woman" may be seen as a constitutive figure of neoliberalism, a discursive construction that compels rigorous interrogation of neoliberal citizenship.

Despite the "regulatory pedagogy" of a popular media culture that "teaches subjects through unspoken means how to conduct themselves," and a broader public discourse that operates similarly but is often more explicit, I join those cultural studies scholars who recognize that popular culture does not simply produce social conformity, and who also emphasize the polysemic nature of all texts or the possibility for "open spaces" where both reader and authorial negotiations take place (Weber 9). With regard to the print mode of popular literature, just as "the multiculturalist publishing boom has not turned writers of color into unwitting pawns of the system, unaware of the rules of the game" that continue to commodify and fetishize Asian Americans (Mannur 85), neither have they become perfectly disciplined subjects, thoroughly incorporated into the regulatory strategies of neoliberal governance. Just as cultural texts are not to be taken as representative reflections of Asian American identity, social experience, or history, neither are they seamless reflections of neoliberal capitalist rationality. Moreover, while neoliberalism aspires to totalization and "seeks to bring all human action into the domain of the market," it is still incomplete and is not without contradictions (Harvey 3). As Brenda Weber has remarked, neoliberalism is "an ideological mandate that mutates—it can itself both make over and be made over" (52).

Asian American Cultural Politics

In the field of Asian American studies, culture, and particularly aesthetic expression, has been understood as the privileged site for the articulation of politics and the demonstration of subjectivity, both panethnic and ethnic. Most scholars, and indeed the prevailing narrative of Asian American cultural politics, attribute this to the field's origins in the activism of the late 1960s, when students, community activists, and intellectuals self-consciously created a politicized racial group identity and formed an Asian American panethnic coalition in which cultural nationalism was often employed to challenge American racism and capitalist exploitation. Wendy Ho's description outlines a primary front in this strategy: "In situating an oppositional stance, cultural nationalists deconstructed the history of dehumanizing and debilitating characterizations of the 'Oriental' in popular and elitist representations. They realized how dominant cultural discourses could contribute to the inequitable circulation of power within mainstream society and within their own ethnic communities" (86). Decrying the exclusion of Asian American self-representation, analysis focused on distorted images and the critique of stereotypes in mainstream American popular culture, upbraiding "over a century's worth of dragon ladies, lotus blossoms, enigmatic assassins, black-clad guerillas, rapacious drug addicts, and sex-starved nerds" (Nguyen and Tu 6). Critics of literature contested Anglo-centric portrayals, the canon, and aesthetic theories of value that caricatured, exoticized, or entirely excluded Asian Americans. In short order, intellectuals incorporated an oppositional stance toward racism and the capitalism that operates through it in the critical framework of Asian American studies, developing a practice of evaluating texts for their "accommodation or resistance" (V. Nguyen, *Race and Resistance* 4).

The other major front in the strategy was the reclamation and production of cultural works that would politically empower ethnic communities and Asian Americans generally. In this political aesthetic, cultural production would stake a clear position against American racism and the exploitation of Asian Americans. It would also showcase the cultural expressions and aesthetic values of Asian ethnic groups in the United States, as well as assert a collective and distinctive Asian American culture, as in *Aiiieeeee!*, the 1973 anthology of Asian American literature edited by Jeffrey Chan, Frank Chin, Lawson Inada, and Shawn Wong. The emerging category of "Asian American literature" became, in fact, a primary site for enacting this cultural politics, and here the parameters of "valuable" work were sharply delineated. As Josephine Park summarizes, "From its inception, Asian American literature limited the kinds of expressions that could be accommodated under its banner: Chinese and Japanese American experience took precedence, and left out of the canon were all those works which did not strike a note of defiance and whose literary expressions were illegible to the stated aims of the movement" (17). In addition to the numerous Asian ethnic groups whose writing was entirely excluded from the new ethnic canon, works by women and gay men who were a part of included groups were at times ignored, or, in cases of commercial success or mainstream critical acclaim, maligned.

This history of Asian American cultural politics is well documented; however, there were also departures from and challenges to the cultural nationalist strategy, the conception of who and what "counts" as authentic in Asian American cultural politics, and the prevailing model of binary critique in Asian American studies.[17] Best known among the cultural controversies in Asian American literary studies are the Maxine Hong Kingston–Frank Chin debates, which were centrally concerned with the role of popular literature.[18] It was resoundingly clear, Sau-ling Wong points out, that the commercial success and popularity of Kingston's 1976 best seller *The Woman Warrior: Memoir of a Girlhood Among Ghosts* automatically marked the text as being "ideologically suspect" to some critics simply by way of association with commodity capitalism ("Necessity and Extravagance" 3). *The Woman Warrior* became the site of a protracted maelstrom that swirled around several tensions in the field's political claims and practices, especially ambivalence about popular forms and the ideological heterogeneity of Asian American cultural production.[19]

To summarize briefly, the debates concerned the tendency of ethnic autobiography toward ethnography or the "Chinatown book," emasculating fetishism, and Orientalism; questions about Asian American identity, sameness, and difference; tensions between cultural nationalism and feminism; and definitions of authentic forms of Chinese American culture and Asian American masculinity.[20] Laura Hyun Yi Kang observes that the decades-long controversy over *The Woman Warrior* initiated in the mid-1970s—the "autobiographical controversy"—has often been treated as "the" defining debate within Asian American literary studies (*Compositional Subjects* 54). Given that Kingston conceived of her book as a novel, but that the publisher (Alfred Knopf) believed it would sell better as an autobiography, one might imagine a very different critical dialogue had critics taken up any number of questions, beyond capitalist objectification and gender war ideology, related to the apparently easy move from one classification to the other (31). Kang regrets that the generic terms of autobiography in which the memoir is typically mapped have confined the literature in ways and have distracted critics from examining the construction and function of "Maxine Hong Kingston" or the "Asian/American Woman" as a writing self within the constraints of larger discursive struggle (56).[21] Inspired by this insight and confident that yet another rehearsal of the Kingston—Chin debates is not necessary, I turn attention toward a range of highly visible fictional narrative genres, historically feminized or gendered, with the aim of tracing the cultural work of contemporary Asian American women's popular literature within the constraints of discourses of neoliberal citizenship and squarely within the context of consumer culture.

The adaptation of popular narrative genres, including not only the maligned autobiography but also and especially the frequently discredited mother-daughter narrative, has played an undeniable role in the emergence of "Asian American women's literature" as an identifiable category in both contemporary literary and popular culture.[22] While no doubt imbedded in many readers' cultural essentialism, the authority granted first to Maxine Hong Kingston and then Amy Tan on the mother-daughter relationship in America was extended to Asian American women writers generally. Some authors capitalized on the market that Kingston and Tan famously helped create by expanding into other feminized forms or "women's genres" of fiction that had the potential to also cross over, reaching a broad female readership and an Asian American "niche" audience.[23] Publishers happily obliged, and titles penned by Asian American women have steadily made their way into the romance, detective fiction, food writing, and travel sections of the bookstore.[24] In fact, one doesn't burst onto the public sphere or "go public," as Michael Warner writes, "simply as an act of will—neither by writing, nor by having an opinion, nor by exposing oneself in the marketplace. The context of publicness must be available, allowing these actions to count in a public way" as demonstrations of and contributions to the meaning of belonging in neoliberal America (6). The social movements of the 1960s, the individual and collective efforts of Asian American authors, and favorable cultural and market forces both inside and particularly outside the academy, created an environment in which "Asian American women's popular literature" would emerge in the contemporary period and participate in the reformulation of cultural citizenship. Changes in political practices and subjectivity brought about by neoliberalism, namely the increasing importance of cultural citizenship, played a part in popular recognition of Asian American women's literature—at least as large a part as Asian American cultural politics or the talents of individual authors.

The rest of this chapter is divided into sections that outline neoliberalism, sketch the development of neoliberal cultural citizenship, and identify recent approaches in Asian American literary and cultural studies that help me theorize a way of understanding genre fiction as chronicles of gendered racial belonging and contributors to discourses of citizenship. In a final section, brief chapter summaries provide a sense of how different genres engage neoliberal citizenship.

Neoliberalism

Neoliberalism became influential as a theory of political economy or market ideology among economists in the United States in the 1960s at the University of Chicago, began to explicitly inform government in the 1970s under the Carter administration, consolidated as economic orthodoxy that guided public policy in the 1980s, and became hegemonic as a social philosophy in the 1990s (Harvey 22).[25] By 2005, David Harvey writes, an emphatic turn toward the policies and logics of neoliberalism can be seen "everywhere," although the development is decidedly uneven and geographically scattered, with the United States, the United Kingdom, and China as the most devoted subscribers (2). The policies of the neoliberal nation-state promote the privatization of public- or state-owned institutions, as well as strong private property and contract rights; the deregulation of industries and trade markets for unfettered competition both domestically and globally; and the withdrawal of the welfare state from social provision in favor of individual market behavior or "freedom" and "choice," responsibility, and entrepreneurialism.[26]

For many, neoliberalism is a synonym for the global consolidation of national economies into a single market system dominated by the liberal democracies of the North. Through macroeconomic policies—trade agreements, loans, and "structural adjustment programs"—of international institutions such as the World Bank, the International Monetary Fund, and the World Trade Organization, and led by the United States and the United Kingdom, the powerful capitalist states of the North have forced open smaller and less powerful national markets to a neocolonial form of resource exploitation by transnational monopoly capital that has devastated the global South, spawned major new labor migration patterns such as the feminization of migration, and deindustrialized "advanced" economies. In short, neoliberalism is "the latest stage of capitalist global structural and hegemonic domination" in which the disparity between the rich and poor is dramatically increasing (Ong 11). This understanding seems accurate given the "accumulation by dispossession" that is evident on a frighteningly massive scale (Harvey 159).

But neoliberalism as a global condition of inequality does not take analysis very far and may even occlude new power relations. Aihwa

Ong convincingly argues that a North-South geographical axis has limited value for specifically understanding the emergence and mutation of neoliberal political rationality in very different postcolonial, authoritarian, and postsocialist settings, including in the economically dynamic region of Asia, an important backdrop for analyzing Asian American women's negotiation of contemporary changes in US citizenship (12). Associated with the British governmentality school, Ong emphasizes in *Neoliberalism as Exception* that neoliberalism is a technology of governing and that neoliberal reasoning is "based on both economic (efficiency) and ethical (self-responsibility) claims," adapts marketplace values to specific locations, and realigns the organization of society, governance, and models of the citizen-subject (11). In this understanding, neoliberalism is a type of governance that centralizes the transformation of ethical systems, deploying dynamic techniques to "remake the social and citizen-subjects" (14). Conceptualizing neoliberalism in this way—as an episteme of mutating governance and subjectivity—is particularly helpful for analyzing the destabilization of and concern for citizenship in the United States in the late twentieth and early twenty-first centuries.

One need not subscribe to a theory of neoliberalism as a *unified* global empire of economic exploitation to be deeply troubled by its devastating economic calculations, specifically the presumption that the market is "an appropriate guide—an ethic—for all human action," and by its efforts to organize every dimension of social life according to market principles or values (Harvey 165). Since neoliberalism "holds that the social good will be maximized by maximizing the reach and frequency of market transactions," globalization has been characterized by a dramatic increase (although uneven flow) of capital, labor, and goods across national borders, zones, and markets (3). In addition to the financialization of everything, or marketplace fundamentalism, the emphasis on commodification in neoliberalism entails the concomitant development of consumerism, or a system that fosters the desire to buy products by promising that they will bring abundance, happiness, and unlimited pleasure. Further, production and what counts as a product expands, since neoliberalism is particularly adept at commodifying knowledge, ideas, identities, and practices—in a word, "culture."

Remaking the social, neoliberal modes of governing rely heavily on the social system of consumer culture, a type of material culture in which people relate to each other through the mediation of market commodities (Lury 1). In this system, commodity consumption signifies or may even constitute modernity, evidencing rationality, free will or choice, and the possession of individual rights (Slater 8–9). Moreover, the definition of political subjectivity or citizenship in consumer cultures includes or is even primarily defined by consumer practices. According to Banet-Weiser, "Consumer citizenship indicates a certain willingness to participate in consumer culture through the purchase of goods as well as a more general affirmation of consumption habits" (73). In addition, Celia Lury argues that consumer culture is "a source of the contemporary belief that self-identity is a kind of cultural resource, asset or possession," but one that is not equally available to all (9).

For some, neoliberal consumer cultures fully replace the political subject with an empowered consumer who acts (by buying or not) only in the best interests of the individual rather than in relation to a larger polity, so the possibilities for democratic political community and collective struggle are greatly diminished. For those like myself who are dubious of the liberal discourse of a strict citizen/consumer divide, the dynamic relationship between citizen and consumer is remade in the formation of neoliberal consumer culture.[27] The national ethos of meritocratic upward mobility in the United States and the very definition of prosperity in the American Dream are predicated in large part, of course, on consumerism, with Americanness or belonging signified specifically in this narrative through home ownership and all of the material goods that come with it. Not surprisingly, the American Dream as a national cultural myth and narrative is experiencing significant instability under neoliberalism and is undergoing revision or rearticulation to accommodate expanded expectations for citizen participation in US consumer culture, a phenomenon I discuss more closely in chapters on mother-daughter narrative and chick lit.

As much as neoliberalism reorganizes the social order and citizen-subjects around consumption, it also reorganizes the labor or production of social life, including the tricky but essential tasks of government. "Responsible" wage earning and self-sufficient family life have come to define full citizenship status and have been codified into public policy in the United States, such as the federal "welfare reform" or the 1996 Personal Responsibility and Work Opportunity Reconciliation Act that excluded noncitizen immigrant families from public support (Fujiwara 38–43). Private individual acts that sustain the self or self-care comprise one leg of the tripartite base of cultural values upholding the neoliberal model of the citizen, with entrepreneurial reinvention or paid labor and market freedom or consumption providing the other primary supports.

The rhetorics of deregulation, privatization, and the wholesale elimination of public programs often suggest the repudiation or "shrinking" of government. But rather than abandoning "the will to govern," neoliberalism is actually concerned with inventing strategies of government, which joins the work of remaking the social with the work of remaking the individual citizen-subject (Rose, "Governing" 53). Following Foucault, Nikolas Rose explains that neoliberal strategies of rule "ask whether it is possible to govern without governing *society*, that is to say, govern through the regulated and accountable choices of autonomous agents—citizens, consumers, parents, employees, managers, investors— and to govern through intensifying and acting upon their allegiance to particular 'communities,'" such as ethnic and racialized communities (61, emphasis in original).[28] In fact, priority is placed on the "regulation of conduct" or shaping self-disciplining subjects who will enact neoliberal market values and perform "good" citizenship roles as both enthusiastic consumers and responsible workers (58). Foucault theorized, in the first volume of *The History of Sexuality*, how political authorities in Europe who sought to manage life in the name of the well-being of populations developed biopower or "power over life." Providing a genealogy of biopolitics or political power over life, Foucault identifies how the strategies that seek management over the bodies of individuals (discipline) and those that seek management over the collective body of a population (regulation) came together by the nineteenth century to create new technologies of power and concomitantly new forms of struggle (Rose, *Politics of Life Itself* 52–54).

In our current era, biopolitics has become increasingly sophisticated with neoliberal models of political subjectivity requiring "populations to be free, self-managing, and self-enterprising individuals," or "entrepreneurs of the self" who can take care of the self and shield the state from responsibility and liability.[29] Repeated emphasis on individual market access as "freedom" and responsibility enables the denial of structural inequalities and social problems, so those who do not succeed purportedly fail by their own shortcomings and their "choices" or conscious departures from neoliberal cultural values, rather than as a result of systemic inequality or even unfortunate circumstance. All are "author of their own misfortune" (Rose, "Governing" 59). In this context, the disavowing ideologies of postracial and postfeminist discourses that claim political movements for racial equality and gender justice are no longer needed have gained currency and flourished alongside the revival of social Darwinism and resurgent American bootstrap ideology. They deny that transnational capital and post-Fordist (nonunion) production create racialized, ethnicized, and gendered spaces, networks, and flows of labor that result in or magnify hierarchies of power and differential access to belonging (Ong 124–32).

More insidiously, the deficiencies of the individual subject have become the object of social preoccupation, rehabilitation, and industry. Neoliberalism posits not only that citizenship is an ongoing project of the self and that individuals carry the responsibility of self-care, but also that all individuals have the full capacity for improvement and are obliged to reinvent or transform the deficient self without public resources or supports. The primary strategy of shifting the goals and obligations of the state to the individual by translating them into "the choices and commitments of individuals" is largely accomplished indirectly through mechanisms that do not carry the imprimatur of "the State" (Rose, "Governing" 58–59) but nonetheless convey neoliberal standards or "templates" for citizenship, especially including commercial media (Ouellette 224). Hailed across neoliberal consumer culture, the deficient yet fully self-reliant subject whose happiness and success, defined in relation to the marketplace, has been compromised, presumably because of the individual's less-than-judicious choices, must strive nonetheless for a better life. Given neoliberalism's politics of "freedom," it is ironic at best, deceptive at worst, and in any case contradictory that neoliberal governmentality maintains a strict morality about the proper distribution of tasks, a specific epistemology of what should be governed, and a particular style or aesthetic of reasoning (Rose, "Governing" 42). Indeed, it is more accurate to say, as Ong puts it, that neoliberal governmentality deploys "a politics of subjection and subject-making" (12).[30]

Cultural Citizenship

Contemporary changes in citizenship and the development of cultural citizenship in the United States in the neoliberal era have involved a "realignment" of the elements, dimensions, or layers that comprise a sense of belonging, and a multiplication of the types of practices required for full membership in the nation, as well as increased demands for established practices. Especially useful for my analysis of Asian American authors' engagements with the reconfiguration of citizenship in popular literature is an understanding of the reordering of citizenship elements as a discursive process of "disarticulation and re-articulation" with neoliberalism (Ong 16). Neoliberalism adapts to and mutates existing regimes of citizenship and other forms of ethical reasoning by negotiating, exploring, and redefining their claims through discursive practices. In this theorization, current shifts in citizenship are the result not of a universal system but of more localized processes within which "neoliberalism interacts with regimes of ruling and regimes of citizenship to produce conditions that change administrative strategies and citizenship practices" (6).

Certainly by the end of the twentieth century, cultural rights were firmly established in human rights discourse; in citizenship studies, cultural citizenship was recognized as the "maintenance and development of cultural lineage via education, custom, language, and religion, and the positive acknowledgment of difference in and by the mainstream" (Miller, "Cultural Citizenship" 231).[31] At the same time, however, cultural citizenship in the United States has undergone significant revision in the process of disarticulation and rearticulation with neoliberalism. "While both conservative critics and culturalist celebrants explain cultural citizenship as the outcome of social movements," Toby Miller asserts, "it must also be understood as an adjustment to economic transformation" (*Cultural Citizenship* 55).[32] In fact, observers often credit the new social movements of the late 1960s and early 1970s with the introduction of cultural citizenship claims into public discourse, but this was also the moment that neoliberalism emerged and became an influential social ideology. By the early 1980s, and with the rise of the New Right, neoliberalism was guiding economic and social policy in the Reagan administration. In Lauren Berlant's influential theorization, the New Right built a coalition of conservative moral activists that deliberately fetishized the family and private life in public discourse to revise American citizenship in a backlash social movement that reacted against the claims advanced in the new social movements (*Queen of America* 31). It moved citizenship practices out of a political public sphere where struggles over inequalities and rights were fought and into an "intimate public sphere" where private acts, values, and feelings associated with normative, heterosexual family life were reframed as the appropriate context for citizenship (123).

In analyzing the privatization of citizenship in the 1980s, Berlant points out that the process was an affective, symptomatic one in which popular media culture and public discourse substituted familial sentiment for political agency, while the primary concern of this "cultural revolution" of the Reaganite right was more accurately the social question of "who will control the vast material resources of the US" (*Queen of America* 97). As noted earlier, the popular culture landscape is at this point saturated with media that urge the public—particularly women and immigrants, or those who most literally reproduce the citizenry—to take responsibility for and undergo private reinvention, largely in the name of the repronormative family.[33] At the same time, Berlant understands the privatization of citizenship as a broader cultural transformation that depoliticizes and infantilizes the citizenry, since the critical knowledge needed for citizens' political subjectivity is contracted and exchanged for passivity, overdependence, and innocence in relation to the state. "Political ideas about the nation are sacrificed to feelings about it" that mirror the feelings people have for their families and particularly their fathers (7). The state then becomes the parent to the child or the infantilized citizen who is protected from the harsh realities of political life. In this study, the privatization of citizenship describes a shift to private acts as citizenship practices, to the ethos of self-care or self-governance, and to individual cultural alignment with the normalizing market values of neoliberalism, including privatization (of public institutions/resources), entrepreneurial reinvention, and consumption.

In reviewing Berlant's influential theorization of the relocation and contraction of citizenship, I mean to reference debates in public sphere theory associated with the Frankfurt School and especially, following Jürgen Habermas, changes in the understanding of publicity and political claims-making in relation to mass culture and specifically the commercial mass media. Habermas observed the major changes in capitalism that took place in the eighteenth century and theorized a vibrant public space or sphere outside the control of the state where rational, critical conversation and democratic exchange took place. This public sphere changed again when the modern development of commercial mass media reduced the democratic public sphere to a space of passive consumption and capitalist competition. Critiques of Habermas have emerged from feminist and queer political theory that rejects the idealization of the public sphere as democratic and open to all. Moreover, critics have argued against a single, totalizing conception of publicness and normalizing notions of rationality, as well as for the importance of counterpublics or marginalized publics that are defined in complex, critical relation to a larger public.[34] One goal of this book is to revisit these debates since the tendency is still to dichotomize, either celebrating and romanticizing the popular practices of the public sphere on the one hand or dismissing them as depoliticizing on the other. An editor's forum in the October 2012 volume of the *Journal of Asian American Studies* briefly takes up questions related to how Asian American studies might engage popular discourse more fully. It focuses on individual academics as public intellectuals or on how Asian American studies may benefit from cultivating scholars who would participate in popular media culture for more critical public-sphere dialogue, providing another indication that reconsideration of the complex role of publicity is especially important at this moment given the substantial development of the media.

A second significant round in the neoliberal disarticulation and rearticulation of cultural citizenship came, in fact, in the context of the technological development of new media, the privatization of telecommunications, and media deregulation and conglomeration; these processes situated the media as a key player in the "New Economy" in the 1980s and subsequent discourses of economic globalization, so that identities, ways of life, and cultural production have become indelibly embedded in privatized media capitalism. Although a good many scholars argue that the Internet and other new media hold the potential for increased participation and an expanded, more democratic public sphere, analysis that more critically centralizes the media often echoes the work of numerous critics such as bell hooks who have been observing for some time the cultural appropriation of racial and ethnic minority cultures by mainstream media that profit from marketing difference in feel-good multicultural texts to white US audiences. Miller argues further that the cultural expression of citizenship claims is centrally important to the organization of inequalities under advanced capitalism through the transformation of culture by "the neoliberal Right" into "a new set of market and ecclesiastical niches and sites of self-governance" or into a technology for managing subjects (*Cultural Citizenship* 179).[35] That is, the practice of publicly claiming rights to inclusion and difference through expressions of culture has been largely displaced by the practice of participating in commercial media culture, through producing but especially through consuming or purchasing expressions of Americanness or "lifestyles" that address and target marginalized cultural groups. Through such practices, cultural identities—both of sameness and difference—are produced and managed, and the subject becomes an appropriately disciplined and regulated citizen of neoliberal consumer culture.[36] This media work is part of the care of the self that neoliberal subjects must master and exhibit as a form of publicity or to be counted as citizens. In Harvey's words, neoliberalization "required both politically and economically the construction of a neoliberal market-based populist culture of differentiated consumerism and individual libertarianism" (42). Understood in this way, cultural citizenship in the United

States now overlaps to a great extent with consumer citizenship, which is perhaps more widely associated with neoliberalism.

The transformation of culture into a marketplace tool of subjection and subjectmaking under neoliberalism is not limited to racial and ethnic cultures. As discussed above, feminist media studies scholars have observed the extent to which the address of girls and women in popular media is now on the basis of gender as a normative cultural identity (white, middle-class, heterosexual American) and as an identity of cultural difference, from males and other females interpellated through marginal racial, ethnic, age, religious, sexual, and familial identifications. Women, who are becoming increasingly powerful consumers with wages, and who also have marketplace needs to satisfy and desires to cultivate, are hailed as cultural citizens and are also instructed that "good" citizenship requires their participation. More than alliance with mainstream commercial culture and normative femininity, neoliberalism in the United States calls on the female subject to perform a set of marketplace activities that is considerably more substantial than what was expected of preceding generations of bourgeois housewives, as well as of the working-class women, immigrant women, and women of color who have historically labored outside and inside the home to support their families.[37] To achieve status as a citizen-subject, the female subject must responsibly reproduce, mother, and care for her children without public resources; secure marketplace advantage for increased future participation; labor as a wage earner in the global economy; and participate in consumer culture. In the symbolic economy of neoliberalism, gender variation is contained and the female subject is semiotically legible as a "woman"—conventionally gendered and marked by normative signs of race and sexuality—only to the extent that she demonstrates conformity to the neoliberal marketplace.

A third reformulation of cultural citizenship and one more explicitly about belonging is identifiable in the anti-immigrant movements of the 1990s. While US citizenship within neoliberalism is a "national capability" that circulates globally and is undergoing denationalization, it is still largely felt, understood, and represented in national terms (Sassen, *Territory* 1); it has also been subject to "renationalization" or to "the politics of closure" that "attempts to restrict citizenship to certain groups, and to exclude others" by assigning differential citizenship status (Fujiwara 24). Part of a discernible historical pattern in the United States, differential citizenship reemerged in the 1990s through the discourse of foreigner racialization as deployed by anti-immigrant movements eager to scapegoat immigrants for economic hardship, grant only partial citizenship, or exclude immigrants from belonging all together, in "the new nativism." What was novel about this movement was not its racism but rather the perception that transnational immigrants posed threats to cultural assumptions about what it means to be American. Reactions took the form of demonizing especially those "immigrants who maintain strong ties to their home countries, sustain transnational families, often travel to and fro, and remain potential sponsors for additional family migrants" (6–7).[38] Moreover, as part of the pattern of labor flows in neoliberal economic globalization, transnational immigrants were increasingly women, specifically Asian women and Latinas. "The heightened visibility of women immigrants materialized in a new nativist construction" that targeted "women and children," Lynn Fujiwara writes, "through anti-immigrant reform movements focusing on reproduction and access to social services," such as welfare and Medicaid (7). The perceived immigrant threat and foreigner racialization took on unprecedented proportions after the events of September 11, 2001, when a series of antiterrorist laws that criminalized immigrants was passed, deportation became policy, and government surveillance and incarceration easily dispensed with civil liberties.[39]

Importantly, the contemporary politics of closure in the United States has been accompanied by immigrant rights movements, liberal and neoconservative immigrant advocacy organizations, and the emergence of actors who claim rights outside of liberal democratic definitions of citizenship. Citizenship, Siu has pointed out, "not only defines who belongs and has rights, but it also serves as site for contesting social injustice and advancing widespread social change" (10). Amid the new nativist backlash against immigrants in the 1990s and drawing on the new social movements' use of culture for galvanizing marginalized groups and claiming full citizenship, as well as earlier struggles for political rights in the United States in the dissident abolitionist and suffrage movements, Renato Rosaldo influentially theorized Latino cultural citizenship. His definition asserts the right of marginalized groups to the maintenance of cultural difference from the dominant national community, and to cultural respect, as well as "to be visible, to be heard, and to belong" as full members of the nation; further, cultural citizenship uses "cultural expression to claim public rights and recognition" and "attends not only to dominant exclusions and marginalizations, but also to subordinate aspirations for and definitions of enfranchisement" (36–37). Claims of belonging are expressed in vernacular cultural practices and also, as Shirley Jennifer Lim emphasizes in her study of Asian American women's public culture from 1930 to 1960, in hybrid use of mainstream forms of culture by subjects distanced from power; indeed, struggles for belonging are found in everyday practices, rather than only in legal discourse or a conventionally defined public sphere of political actors (8). Finally, recognizing "the partial language, epistemology, aesthetics, rituals and pleasure" of a narrowly delimited political field and exclusionary public sphere, and citing a combination of ideological and material forces that includes the new social movements, migration, religion, the waning relevance of the nation-state, and the growth of mass media and communication technologies, Liesbet Van Zoonen understands popular culture as a crucial dimension of contemporary political citizenship and "a battleground where demands for rights and duties are fiercely asserted and denied" (8).

Neoliberal cultural citizenship has particular historical as well as contemporary significance for Asian American women. In an analysis of the temporal and discursive tenacity of gendered racial national exclusion and the legal concept of derivative status, Rhacel Salazar Parreñas and Winnie Tam observe that Asian American women have most often had to gain entry and legal citizenship in the United States through men (Asian and non-Asian) as "picture brides" and "war brides," for example, and through "family reunification"; and the citizenship of Asian immigrant women remains contingent upon how well they conform to normative ideologies or hegemonic cultural values of femininity and domesticity as demonstrated through family formation and maternal labor, as the Pew Center Report illustrates (113). Eithne Luibhéid and several other scholars have pointed out that, although the Immigration and Nationality Act of 1965 "finally eliminated the explicitly racist immigration standards of the National Origins Act of 1924" and made official citizenship legally possible for a majority of Asian immigrants for the first time in US history through abolishing Asian national origin quotas, its preference categories (which allocated 74 percent of slots to family reunification, 20 percent to workers, and 6 percent to refugees), were both racially discriminatory and heteronormative, with specific effects for women that maintained the legacy of regulation in immigration laws from the era of exclusion (22).[40]

Family reunification policies have always "codified a heteropatriarchal sexual and gender order and facilitated the exclusion of women who violated or threatened it. At the same time, heteropatriarchal policies also produced racial, ethnic, and class exclusions" (Luibhéid 8). In fact, the 1965 act resulted in *more* regulation rather than less, with deriva-tive status and the cultural unit of the normative family still firmly entrenched as "the primary ideological apparatus, the central system of symbols, through which the state contains and manages contradictions in the social structure" (Robert Lee 7).[41] Moreover, in concert with the large-scale migration patterns of neoliberal globalization and the labor requirements of the US economy, the act's preference categories "pro-duced a racialized and gendered [female] noncitizen immigrant work-force for domestic and low-end labor markets in the US" (Eng 31), and an elite class of educated professionals, for a two-tiered immigration pattern that unexpectedly and dramatically remade "Asian America" into a predominately immigrant population (Fujiwara 25). An important context for the changes addressed in *Asian American Women's Popu-lar Literature* is the current reality of everyday struggle for citizenship rights by Asian women who are pulled to the United States for low-wage employment and who stand in stark contrast to the transnational elites and professionals entering through very different circumstances and possessing considerably greater resources to contend with the volatile terrain of neoliberal belonging.[42] Recognizing that some women have affiliations with two or more nations or even other forms of political community, as in transnational, flexible, and diasporic citizenships, we should understand citizenship as "multilayered" or multiscalar, having local, ethnic, national, and supranational resonance.[43] At the same time, we must recognize that claiming social belonging in the nation and/ or inclusion in the territorially based nation-state may be a matter of survival, particularly for undocumented workers, asylum seekers, and refugees.[44] As Saskia Sassen maintains, it is inside the national "that the most complex meanings of the global are being constituted," and the nation remains crucial for understanding new forms and practices of belonging (*Territory* 1).

In addition to legal citizenship requirements to conform to norma-tive cultural ideologies of femininity, domesticity, and sexuality through state-mandated family formation, Asian American women were com-pelled to establish social belonging in the mid-twentieth-century indus-trial era, Shirley Jennifer Lim discovered, by appropriately displaying gender and femininity through the production and consumption of dif-ferent modern cultural forms, including sorority membership, beauty pageants, magazines, films, and parades (9). In the postindustrial era, I assert that an even more robust neoliberal cultural citizenship demands Asian American female participation in mainstream cultural narratives and popular media forms to claim and establish belonging. As McRobbie explains the new sexual contract of feminine modes of citizenship in contemporary neoliberal consumer culture, "The visual (and verbal) discourses of public femininity ... come to occupy an increasingly spectacular set of sites, events, narratives, and occasions within the cultural milieu" (*Aftermath of Feminism* 60). While the destabilization of citizenship under neoliberalism has had exclusionary effects for Asian American women, it has also paradoxically enabled a new level of visibility for belonging because it requires public "evidence" of Asian American women's adherence to the market fundamentalism of neoliberalism that has pervaded social life and thought and come to define Americanness. This book examines the imperative to participate in mainstream culture and complicates what is often taken as evidence of citizenship since I demonstrate how several texts stake various positions, presenting different combinations that simultaneously affirm Asian American women's cultural citizenship and question what it and other forms of neoliberal belonging mean for them as gendered racial subjects.[45]

Reading Neoliberalism in Asian American Women's Popular Literature

Asian American Women's Popular Literature is indebted to a critical tradition in the study of Asian American women's literature and Asian American feminism that cautiously employs "Asian American women," deploying it as a mediated category of identity. Ground-breaking critics such as Elaine Kim, Amy Ling, Shirley Geok-lin Lim, and King-kok Cheung were among the first to "cast doubt" on the unity of identity and generic categories in Asian American literature, all the while insisting on the significance of the literature (Lim, Tsutakawa, and Donnelly 11). The scholarship on Asian American women's literature has consistently questioned the conventional canonical divides that tend to marginalize or occlude it, divides between fiction and nonfiction, authentic and "fake" culture, and literary and popular forms. At the same time, it has objected to the spectacular fetishization of Asian women on the one extreme and their erasure on the other.[46] In many cases, this scholarship has taken the mandate of oppositionality understood as antiracism to the more heterodox level of rejecting binaries themselves, providing an antifoundational basis for the development of the critical concept of "heterogeneity" in Asian American studies as it was initially expressed in the 1990s and as it is now widely accepted. In addition to the influential work of Lisa Lowe, scholars such as Traise Yamamoto, Susan Koshy, Kandice Chuh, and Laura Hyun Yi Kang have questioned, respectively, the constructs "autobiography," "Asian American literature," "Asian American studies," and "Asian American women" as "masks," "fictions," a "subjectless discourse," or "compositional subjects." These scholars consider the field a form of critique that continually redefines the political, a framework that well serves the challenge of understanding the contemporary reformulation of citizenship. As Leslie Bow observes, Asian American women's literature operates as a site "where questions can be posed about the gendered relationship of the individual to the state, about the status of the subject defined by group affiliation, and about exclusions that produce national unity" (35).

Although Asian American studies initially saw little value in popular culture, even when produced by Asian Americans, the deconstruction of images created a base upon which inquiry could maintain connections to earlier priorities and build: "By examining these images in the historical specificity of their production, circulation, and consumption, scholars and critics have demonstrated the salience of popular culture as a realm of political conflict and an important force in shaping the material and social realities, but also the imaginative inner lives, of Asian Americans" (Nguyen and Tu 6). In the 1990s, in the context of unprecedented publication by Asian American authors, the rise of cultural studies, the development of anti-identitarian queer theory, and the shift in American studies toward more transnational concerns, several scholars reevaluated the prevailing critical apparatus in Asian American studies and initiated what I call "the reluctant turn toward publicity." Viet Nguyen influentially advanced the thesis that Asian American studies had been limited by reading "for signs of resistance or accommodation" to racism and capitalism. The binary critical approach resulted in an intellectual barrier that could not appreciate the ideological heterogeneity of Asian Americans and Asian American literature alike (*Race and Resistance* 5–6). Such a framework obscures, Nguyen asserts, the mutual interdependence of and movement between the "bad subject" who refuses interpellation into the social order and the subject who is accommodating; the "flexible strategies" that subjects, including authors, commonly use to negotiate constraints and ethical dilemmas of social conditions under consumer capitalism; and the commodification of Asian American identity within global capitalism (144–45). The misreading of a substantial amount of cultural production has been the result not only of a well-intended but rigid ideological practice but also a political unconscious that disavows uncomfortable contradictions, chiefly the contradiction between using the symbolic capital of race and resistance to institutionalize Asian American studies but firmly rejecting the social and political value of other forms of panethnic entrepreneurship, or the practice of "trading in race" (4–6).[47]

Recent reading practices bring attention to texts that accommodate or are complicit with structures of power, without necessarily "retooling" them as subversive in the familiar fetishization of resistance that has become a default alternative (Chang 68). Or, processes such as "accommodation," "assimilation," "inclusion," and "Americanization" have been retrieved from the dustbin of rigid interpretation for more nuanced analysis. Scholars acknowledge that, rather than being entirely free agents of creative expression and political vision, "authors' choices are constrained by the discursive fields they enter" (P. Chu 31) and texts are shaped by a process of negotiation or "the complex interplay between authorial design, available social space, and accessible cultural resources" (Ling 30).[48] For example, Anupama Jain argues that especially in the context of contemporary global migration and diasporas, anxieties about belonging and identity are endemic; as well, "'becoming American' should be interpreted as a process in which there is always some aspect of volition, adaptation to the country combined with the maintenance of ethnic or other identifications predating immigration, an inevitable ambivalence about transformations that are engendered by migration" (20).

The studied neglect of popular culture has given way to a more thorough critical recognition of the heterogeneity of Asian America, one that resists the presumption of racial minorities as resistant or uniformly "bad subjects," what Vijay Prashad has called "the illusory search for coherence" in identity politics (132), and Viet Nguyen considers the "disavowed essentialism of racial identity" (*Race and Resistance* 145).[49] Collections as well as monographs have expanded the scope of Asian American cultural studies well beyond a critique of stereotypes or depictions of Asians in American popular culture. They analyze, the editors of *Alien Encounters: Popular Culture in Asian America* write, "specific moments of uneven engagement that might manifest themselves as complicity, confrontation, or both, and that differentially interpolate Asian Americans as consumers and in some cases producers and workers" (Nguyen and Tu 3).[50] My understanding of genre fiction as chronicles of gendered racial citizenship and as contributors to discourses of neoliberal citizenship leans on studies that analyze popular genres of literature as varied as memoir, science fiction, chick lit, the cookbook, and the thriller for formal signifiers as well as for the ideological work they perform.[51] As Maureen Reddy has written, "The codes and conventions of each genre are intertwined with the codes and conventions of the society in which the literary texts are produced, making genre fiction an especially useful arena for investigating race and gender" (*Traces, Codes, and Clues* 1–2). The distinctive frameworks of popular genres are "instantly recognizable" but also negotiable, with certain codes and conventions more available than others for complex revision (McCann 42). Generic categories and characteristics are useful as a discourse or "a way of imagining and representing certain stories, characters, settings, or problems," and less productive when understood solely as fixed rules, commercial classifications, or literary fields (Mizejewski 202).

Christine So calls for a reading practice that "looks more closely at how Asian Americans enter and appropriate US mainstream culture and ideologies" because, rather than "ignore or discount the history of racialization, exclusion, and alienation of Asians in the United States, … it charts more fully how Asian Americans make an appearance in the American imaginary" (6, 8). Erin Khuê Ninh provides an unflinching analysis of texts that address "the political-economic structures of power obtaining between parents and daughters in the immigrant family," which seems to operate as a "sort of cottage industry, for a particular brand of good capitalist subject: Get your filial child, your doctor/lawyer, your model minority here" (6, 2). Indeed, the contradictions of and ambivalences around Asian American success, including those discernible in popular literature, have become part of the political consciousness of the critical apparatus in Asian American studies, and this will no doubt continue as reconceptualizations of "failure" gain traction to contend with the contemporary context of politically untenable neoliberal definitions and mandates for success (V. Nguyen, *Race and Resistance* 147).[52] This is crucial because, although the figure of the Asian American female subject often circulates in public discourse as "success," the reality is far more complicated when the operations of success/failure models are applied to specific Asian ethnic groups and social contexts. As Minh-Ha T. Pham explains, "It is precisely because of the varied and complicated ways in which Asian Americans have both voluntarily and involuntarily embodied 'success' that there is an urgent need for Asian Americanists to critique the ideologically laden frameworks of success/failure as an apparatus of racial meaning and difference" (331).

Situated at the crossroads of Asian American literary studies, feminist media and cultural studies, and citizenship studies, *Asian American Women's Popular Literature* draws on a repertoire of recent reading practices. It refuses the false choices presented in the conventional binaries of aesthetics or politics, race or gender, resistance or accommodation, success or failure. My reading method is thus indebted to post-structuralism and interdisciplinarity, although the primary texts I discuss in detail are all contemporary novels. Some of the novels in the archive are commercially prosperous books or novels that have been critically acclaimed, while others ally themselves with enterprising genres and adjacent popular media, but in all cases they are palpably self-conscious of the connections between the commercial and the literary.

Because *Asian American Women's Popular Literature* explores how several Asian American women writers engage specific discourses of neoliberal citizenship through popular genre fiction, contextualization is important to my methodology. As the preceding sections of this chapter have suggested, the current transformations in belonging must be read through the structuring inequalities of gender and racial hierarchies; the histories, policies, and processes of migration; and the ideologies and commitments that reckon with neoliberalism. While the mother-daughter narratives I consider in chapter 2 depict the recent past of their narrators' childhoods, or the beginnings of the neoliberal era in the 1970s, all of the novels in the archive were published after neoliberalism became hegemonic as a social philosophy in the 1990s and before the economic downturn began in late 2007. The archive provides snapshots of two roughly specific historical moments, one in the mid- to late 1990s and the other in the early to mid-2000s, in which struggles and anxieties over the meaning of the American Dream and Americanness or belonging within the United States, especially in relation to race and gender categories, were salient for a set of Asian American women writers.[53] As with all Asian American cultural production, popular literature should be contextualized in both ethnic histories and in panethnic politics, or within "Asian America" as a discursive construct that is mobilized in various ways and by different agents. I retain "Asian American literature" as part of an argument about authors' engagement with the marketplace, which complements recent scholarship that has turned toward ethnic specific formations. While I attend to the history and contemporary context of Asian American women's contingent political or formal citizenship, I focus on citizenship as a social process involving cultural practices and productions, since it "is a qualitative experience produced and sustained by everyday interactions and practices that enact inclusions and exclusions" (Siu 7). Similarly, because political citizenship is now understood as inseparable from and intertwined with social and cultural dimensions, I follow the recent practice of scholars who use "citizenship" and "belonging" interchangeably.[54]

With the understanding that popular culture is a fundamental site of struggle and a primary site for the production of citizen-subjects and citizenship discourses in the United States, I situate textual analyses within contemporary social life in the United States, identifying how the specific mandates of "good citizenship" as defined by neoliberal marketplace values may be manifest and to what extent popular genres may be characteristically neoliberal. Reading less for character development, psychological interiority, and unlimited rereading than for the denotative and connotative meanings of the language of the marketplace, this study maps the symbolic and semiotic representation of neoliberalism. More specifically, in generic conventions and innovations I trace the process of disarticulation and rearticulation of citizenship with neoliberalism, detailing how texts negotiate and represent biological, consumer, cosmopolitan, and transnational citizenships. Each of the next four chapters is devoted to a different popular genre and analyzes works for how they negotiate the constraints of a specific discourse of neoliberal citizenship at a particular historical moment. I contextualize mother-daughter narratives and the mandate to manage fertility and family in neoliberal maternal discourse; chick lit and the necessity of gaining qualifications for participation in the marketplace in postfeminism; detective fiction and the imperative to work in the New Economy; and food writing and the mandate to participate in global consumer culture in the transnational discourse of globalization.

In my reading of Asian American women's popular literature, I employ a nuanced understanding of genre, emphasizing that genres are as dynamic as they are stable, and that texts often, perhaps always, participate in more than one genre. Following Patricia Chu, who expands the methods of Asian American and feminist literary studies in her influential *Assimilating Asians: Gendered Strategies of Authorship in Asian America*, I read the adaptation of genres as strategies that register Asian American women's particular relation to the social order, underscoring "the agency of Asian Americans as authors," as well as citizens (11). I also build on Brian McHale's view of the "reciprocity" between literary and popular genres, providing an additional response to concerns about the inadequacy of a canonical framework and a hierarchy of forms for appreciating Asian American cultural production (quoted in Merivale and Sweeney 5). Further, my understanding of popular literature includes how genres are particularly dynamic during periods of intense change, since to be legible as popular genres they must engage dominant social knowledge (Hariman 19). Most importantly, and with a focus on authors' textual negotiation of citizenship discourses as instructive narrative practices, my inquiry heeds concerns about the critical tendency to read texts "in the manner of an insurance adjuster" (Jun 5). *Asian American Women's Popular Literature* aims to balance the critical goal to profile "Asian Americans as agents in the production of popular culture" with awareness of how popular texts may compel and shape neoliberal citizen-subjects in the model of the aspiring individual that dares not fail (Davé, Nishime, and Oren xiv, 1–2). As Yoonmee Chang has observed, "Asian American literature is apparently complicit, vocally oppositional, oppositional but reabsorbed, subversive by being complicit, confounded, and ambivalent, as well as a mixture of several of these positions in shifting combinations" (68). With such a variety of possible textual strategies and effects at play, I identify a range of generic innovations and recognize that they are not all or uniformly interventionist or do not necessarily intervene in the ethical ways scholars may prefer.

Asian American Women's Popular Literature does not present a theory of Asian American women's popular literature and demonstrate it through analysis of textual examples or representatives of Asian American citizenship discourse; nor do I assume that all Asian American women writers are especially concerned with changes in belonging. In fact, texts are included in this study because of the insight into neoliberal modes of citizenship that their particular narrative practices provide. I nevertheless observe that these authors are uniquely situated in relation to discourses of neoliberal citizenship because of a social history of gendered racial exclusion, and because Asian American women are now often positioned "as idealized subjects of a neoliberal world order" while simultaneously targeted in new forms of exclusion (Jun 9). It is my firm conviction that literature can help us understand recent changes and may well enable new epistemological visions of belonging. *Asian American Women's Popular Literature* focuses on fictional print narratives, locates them in a neoliberal context that blurs distinctions among cultural, political, and consumer practices, and moves beyond interpretations of literature as aestheticized tools of liberal nation-building or as unequivocal affirmations of cultural citizenship.

Chapter Overview

Chapter 2, "Asian American Mother-Daughter Narrative and the Neoliberal American Dream of Transformative Femininity," recontextualizes this most identifiable and feminizing genre of Asian American women's literature in the citizenship discourse I call "neoliberal maternal discourse" and offers an alternative to shallow sentimentality for understanding the popularity of mother-daughter narratives. Rather than part of a "mass genre" of sentimental realism that fully contains women's citizenship, as Berlant suggests in *The Female Complaint*, mother-daughter narrative also operates as a space within neoliberal maternal discourse for contending with a model of gendered cultural citizenship that centralizes bourgeois motherhood as transformative. The chapter begins with the public controversy over Amy Chua's *Battle Hymn of the Tiger Mother*. Discussion highlights the imperative for women in the United States to culturally display that they "exercise biological prudence" or biological citizenship and embrace consumer-based practices for the sake of the family and the nation (Rose, *Politics of Life Itself* 24). Adaptations of the popular form in Patti Kim's *A Cab Called Reliable* and Lan Cao's *Monkey Bridge* exhibit their authors' Americanness and thematically recognize the importance of participation in mainstream culture for Asian immigrant women's belonging. However, through plots that fracture mother-daughter relationships they also resist interpellations of Asian American women as "good citizens," as in the mediating figure of the maternal model minority. Building on feminist, queer, and critical race theory, I argue that these novels address the differential biopolitics of neoliberal cultural citizenship for Asian American women (S. Sharma 139). If Patricia Chu finds in the mother-daughter narrative a utopian family romance that affirms cultural citizenship, in the hands of these authors' flexible strategies the genre is also a site for questioning the reinscription of the maternal romance as a viable route for belonging.

Chapter 3, "Romancing the Self and Negotiating Postfeminist Consumer Citizenship in Asian American Women's Labor Lit," deepens my argument that Asian American women's genre fiction moves beyond affirmations of cultural citizenship to engage various discourses of neoliberal belonging. Here I contextualize innovative chick lit by Asian American women within postfeminism and show how the novels contribute to the understanding of consumer citizenship. I emphasize that postfeminist cultural texts, and specifically the generic revisions of chick lit, deploy "a variety of positions with respect to feminism," rather than always a neoliberal rubric that unequivocally lays out the "pastness" of sexism, racism, and class inequality (Tasker and Negra 8). Similar to the genre as a whole, "labor lit" registers the demands for women's flexible labor as its occasion, but unlike most chick lit, labor lit foregrounds the negotiation of work and romance and chronicles the challenges that women regularly face in the workplace. Further, instead of fantastically resolving the inequitable conditions of employment, Michelle Yu and Blossom Kan's *China Dolls* and Sonia Singh's *Goddess for Hire* reveal untenable contradictions, even if they do not entirely repudiate consumer citizenship. In search of meaningful professional careers, the heroines of these novels encounter a marketplace in which production and consumption are intertwined, and good citizen-workers are "flex subjects" who continually cultivate and reinvent the self by demonstrating marketplace expertise (Weber 39). That is, in addition to the qualifications specific to occupations, they must display "romantic consumerism" or taste distinctions about the ever-expanding range of commodities available under neoliberalism (J. Collins 186). The novels illuminate that for Asian American women the romance with the laboring self fits squarely within the ideology of the American Dream that assigns Asian Americans to contingent belonging. Analysis of Asian American labor lit underscores that the genre registers not only the gender, commercial, and domestic concerns of the novel's roots but also contemporary concerns, including the racialized labor of consumer citizenship for Asian American women.

Turning toward the global dimensions of American belonging in "Neoliberal Detective Work: Uncovering Cosmopolitan Corruption in the New Economy," chapter 4 describes how the detective fiction of Sujata Massey and Suki Kim engages the terms of the "New Economy," a discourse of neoliberal cosmopolitan citizenship that demands that labile subjects work for the information-driven global economy. With its generic commitments to ontological and epistemological questions, including detection and investigation, the detective novel lends itself to an interrogation of social conditions, and, in this analysis, neoliberal claims of ethical prosperity resulting from global flows of labor, culture, and information. Massey's *Girl in a Box* and Kim's *The Interpreter* respectively trace Japanese American and Korean American female characters as cosmopolitan citizens whose labor in state-sponsored international espionage and court interpretation is instrumental in the exchange of information and the regulation of the global economy. While these occupations at first glance appear glamorous, they are low-paid and insecure, suggesting that such labor is part of the larger pattern of the

feminization of migration. More startling, the protagonists uncover corruption on a massive scale and learn about the lethal dimensions of the
New Economy. The novels recycle narrative codes to intervene in the
ethically ennobled discourse of neoliberal cosmopolitanism that appropriates the culturally complex or global "American" laboring subject.

Chapter 5, "Food Writing and Transnational Belonging in Global
Consumer Culture," examines how belonging is produced and where
it resides in the transnational citizenship discourse of globalization.
Extending my argument to a text that rigorously resists generic classification, I analyze Ruth Ozeki's *My Year of Meats* as a type of fiction
that engages the neoliberal citizenship mandate to participate in global
consumer culture and become a transnational but still identifiably
American subject. I theorize that the novel remediates various formats
of food writing or culinary discourse, such as food television, memoir
cookbooks, and documentary film. Trading in the culinary cultural capital of global food tourism, the organic and slow food movements, and
celebrity chef restaurants, *My Year of Meats* signifies transnational taste
distinctions and addresses transnational class formations that remain
invested in neoliberal American cultural values and historical relationships between nation-states. At the same time, Ozeki's novel explores
distinct possibilities for popular literature as a site for ethical debate and
as an agent of social change.

Through a brief reading of Mira Nair's adaptation of Jhumpa Lahiri's
The Namesake (2003), I conclude *Asian American Women's Popular
Literature* by emphasizing how the discourses of neoliberal citizenship
that constrain Asian American women's belonging have paradoxically
"allowed" Asian American women writers' works "to count in a public
way" (Warner 63). Rather than attribute the popularity of "Asian American women's literature" primarily to the spectacular desires of consumer
culture, I emphasize that changes in the function of literature and
debates surrounding contemporary citizenship have played major roles,
enabling a legibility for writers who are responding to social formations
under neoliberalism.

2 / Asian American Mother-Daughter Narrative and the Neoliberal American Dream of Transformative Femininity

Like every Asian American woman in her late twenties, I had the idea of writing an epic novel about mother-daughter relationships spanning several generations, based loosely on my own family's story. This was before Sophia was born, when I was living in New York, trying to figure out what I was doing working at a Wall Street law firm.
—AMY CHUA, *BATTLE HYMN OF THE TIGER MOTHER*

With the January 2011 publication of the essay "Why Chinese Mothers Are Superior" in the *Wall Street Journal*, Yale University law professor Amy Chua created a media spectacle about mothering in the United States that starred Asian American women. Obviously designed to provoke a dispute that would attract high-visibility exposure from such publicity venues as the *Today Show*, the article is composed of "controversial sections" from *Battle Hymn of the Tiger Mother*, Chua's memoir about raising two daughters to become culturally sophisticated, diligent, and "successful" Americans. It includes the observation, for example, "Western parents are concerned about their children's psyches. Chinese parents aren't. They assume strength, not fragility, and as a result they behave very differently." The desired firestorm quickly formed, with an intense tornado of Internet postings and articles expressing outrage, disbelief, and personal attacks against Chua as a "narrow-minded, joyless bigot"; there were even death threats (Liu). Other Asian American women were swiftly called in for their opinions on Chua's memoir, with commentary by such mother-daughter relationship experts as television-news-reporter-turned-HapaMama-blog-writer Grace Hwang Lynch and novelist Gish Jen.

The purpose of opening with this rather sensationalist tale is not to condemn Chua and her model of mothering nor to defend Chinese or Asian American mothers. Neither does this chapter take primary aim against the commodity fetishism of "mass culture" that alternately idealizes and demonizes mothers, even if *Asian American Women's Popular Literature* uses a decidedly critical approach to neoliberal capitalism and its cultural formations. Instead, this controversy exemplifies my assertion that the Asian American mother-daughter narrative, whether memoir or fiction, participates in a much broader conversation about mothering or what I describe as "neoliberal maternal discourse" that is also, and perhaps even more fundamentally, a conversation about neoliberal cultural citizenship or the mainstream practices and expressions that currently define what it means to be an American. Chua's memoir converses with such varied media "texts" as the personas of Michelle Obama's "Mom-in-Chief" and Sarah Palin's "Mamma Grizzly," the films *The Kids Are All Right* (2010) and *The Twilight Saga: Breaking Dawn* (2011), the reality shows *16 and Pregnant* (2009–) and *Secretly Pregnant* (2011–), and the Casey Anthony trial. This chapter explores the racialized dimensions of neoliberal maternal discourse (NMD) and specifically how Asian American mother-daughter novels may contribute to this often rousing and always complex exchange.

Whether by example or counterexample, fantasy or cautionary tale, or a combination of extremes, the narratives and texts that comprise NMD detail a version of contemporary Americanness for female subjects largely defined in the national imaginary by an ideology of femininity—a transformative femininity—that centralizes bourgeois motherhood, which is defined here as consumer-based affective and material practices associated with the white, middle-class nuclear family.[1] Put another way, NMD addresses a repronormative model of cultural citizenship for women characterized by "striving" and "responsible" participation in motherhood and consumer culture.[2] As overlapping and feminized domains, motherhood and consumer culture are popularly regarded in the contemporary United States as empowering and transformative, promising to positively regenerate the individual, the family, and the nation but also needing careful self-discipline, since they depend upon women's labor, paid and unpaid, material and affective. Neoliberal maternal discourse offers an important site for understanding changes in belonging and specifically the biological imperatives of gendered cultural citizenship, because the "reproduction of society takes place constantly through countless reiterative practices, many of which are structured as simultaneously productive and consumptive in nature" (Franke 189). Or, as Ruby C. Tapia has recently observed, US citizen-subjects are born and reborn through different maternities in the racialized productions of the maternal in public discourse (24).

Recontextualizing Asian American mother-daughter narratives within the constraints of neoliberal belonging, this chapter's analysis of

Patti Kim's *A Cab Called Reliable* (1997) and Lan Cao's *Monkey Bridge* (1997) starts with the premise that to claim full citizenship in the United States, female subjects, and especially women of color who are distanced from power, are compelled to participate in bourgeois motherhood. As importantly, women must publically display their cultural alignment with neoliberal values through producing and/or consuming transformation narratives about bourgeois motherhood, or updated fantasies of the American Dream, such as *Battle Hymn of the Tiger Mother*. As Ann Anagnost observes, the middle-class display of affective maternal labor "has become increasingly marked as a measure of value, self-worth, and citizenship in ways that beg an analysis of its specific formations" (142). Surely, the cultural preoccupation with reproduction exhibits public anxiety about an unpredictable future given the uncertainties of contemporary social life, and interpreting the cultural projection of anxieties symptomatically helps us recognize the meaning of the exclusion or demonization of all those who appear to threaten the social future by choosing not to reproduce. It also helps in understanding the terms of belonging for those who do reproduce (for) the nation, not simply as "a choice" but in relation to a discursive formation wherein subjects are produced through regulation, discipline, and resistance. Rather than part of a homogenous mass genre of sentimental realism that thoroughly contains women's claims to US citizenship and appeals only to disciples of normative white femininity, the mother-daughter narrative also functions as a space within NMD where subjects wrestle with neoliberalism's increased demands for consumption and labor from women, specifically the mandate to responsibly manage fertility and family through marketplace activities.[3] As part of NMD, the mother-daughter narrative in the hands of Asian American women writers has been important both in affirming the cultural citizenship of Asian American women and in articulating its limits, contributing insight into contemporary reformulations of citizenship that insist on recycling national myths of Americanness.

Neoliberal Maternal Discourse and Cultural Citizenship

> *In addition to witnessing the politics of woman's discipline to the norms of*
> *proper motherhood, it is important to recount this moment as a case study*
> *in the process of nation formation and its reliance on manipulation of the*
> *identity form to occlude the centrality of reproduction to the processes by*
> *which the nation rejuvenates itself.*
> —LAUREN BERLANT, *THE QUEEN OF AMERICA GOES*
> *TO WASHINGTON CITY*[4]

Reiterations about the reproduction of society within NMD, which began to coalesce in the 1970s, do seem countless and provide a cacophony of statements, "a deafening roar" of cultural narratives and media texts, about motherhood (Hewitt 132). As the section above suggests, I conceptualize this discourse expansively as popular constructions of feminine subjectivity that address the maternal in visual media forms both old and new, political rhetoric, and public controversies, as well as various print modes and genres, such as the memoir and the novel. Neoliberal maternal discourse overlaps with but significantly extends outside the "matrilineal discourse" described in Asian American literary studies, which focuses on Asian American female authors, maternal presences or surrogate mothers, and daughters' perspectives; NMD also goes well beyond "maternal discourse" as established in feminist literary studies, which focuses on contemporary women's writing that foregrounds the mother as intersubject with the daughter, is written from a mother's perspective or point of view, and features a mother's voice.[5] In this broader popular discourse, women are often represented as members of the nation only to the extent that they adhere to a model of motherhood that adopts the striving ethos, rhetorical tropes, and cultural practices of the neoliberal marketplace, including, most prominently, privatization, entrepreneurialism, and consumption (Ong 6). At the same time, this is most definitely not a seamless discourse and includes contributions that trouble or even contest the model. As E. Ann Kaplan influentially observes, the imaginary or mythic mother erupts in popular cultural discourse when changes in social formation produce new threats (15).[6] Given neoliberalism's investments in changing governance, citizenship, and subjectivity, we should understand NMD as a public response to these changes and a site for managing anxieties about them as well as providing affective experience, although not always the comfort of containment, in the cultural sphere.

Illustrating the interplay between popular culture media forms and formats, and the dissolving boundaries between culture, commerce, and politics, NMD is a deeply developed formation of print, visual, and digital intertexts. Although the narratives that link transformative femininity and belonging in NMD are not always books authored by women, I do not mean to suggest that the print mode is declining or is less important than other forms.[7] On the contrary, and particularly given the concomitant development of popular literary culture in the United States in which women are often the predominant readership or audience, books and particularly the novel are central in this discourse.[8] Further, *Asian American Women's Popular Literature*'s contention that Asian American women's popular literature has been important for the legibility of Asian American women's citizenship and that it has contributed to the contemporary reformulation of belonging is in large part based on the premise that authorship is one of several methods of displaying participation in mainstream culture as mandated by neoliberal cultural citizenship.

The wide range of fiction and nonfiction written by women about mothers, mothering, and motherhood that finds its way into public consciousness, whether as print texts, e-books, or filmic adaptations, is breathtaking. Neoliberal maternal discourse includes inspirational tales recounting difficult journeys, popular feminist texts that valorize the maternal, and acclaimed works about traumatic or untenable circumstances for mothering and daughtering. The popular genre fiction about motherhood dating from the early 1990s, sometimes referred to as "mommy lit," and not necessarily written by women, also figures prominently, as do blogs and websites that provide consumer parenting advice and self-help narratives that are typically preoccupied with working mothers and that ever-elusive "work-life balance" (Hewitt 122).[9] The "new" mommy lit has a spectacularly visible presence and includes autobiographical writing, especially the form of "the memoir" that commercial coaching websites such as *The Momoir Project* exhort, digital media texts or Internet mommy lit, online blogs and zines, and the community spaces of the "maternal feminist revolution."[10]

Susan Douglas and Meredith Michaels have recently characterized the popular media representation of mothers and motherhood that has permeated social life in the United States since the 1970s as a "postfeminist media obsession" with the idealization of motherhood (9). They call it the mythology of "the new momism," and largely attribute it to the emergence of mothers as a primary consumer market in advanced capitalism.[11] As a strict set of ideals, norms, and practices, the new momism is an ideological backlash against changes in the primacy of the maternal role for women in the family and specifically the increasing importance of women's wage labor. The new momism appears to celebrate motherhood, they explain, but presents standards of perfection that prey on anxieties to sell products and services, often through media controversies such as "the Mommy Wars" (4–5).[12] In *The Mommy Myth*, Douglas and Michaels examine "how the images of motherhood in TV shows, movies, advertising, women's magazines, and the news have evolved since 1970, raising the bar, year by year, of the standards of good motherhood while singling out and condemning those we were supposed to see as dreadful mothers" through the relentless recuperation of retrograde racial, class, gender, and national ideologies (14).

The relationship of feminism to popular culture's representation of contemporary motherhood has been a concern for scholars. While Douglas and Michaels locate the emergence of the new momism in the context of the US women's movement of the 1970s, they argue that it has become the central justifying ideology of postfeminism. Others have questioned to what extent "alternative" feminist mothers of the third wave have also adopted the idealization of motherhood in neoliberal marketplace terms (Thompson). As early as 1994, Suzanna Danuta Walters attributed the increasing prominence of the mother-daughter relationship in US popular culture (film, television, fiction, and magazines) to the influence of the women's liberation movement and academic feminism, but she regretted that it brought little change to dominant discourse and continued to reductively focus on the easily consumable, binary psychological destinies of "blame or bond" between mother and daughter (188, 223–34).[13] New terms such as "neoliberal feminism" (Grewal 28) and "consumer feminism" (Zeisler 105) have also been coined to name the close associations between popular discourses of female and maternal empowerment and consumer culture. These observations indicate how NMD functions in relation to a variety of feminisms, how effectively neoliberal market processes are able to incorporate political subjectivities and citizenship practices into "lifestyles," and indeed how neoliberalism as an ideology disarticulates and rearticulates other political rationalities or ethical regimes, such as feminism, as discussed in chapter 1.[14]

The model of cultural citizenship for women taken up in NMD is related not only to changes in the family that may be linked to feminism but also to recent changes in US citizenship that moved practices out of a political public sphere and into an intimate public sphere where private acts, values, and feelings associated with normative, heterosexual family life became the appropriate context for citizenship.[15] As Lauren Berlant influentially argues, the shift to privatized citizenship was a piece of "the cultural revolution of the Reaganite right," since it deliberately fetishized the family and private life in public discourse to revise American citizenship (31). A "tableau" of family, mother, and babies emerged as a national imaginary and "became the new sentimental icons of national culture" (123). Accordingly, Berlant connects the privatization of citizenship to a reinvigoration of the fantasy of the American Dream, which "fuses private fortune with that of the nation: it promises that if you invest your energies in work and family-making, the nation will secure the broader social and economic conditions in which your labor can gain value and your life can be lived with dignity" (4).

Updating narratives of the American Dream has been the focus of a great deal of energy across the neoliberal cultural landscape, even as social mobility has spiraled downward. Although we might imagine that such narratives would be a harder sell, as fantasy, family narratives of upward mobility seem to become increasingly compelling the further from reality they operate. Moreover, in neoliberal governance, when material conditions contradict dominant ideology, national myths and symbolic narratives take on an even more crucial role.[16] In this context, "reinhabiting structures of family and kinship" has become a strategy for a variety of neoliberal citizenship claims; it is the basis upon which gay men and lesbians have "come out" into the polity, for example, in the contemporary United States, most visibly since the 2003 decision protecting the privacy rights of same-sex couples in Lawrence v. Texas (Eng 27). In his study of queer liberalism, David Eng joins several other scholars in asserting that "good citizenship" has come to be even more explicitly defined through the conjugal marital couple and the heteronormative nuclear family, which is the racialized, property-owning building block of the "free market" global order (25).[17]

As the epigraph for this section indicates, the tableau of family in US popular culture of the late twentieth century was part of a sentimental manipulation of the identity category "woman" that occluded "the centrality of reproduction to the processes by which the nation rejuvenates itself" (Berlant 98). While manipulation still abounds, I suggest that at this point we are dealing with a somewhat different moment of struggle in which NMD continually *projects* the repronormativity prescribed for females and upon which the neoliberal nation state relies, in part illustrating and communicating the importance of displaying a transformative femininity for women's citizenship in the contemporary United States. Moreover, although the privatization of citizenship under neoliberalism still attempts to deflect attention away from the exploitation of women's reproductive labor, public discourse also registers the return of the repressed narrative of maternal labor for the family/nation. The desire for privatization in the neoliberal national imaginary is not fulfilled but is instead figured as a public repetition compulsion, potentially exposing a major contradiction in contemporary US capitalism and updated fantasies of the American Dream. Given the historical and contemporary trauma of women's national exclusion from liberal citizenship, particularly for Asian American women, NMD produces no narrative closure on the privatization of citizenship, repetitiously and symptomatically registers widespread anxiety about and discontent with the social conditions and value of mothering, and operates as a site for contending with the reigning model of gendered cultural citizenship that centralizes bourgeois motherhood as a transformative route to belonging in America, despite decreasing access to it.

As a contemporary biopolitical formation and site of political power and struggle over life, NMD projects and negotiates biological citizenship, and we should recognize strong links between the current model of cultural citizenship and biological citizenship, which is a neoliberal technology of self-governance in which "individuals themselves must exercise biological prudence for their own sake, that of their families, that of their own lineage, and that of the nation as a whole" (Rose, *Politics of Life Itself* 24). As Sarah Sharma reminds us, however, theorizing biopolitics as differential is necessary both to recognize complexity and multiplicity and to "consider the various technologies of power and self and the affective dimension of these investments and reductions into human life" (139). The biopolitical regulation of life "reduces *certain* life to bare life. At the same time it also invests in the lives of others, as in the maintenance of lifestyles" (139, emphasis in original). Similarly, Teresa Brennan understands that, along with the disciplined and regulated body, the biopolitical formations of neoliberalism create a "bio-deregulation of the body" for marginalized subjects who lack time, food, rest, and otherwise live with insecurity (20–24). Building on feminist, queer, and critical race theory, I argue that *A Cab Called Reliable* and *Monkey Bridge* help us understand the differential biopolitics of neoliberal cultural citizenship for Asian American and Asian diasporic female subjects. Before discussing the texts themselves, I pause briefly and return to Chua's memoir and to NMD as a racialized formation with specific relevance for Asian American mother-daughter narrative.

Asian American Mother-Daughter Narrative
and Neoliberal Maternal Discourse

> *Chinese-Americans, when you try to understand what things in you are*
> *Chinese, how do you separate what is peculiar to childhood, to poverty,*
> *insanities, one family, your mother who marked your growing with stories,*
> *from what is Chinese? What is Chinese tradition and what is the movies?*
> —MAXINE HONG KINGSTON, *THE WOMAN WARRIOR:*
> *MEMOIR OF A GIRLHOOD AMONG GHOSTS*

Beginning perhaps with the 1975 award-winning publication of *The Woman Warrior: Memoir of a Girlhood Among Ghosts,* and certainly since Amy Tan's novel *The Joy Luck Club* became a best seller in 1989, the mother-daughter narrative has been the most direct route to a mainstream audience for Asian American women writers, with motherhood as well as daughterhood explicitly part of that path.[18] In an article titled "Daughters of America," one reviewer of *The Joy Luck Club* observed that, "whether by a quirk of literary fate or because it is their psychological destiny, Chinese American women seem to have won the world rights to the mother-daughter relationship" (quoted in Grice 65–66).[19] Cultural authority on the mother-daughter relationship in the United States then extended to Asian American women writers generally. Some authors capitalized on the market that first Kingston and then Tan famously helped create by expanding into other "feminized" forms that had the potential to cross over, in the sense that they might reach both a more general female readership of a particular popular genre and a specifically Asian American audience. Of course, attributing the authorial choice by Chinese Americans or Asian Americans to write mother-daughter narratives, and their subsequent marketplace success, primarily to psychological or creative hard-wiring is clearly far too reductive and is palpable as cultural code for an essential racial trait, even within the rhetorical context of a postracial neoliberalism that advocates "color-blindness."

In fact, such essentialism was one reason for the very strong response, even outrage, over Chua's memoir.[20] *Battle Hymn of the Tiger Mother* uses the construct "Chinese motherhood" to refer to a neotraditionalist model of parenting that Chua defends, despite its drawbacks. As Latoya Peterson points out on her website *Racialicious,* Chua tries to broaden the definition of her terms:

> I'm using the term "Chinese mother" loosely. I recently met a
> supersuccessful white guy from South Dakota (you've seen him

on television), and after comparing notes we decided his working-class father had definitely been a Chinese mother. I know some Korean, Indian, Jamaican, Irish and Ghanaian parents who qualify too. Conversely, I know some mothers of Chinese heritage, almost always born in the West, who are not Chinese mothers, by choice or otherwise. (quoted in Peterson)

However, the "tongue-in-cheek explanations of cultural differences" and oscillation from metaphorical figure to anecdotal example go too far for Peterson, as they did for many of the over six thousand readers who posted online comments to Chua's article in the week following its publication (Peterson).

The chord that Chua struck and that catapulted the book to seventh on Amazon.com in just a few days helps to illuminate how the demands of the marketplace have shaped Asian American mother-daughter narratives and what kinds of cultural work they may perform in the national imaginary (Yang, "Mother Superior?"). The text is no simple idealization of a Chinese American mother's efforts to raise two multiracial daughters, and at certain moments in the text Chua does not uphold neoliberal values or illustrate consumer-based affective or material practices. This is evident, for example, when she insists that her daughters make their father a genuinely sincere birthday card rather than buy one, or when Chua does not permit sleepovers, a ritual site for the production of normative, consumption-based femininity.[21] Even if texts do not fully and faithfully stage bourgeois motherhood, however, they may manufacture it extratextually by creating desire and enabling readers' consumption of texts that do provide a narrative of transformative femininity in the context of neoliberal maternal discourse.[22] Indeed, *Battle Hymn of the Tiger Mother* once again positions the figure of the Asian American woman as a model American citizen, the *maternal model minority*, under the limelight. Related to the sexual model minority that Susan Koshy has theorized, in which the mediating figure of the Asian American woman becomes "emblematic of the perfect match between family-centrism and sex appeal," the maternal model minority is emblematic of a match between ideal motherhood and neoliberal capitalism's values of privatization, entrepreneurial reinvention, and consumerism, which combine for the normalizing reproduction of the nation (*Sexual Naturalization* 16–17). In another powerful rearticulation of Asian American femininity, and similar to the sexual model minority that "buttress[ed] and reviv[ed] a besieged ideal of the *American* family," the maternal model minority helps manage a cultural struggle over shifting narratives of the American Dream under a neoliberal political economy that relies upon new forms of feminized labor, consumption, and subjectivity (17, emphasis in original).

The figure of the maternal model minority, appearing most recently in the Tiger Mother, is positioned in the racial field of popular neoliberal maternal discourse in triangular relation to, on the one hand, the figure of the high-powered career woman, typically coded white, who has repudiated motherhood entirely or at least as her primary identification and social value.[23] This figure was the demonized side of the Mommy Wars media spectacle in the late 1980s and early 1990s that positioned working women against stay-at-home mothers and has been cinematically revived in characters such as Miranda Priestly (Meryl Streep) in the 2006 film *The Devil Wears Prada*. On the other hand, the maternal model minority plays opposite the figure of the "bad mother," often coded black, who both refuses to responsibly mother and refuses to labor in the marketplace. This figure was the scapegoat of "welfare reform" in the 1990s and more recently appeared in 2009 as Mo'Nique's character Mary in *Precious* (Harris-Lacewell). A version of the "Welfare Queen" is now also figured in the "alien" mother who does not properly regulate fertility and threatens to become dependent on the state, such as the immigrant mother of the "anchor baby" or even the cyborg "Octomom" Nadya Suleman. These stereotypical and racialized figures have specific cultural histories that emerge from distinct material forces, but they similarly stake out the most reductive space within the representational politics of contemporary popular culture that traffics in a social pedagogy that reflects the neoliberal values of gendered cultural citizenship. The "cultural difference" of the figure of the Asian American maternal model minority positions her between extremes within this racial field, where she balances motherhood with employment to prudently manage family and fertility.

The racialized, gendered, and nationalist ideological battles of the Mommy Wars have publically operated since the late 1980s as thinly veiled rationales for the exploitation of women's labor, unpaid and paid, and this has become even clearer in the past few years as new versions emerged in recessionary culture that called for women's sacrifice to and makeover responsibility for economic recovery. The inflection of the economic crisis is actually central to Chua's book since it focuses on social instability as the backdrop to "the risks she is willing to take to invest" in the future of her daughters.[24] As Clare Jean Kim influentially theorizes, the persistence and continuation of racial triangulation is matched by specific historical formations, with the contemporary model minority manifestation first emerging in the mid-1960s with immigration policy and economic changes (118–20). While Asian Americans are positioned as models relative to African Americans in a black/white binary of racial dynamics that reroutes African American claims to equal rights and full citizenship, the model also rests on the presumption that Asian Americans are "culturally distinctive" or immutably foreign in relation to white Americans. This claim has been revamped in various ways in the past forty years in periods of racial change and cultural instability when codes that celebrate marginality have been modified in divisive politics that continue to ostracize Asian Americans, in what may be called the double discourse of the model minority thesis.

Indeed, model minority cultural assumptions of "distinctive" family solidarity, diligence, respect for education, and self-sufficiency align with the privatization of citizenship under neoliberalism to revive the trope of the purportedly apolitical Asian American who is "too busy getting ahead and making money to care about politics" (C. Kim 118). Shifts in belonging that privilege "autonomous, responsible choice-making subjects who can serve the nation best by becoming 'entrepreneurs of the self'" recuperate standard scripts of Americanization since they valorize affluence; are indebted to the property-owning, rational, bourgeois subject considered ideal in liberalism; and assume upward mobility (Ong, *Buddha Is Hiding* 9). In short, the contributing and striving neoliberal citizen "fits snuggly with the independent, self-supporting image of the model minority" (Das Gupta 55). Koshy indicates as well that the feminized figure of the model minority monitors and manages unruly whiteness. In NMD, maternal model minorities instruct all female worker-consumers to update their "skill set" for an advanced-capitalist marketplace in which they must participate in the transformations of motherhood and consumer culture and reproduce the social order to become good citizens, as my readings of *A Cab Called Reliable* and *Monkey Bridge* will show.

Generational Variations on a Theme

> *It's ultimately my responsibility—my strict Chinese mom told me "never blame other people for your problems!"*
> —AMY CHUA, "WHY CHINESE MOTHERS ARE SUPERIOR"

Hovering between the literary and the commercial, the marginal and the mainstream, Patti Kim's *A Cab Called Reliable* and Lan Cao's *Monkey Bridge* address the American Dream as it is being reimagined in the neoliberal era, registering reconfigurations of the gendered racial belonging, contingency, and exclusion of Asian American women. Both books received immediate attention upon publication and were similarly included in Linda Lesher's *The Best Novels of the Nineties: A Readers' Guide;* while Kim received the 1997 Towson University Prize for Literature and was nominated for the Book-of-the-Month Club's Stephen Crane award for First Fiction, Cao's novel was reviewed in high-visibility venues, such as the *Christian Science Monitor.* Isabelle Thuy Pelaud points out that Cao's *Monkey Bridge* was the first Vietnamese American work to be reviewed in the *New York Times*, and by no less than the influential literary curator Michiko Kakutani (139). No doubt because the mother-daughter story is suspended and replaced with a father-daughter story in *A Cab Called Reliable, Monkey Bridge* drew more frequent comparisons from critics to the famous earlier narratives by Kingston and Tan.[25] Primarily told from the point of view of daughters, centrally concerned with recuperating diasporic mothers, and representing protagonists as authors, both texts illustrate characteristics of Asian American mother-daughter writing as described by Wendy Ho, Helena Grice, and Patricia Chu, respectively.[26] While *Monkey Bridge* features a mother who is emotionally distant and receding further from her daughter, *A Cab Called Reliable* is a story with a physically absent mother at its center. As the daughters recall their desire to recover their mothers, they provide rather unflattering portraits of their mothers and even more condemning representations of themselves.

Reminiscences of narrator-protagonists' immigration, early education, and youth, these fictional texts clearly draw upon the novel of female development or the bildungsroman, and also may be considered distant descendents of the sentimental and domestic novels, all popular forms that have been understood to interpellate readers into normative gender, class, racial, and national subject positions (P. Chu 14–15). Realist mother-daughter writing that makes use of the bildung narrative has been devalued in Asian American literary studies as individual and familial stories of reconciliation that serve as allegories for the formation of the citizen who relinquishes difference, and as stories that elicit reader identification with "an idealized 'national' form of subjectivity" (Lowe 98).[27] Some scholars have nevertheless appreciated the generic revisions and adaptations that Asian American authors make and the possible alternative purposes for using realist forms.[28] They have either questioned the idea that entire mediums, such as print texts; entire forms, such as the novel; or entire aesthetic modes, such as realism and naturalism, are inevitable "accomplices in bourgeois nationalist totalization" that "necessarily produce 'mimetic' results," in readers (Ling 21). Newer approaches build upon the understanding that realist narratives such as the bildungsroman may be "site[s] for both the construction and the contestation of cultural meanings," neither wholly complicit nor purely resistant (S. S. Wong 130). Jinqi Ling and Patricia Chu, for example, understand the authoring of realist works as textual practices that participate in a range of strategies and negotiations and locate Asian American writing as an active agent in the cultural formation of history.[29]

In addition to the bildungsroman and other realist forms, the contemporary Asian American mother-daughter narrative is associated with hybridization. While genres are less stable than many critics acknowledge, I consider the mother-daughter narrative an especially enterprising genre, well suited for registering the shifting sands of political subjectivity under neoliberalism. Alluding to and borrowing tropes from *The Woman Warrior, A Cab Called Reliable* and *Monkey Bridge* similarly defy neat literary categorization.[30] *A Cab Called Reliable* and *Monkey Bridge* also draw liberally from the conventions of various genres and modes and detail a context of convergent popular culture media forms. The story told in *A Cab Called Reliable* is a fictional multigenre mother-daughter narrative, a pastiche that remixes excerpts of the narrator's childhood poetry and fiction with letters, memoir, biographies of the narrator's female relatives and ancestors in Korea, historical and ethnographic sketches of Korea, and photographs of her mother, brother, and a friend. Among other sources that typically carry relatively stable indexical bonds to "reality," the narrator's presentation of photographs alongside more obviously fictional elements blurs distinctions between fictional and nonfictional texts and points to the constructed nature of all cultural narratives, even if the cover of *A Cab Called Reliable* declares that it is "*A Novel.*"[31] Without photographs but with more expository consideration for how various popular media such as film and television shape national subjects, *Monkey Bridge* also calls attention to the instability of realist narrative through the repeated interruption and revision of Mai's story by Thanh's point of view through the insertion of her diary entries and letters into the text.

Generic hybridity, intertextuality, and pastiche indicate that both novels are explicitly paranarrative or interested in how narratives are constructed and how they produce subjectivity, community, and national belonging within contemporary convergence culture. Such techniques seem to explore the possibility of disrupting hegemonic codes, and both texts do represent the American Dream, Orientalism, and model minority racialization as powerful ideological forces that may at times be contested. Moreover, *A Cab Called Reliable* and *Monkey Bridge* extend the notion that Asian American women's literature is "the fiction of matrilineage" (Grice 35). To the reclamation of erased, silenced, or absent Asian American women forebearers, they add widely recognized Asian American authors of mother-daughter texts from an earlier generation who may be contextualized in relation to contemporary NMD.

At the level of authorship, Kim and Cao demonstrate their cultural citizenship through writing and modifying mother-daughter print narratives, a mainstream cultural form that appropriately displays transformative femininity. They also make self-conscious use of the strong association of Asian American women, post-Kingston and -Tan, with expertise on mother-daughter relationships and the cultural capital of authoring "high pop" multicultural literature by presenting narrators who have likewise authored texts in the recent past of the diegesis, when they were growing up (Middleton Meyer 94). Kim's Ahn Joo first took up creative writing as a child to manage the grief of her mother's absence, while Mai's story about her mother's mental illness begins with a foreshadowing flashback to Mai's volunteer work at a Saigon hospital where she transcribed "battlefield memories and dying declarations" (Cao 12). As demonstrated by their expertise as narrators, as the two protagonists were growing up they honed cultural skills and adapted cultural narratives, especially the neoliberal American Dream of transformative femininity. While the narrator-daughters do not literally become maternal model minorities, they promote and at times adopt the practices of bourgeois motherhood that they desire but do not see in their mothers, deploying the neoliberal tropes of individual agency, choice, and responsibility, and matching motherhood with the neoliberal cultural values of privatization, entrepreneurial reinvention, and consumerism.

At the same time, I contend that these novels ironize the authorship of mother-daughter narratives as an empowering route to belonging by undercutting their own narrators, since their reminiscences betray a failure to remain in relation to their mothers. The family plot that typically figures belonging ultimately unravels in these novels as narrator-daughters recall how they harshly judged their "bad" mothers for not conforming to neoliberal rationalities. Kim and Cao modify mother-daughter narratives by offering novels that do not fully endorse the sanctity of bourgeois motherhood as a sentimental narrative code of neoliberal cultural citizenship or even Asian American revisions of it. More specifically, *A Cab Called Reliable* and *Monkey Bridge* suspend the transformations—of both mothers and daughters—so often central in the mother-daughter narratives featured in NMD, neither fully rejecting or accepting them, and draw critical attention to the current reconfiguration of the American Dream. In identifying this narrative practice, I reference Anne Cheng's influential theorization of Asian Americans as suspended between rejection and incorporation in a nation that depends upon "exclusion-yet-retention of racialized others" (10). In this melancholic dynamic, which has developed in the United States from a history of racism that contradicts national democratic ideals, a dominant white national subject continually feeds off of or consumes the racial other it mourns and denies, while the racial other is suspended in a marginal space in relation to the nation.

A Cab Called Reliable and *Monkey Bridge* do not end in happy resolution in which mother and daughter mirror white, middle-class women and reassure readers that Asian American patriarchy can be resisted and Asian American difference can be "overcome" or "healed," as literary critics have contended in charges of "sugar sisterhood" (S.-L. Wong, "Sugar Sisterhood") and "model minority discourse" (Palumbo-Liu, *Asian/American*). Nor do the mothers and daughters mirror each other through completing similar emotional searches for inner strength, literally revisiting the motherland for cultural identification, or even suffering through feminized impoverishment to arrive at mutual middle-class comfort in the United States, plot developments Patricia Chu has identified in Asian American mother-daughter bildungsromane. Instead, these texts end with mother and daughter worlds apart: they closely scrutinize the narrators who exhort their mothers to adopt the striving cultural practices of bourgeois motherhood and become maternal model minorities, and they examine the ways in which the narrators embrace and display repronormative family practices, entrepreneurial reinvention, and participation in consumer culture. Through contrasting conceptions of maternality, embodied by different generations, *A Cab Called Reliable* and *Monkey Bridge* negotiate and present a variation of the Mommy Wars. Unlike so many other representations in NMD, however, these novels present no victors.

A Cab Called Reliable is told from the first-person perspective of Ahn Joo Cho, a young adult character who immigrated to Arlington, Virginia, from Pusan, South Korea, with her mother, father, and younger brother when she was in the first grade. Kim's ironic stance toward her narrator and perhaps toward the mother-daughter narrative as a sort of cultural vehicle for belonging is announced in the novel's title and immediately introduced by Ahn Joo, who begins by retelling the story of the day in third grade when she returned home from school to find her mother and brother leaving the family in a taxi whose company brand name, painted on the car door, was "Reliable," a word she did not recognize. As Ahn Joo recounts how she struggled to understand her mother's apparent return to Korea and how she tried to salvage some kind of connection with her through the stories she learned to craft as a budding creative writer, the narrator discloses a family torn apart by domestic violence and the unfulfilled fantasies of American Dream transformation. The novel vividly recalls the Cho family's first years in the United States when Ahn Joo's abusive and alcohol-addicted father was an underpaid laborer and her mother washed dishes, delivered newspapers, and babysat to support their family. After two years and discovering that life in the United States was worse, not better, than life in Korea, Ahn Joo's mother left, while her father persisted, cycling through a series of jobs welding fences; selling hotdogs to tourists on the Washington, DC, mall from a vending truck; and eventually opening his own lunch counter. The novel ends when Ahn Joo is in college and on the day that she herself leaves her father to live on her own as an adult.

Cao's *Monkey Bridge* similarly focuses on the cleavage between the narrator Mai Nguyen and her mother, Thanh, both refugee Vietnamese who settled in the immigrant community of Little Saigon in Falls Church, Virginia. As described by this first-person narrator, the tension became a serious conflict when Mai began to prepare for college at seventeen and Thanh suffered a stroke. Thanh had been withholding from Mai their family history and the details of her departure from Viet Nam three years earlier in 1975. The plan was for Thanh to come to the United States with her father, Baba Quan, and join Mai, who had left a few months earlier with the help of the American Colonel and family friend Michael MacMahon ("Uncle Michael"). But Thanh arrived alone, with no real explanation of Baba Quan's absence. In an effort to restore her mother's health, Mai attempts to relocate Baba Quan, reconstruct her family narrative, and revise familial roles with the cultural skills and resources she has gathered as a new and aspiring American. At the end of this process, which is revealed to be entirely inadequate, Mai learns that Baba Quan is not her biological grandfather and that her mother has fabricated much of the family history. If Patricia Chu finds that the mother-daughter narrative is a utopian family romance that affirms cultural citizenship, *A Cab Called Reliable* and *Monkey Bridge* are closer to dystopian cautionary tales about reproducing the maternal romance as a route to belonging. Although these are in some ways pessimistic plots, they clarify that cultural citizenship practices need not fully endorse the repronormative nuclear family that prevails in American Dream narratives and neoliberal citizenship discourses alike.

Striving for Authorship of the American Dream in *A Cab Called Reliable*

In the story she narrates in *A Cab Called Reliable*, Ahn Joo describes how she became an astute critic of late-twentieth-century America as she made her way through the US public school system in the 1970s, and she highlights how she ultimately rejected many of the governing assumptions of her education.[32] As Elaine Kim writes, *A Cab Called Reliable* makes Ahn Joo's "miseducation clear" (88). I emphasize that the novel goes beyond a critique of liberal multiculturalism in schooling and beyond the plot of the bildungsroman that focuses on formal education, since I read it as a bracing challenge to the American Dream, including ironic commentary on Ahn Joo's own adoption of a neoliberal model of gendered cultural citizenship that was unavailable and untenable for her mother.[33] Education structures Ahn Joo's bildung narrative and is central to her story, with the first sentences of the novel situating the place and time of her story in relation to "Sherwood Elementary School" (P. Kim 1). Subsequent chapters proceed chronologically, often beginning with a new academic year, the introduction of her teacher, a description of Ahn Joo's relationship with the teacher, and an evaluation of what she learned that year. Ahn Joo narrates the difference between what she was taught as she was growing up and what she learned in a defiantly proud tone that conveys how she resisted late-twentieth-century versions of US Orientalism, model minority racialization, and normative femininity. But her poetic efforts and fiction writing illustrate that the technologies of power at play in school still have their effects. Her resistance and analytical skills, however critical, broke down in her own representations of her mother, which reinstall familiar stereotypes and the figure of the maternal model minority. The text embeds a mother-daughter tale about cultural citizenship in a mother-daughter narrative, communicating what is and what is not possible given imperatives for participation in mainstream cultural narratives in neoliberal citizenship.

Ahn Joo's narrative carefully documents the quotidian Orientalism she encountered, from the school crossing guard who asked her where she was from, to classmates who thought that Ahn Joo and Sun Joo, a new student with the same middle name, must be related, to the string of teachers who assumed hers was the ideal immigrant experience from "third world oppression" to "American opportunity." This documentation is paired with a recollection of Ahn Joo's increasingly irreverent attitude when, for example, she was called upon to recite the Pledge of Allegiance, and required to read from the textbook *Our Western Civilization*. By the time she entered Weston Junior High, where she was misplaced in a gifted and talented trigonometry class because she was "quiet, looked Chinese, and wore glasses," Ahn Joo overtly contested the model minority thesis that so thoroughly informed her education (P. Kim 100). The narrator recalls that she rebelliously (or self-destructively) cheated and deliberately failed her academic subjects in order to be categorized as a "troubled adolescent" by Mrs. Hubbel, a reluctant counselor who told her, "[Y]ou were not meant to be a delinquent" (97–98). Ahn Joo was also critical of the imposition of heteronormative femininity and "the clusters of fours and sixes" or the cliques of girls that excluded her and whom she searingly characterized as superficially preoccupied with "kiwi-flavored lip gloss, the hemline of their skirts, love notes folded into the shape of stars" (100).[34] Rather than trying to conform, Ahn Joo disrupted their circles, confronting the "simpletons who decorated other simpletons' lockers with streamers and balloons . . . to ensure the returned favor on their own birthdays" (101). She stole a bottle of perfume from a cheerleader's locker, wrote pornographic love letters to a girl who read romances in the cafeteria, and "kicked the soccer ball into Jane Jordan's face when a game wasn't in session" (98–99). Ahn Joo tells the reader that these were deliberate, unruly acts, which she believed would demonstrate her agency and superiority to the "pigs living in mediocrity" (100).

Although Ahn Joo was sympathetic when her father pleaded for her to "[*s*]*tudy hard, place first in your class, become a doctor or lawyer, take care of me, make money, make my suffering pay off, make my sacrifice worthwhile*," as narrator she refuses to corroborate the "strong family ties" of the idealized Korean family in which "all lived happily together," as described in the *World Book* encyclopedia in her sixth-grade classroom (125, emphasis in original 83). In addition to the poverty, alcoholism, and physical abuse in her family in the United States, Ahn Joo reveals a long history of family violence, mental illness, and betrayals in Korea, and subtly alludes to the context of US militarism in Korea, even though it was entirely excised from the official sources she consulted at school as a child. Throughout her recollection of her formative years, the narrator is careful to refute the discourses that interpellated her as model minority, "American feminine," and "dutiful Asian daughter," even when reproduced by her father. As if to punctuate her resistance, the novel ends with Ahn Joo recounting how she left her father's Potomac home to pursue her individual dream of becoming a writer.

But the novel ironically contrasts Ahn Joo's story of her critical agency and resistance to mainstream ideologies and cultural scripts of success with the parallel story of her development as a writer, which highlights Ahn Joo's juvenilia, where she creatively attempted to transform her mother, who did not align with the dominant ideology of motherhood. However much Ahn Joo condemned the racism, standards of white femininity, and cultural imperialism that marginalized her, she attributed her sense of alienation and feelings of loneliness while growing up primarily to what she considered her mother's selfish abandonment. She initially mourned and coped with her feelings about the trauma at home by writing therapeutic poetry, such as "Tears in the Toilet," titled for her mother's frequent retreat to the relative safety of the bathroom. In "Reliable," an ironic poetic meditation and a vocabulary-building exercise written soon after her mother's departure, each letter of the title word begins a separate stanza, with the second "L" describing her mother's love:

> L is for love. My mother used to sing Korean love songs. One was about the love for a river. Another was about the love for a mountain. And another was about the love of a mother. She sang about chrysanthemums, barley fields, and whispering winds. She knew many songs by heart. But only one line to only one song was taught to me: "It's not love if you can't let me go." (P. Kim 24–25)

While "Reliable" again acknowledges Ahn Joo's troubled family in a first stanza that laments how much she missed her mother and brother who "went away," in this poem the persona omits all reference to violence. It seems to blame her *un*reliable mother through a metaphorical representation of her love as abstract, detached, and unknowable—an unmistakable representation of the racial stereotype of the inscrutable Asian. Ahn Joo shared the piece with her third-grade teacher, Miss Washburn, who was moved to pitying tears and chose the title as the vocabulary word of the week, displaying the poem on the classroom bulletin board. But Ahn

Joo discovered that this failed maternality was not the sort to publicize, so she traded her definition of "reliable" for another student's definition of "exotic," underscoring the lesson that this portrait of her mother was too far removed from mainstream bourgeois motherhood to be easily consumed.

Thereafter, for school officials and fellow students alike the young Ahn Joo fabricated elaborate lies about her small family and tragic explanations of premature or accidental death for her mother's absence. Soon she created flattering representations of a striving mother in her creative writing, which helped her manage her own painful feelings and the normative familial sentiments and acts that were expected for belonging, since these works appropriately displayed her mother's gender and femininity. Indeed, Ahn Joo quickly learned to adapt popular tropes and narratives, studying and incorporating the meaning of new words such as "martyr" in imaginative works that vividly reflected an idealized mother and a form of child-rearing which Sharon Hays has named "intensive mothering." As the dominant ideology of mothering in the United States since the mid-twentieth century, this model "tells us that children are innocent and priceless, that their rearing should be carried out primarily by individual mothers and that it should be centered on children's needs, with methods that are informed by experts, labor-intensive, and costly" (Hays 21).[35] In its recent elaboration in the new momism, intensive mothering conveys that "no woman is complete or fulfilled unless she has kids, that women remain the best primary caretakers of children, and that to be a remotely decent mother, a woman has to devote" herself entirely to her children (Douglas and Michaels 4). It is typically presented as a universal or naturalized standard, but this ideal of motherhood in the United States is a myth reserved for a subset of privileged, white American women, evidenced through consumption, central to conceptions of femininity, and now a requirement of a citizenship model in which rights and practices are framed as consumer choices (Thompson). Although "it has never been followed in practice by the majority of parents, the model of the white, native-born middle-class has long been and continues to be, the most powerful, visible, and self-consciously articulated" (Hays 21).

While Ahn Joo recalls that anything she wrote about Korea impressed her teachers and peers, the selection of poems and stories that are reproduced in *A Cab Called Reliable* and that brought her positive attention are sentimental mother-daughter narratives in which Ahn Joo reconstructed her mother as a bourgeois maternal figure in the mold of intensive mothering—a maternal model minority who emulates and manages repronormative white femininity. The novel also makes plain that Ahn Joo was tutored in school to glean material from "official" authorities, rather than from her own experiences or knowledge of Korean or Korean American culture. Given this context of discursive constraints, after a few years of aestheticizing, fictionalizing, and narrating her mother and their relationship in poetry and short stories, Ahn Joo learned specifically which portrayals of femininity would appeal to her mainstream audience and mastered the appropriately deracinated "knowledge" of Korea that it expected to have affirmed. In response to the theme of "My Family," for example, Ahn Joo researched details about Korea at school and penned "The Voice of My Mother," which won first place in the Young Writer's Award contest in sixth grade. Collapsing two cultural registers, the prose poem is composed of a selection of Korean colloquialisms, maternal advice, and protective warnings that reflect the tenets of intensive mothering. It earned Ahn Joo her teachers' sympathy, applause from classmates and their parents, and the gift of a typewriter from her father. What began as a therapeutic strategy for coping with the loss of her mother became the active management of dominant discourse and a sort of "ethnic entrepreneurialism" through which she could present her mother and herself as "successful" Americans in exchange for a sense of social belonging, as well as maintain some measure of connection with her mother.[36]

Ahn Joo also experimented in performance art, creating the persona of "Palmer," replete with a matrilineal heritage of gifted palm readers extending back through a devoted mother to a great-great-grandmother. She sold "futures, fortunes, and tales during lunch and recess" to the delight of her classmates, who heard the promise of transformation in the narratives she created (P. Kim 60). Ahn Joo became wildly popular by telling her classmates what they wanted to hear and feel, kneeling before them to trace the line of the heart in each palm, despite charging them a quarter and limiting services to one fortune per student. More than a reclamation of absent forbearers or even a reconstruction of her relationship with her mother, Ahn Joo's genealogical narrative and the legacy of Palmer function in the novel as a parable of bourgeois motherhood. It exemplifies how mothers should align with neoliberal values and reproduce responsible subject-citizens who are also able to skillfully reinvent themselves through striving entrepreneurialism. Encouraged and rewarded at school through a creative education that involved affective and ideological self-discipline, Ahn Joo wrote mother-daughter narratives that transformed her mother to fit the mold of the maternal model minority, rewrote their relationship, and reinvented herself as heir to maternal marketplace responsibility.

Ironically, during her most rebellious period in junior high, Ahn Joo expanded her maternal reinventions to visual narrative. While frantically searching for information about her mother, she found three photographs in her father's dresser and again reimagined her mother as an idealized figure: she created dialogue with interlocutors in which her mother gave virtuous middle-class explanations about education for why Ahn Joo remained in the United States, practiced posing like her mother, and "tried to live in a world that was black and white" (P. Kim 102). Similar to her earlier creative works and the matrilineage she traced in her palmistry, the narrative Ahn Joo composed from the photographs reconstructed her mother's life in the biopolitical terms of conventional gender ideology. Visually, the photographs of her mother (fig. 2.1) are represented in a three-page sequence for a chronological narrative that reflects the repronormative temporality of transformative femininity, with the first depicting her as the big sister of a pouting younger brother, the second an innocent schoolgirl with dimples and averted glance, and finally an attentive mother on a family outing at the beach. Assumptions about socialization, life cycle, and women's "biological clock" are naturalized in this sequence for the reproduction of the nuclear family in normative time, which depends upon the temporalities of family, reproductive, and inheritance time (Halberstam 5). Although the photographs are presented as visual evidence of a bourgeois mother's biography, readers know that they are part of Ahn Joo's childhood fantasies, or a nostalgic transformation that has not taken place in the fictional world of the novel; more accurately, the diasporic mother has been refused entrance into the social order, which does not resemble its representation in mainstream cultural narratives.

A series of eleven unsent and mostly unfinished letters to her mother confirm Ahn Joo's alignment with the neoliberal tropes, scripts, and cultural values that claim to signify Americanness. The first few are informational and formal in tone, notifying her mother of their new address and telephone number in Potomac. The letters become progressively more descriptive, providing details about their improved lives, the large size of their townhouse, her father's success in business, and her plans to study literature and creative writing in college. They are written as testimonies, especially to how Mr. Cho had "changed beyond recognition," and read like American Dream narratives with the transformation of the striving

FIGURE 2.1. Ahn-Joo uses photographs of her mother to produce narratives about transformative femininity. Photographs courtesy of Patti Kim.

individual into the responsible economic citizen who participates in production and consumption as their recognizable plot point (P. Kim 106).

The letters similarly reveal Ahn Joo's investments in intensive mothering and the maternal model minority figure, particularly through how they interpellate her mother as a "failure," in contrast to "all good mothers" (108). The most revealing letter is one in which she castigates her mother for leaving:

> As a young woman, I now see that you suffered greatly living with Father. You suffered greatly living with me. Your life here was torturous. You were unhappy, and what is greater or more rational than having as one's sole purpose in life the fulfillment of one's own personal happiness? And when you were given the opportunity to pursue a happier, more self-satisfying, comfortable and complacent existence without me, you didn't hesitate. Your choice did not exactly heighten my hope for humanity nor was it one I would characterize as heroic, admirable, or meritorious. Your choice was that of any feeble-minded, well-fed, common woman. (107–8, emphasis in original)

Ahn Joo's emphasis on her mother's "choice" to leave the United States echoes the marketplace fundamentalism or "free market" principle of neoliberalism in which the American Dream of individual success is purportedly available to anyone who takes personal responsibility, works hard, and makes rational economic choices. Survival and prosperity are always choices in the neoliberal worldview, reflecting the enhancement of one's human capital; hardship in this model results from "a lack of

competitive strength or because of personal, cultural, and political fail-
ings" (Harvey 157). Indeed, in this letter Ahn Joo condemns her mother
for not being ambitious enough and for not correctly choosing a genuine
renovation that would align with transformative femininity and bourgeois motherhood, or the mandates of cultural belonging. In Ahn Joo's
evaluation, her mother took the easy way out and opted instead for comfortable individual happiness.

In this scathing missive, the gendered racial subject is held indi-
vidually responsible, while the individual costs that Asian diasporic
and immigrant women must pay in pursuit of the American Dream
remain invisible, since the daughter ignores her mother's labor to support the family. Further, Ahn Joo snarkily discounts the physical and
emotional abuse in the family that jeopardized her mother's personal
survival and blithely displaces it, reconstructing her reason for leaving as a more benign unhappiness. Similar to Ronyoung Kim's *Clay
Walls* (1984), a female bildungsroman in which a Korean immigrant
family's efforts to fit a middle-class model result in the household
as a site of both economic exploitation and physical violence for the
mother, *A Cab Called Reliable* links structural inequalities, discourses
of power, and violence in the family but also draws attention to their
subject effects on the narrator who cannot make the same connections. Unable to acknowledge the social conditions that disallowed the
personal "choice" of transformative femininity for her mother, and
constrained by the gendered racial ideological terms of the neoliberal
American Dream in understanding her mother's return to Korea, Ahn
Joo regards her departure as a refusal of the imperatives of neoliberal
citizenship. Ahn Joo represents her not as an individual who takes
responsibility for personal safety, but as an individual wholly responsible for the family's fragmentation.

When Ahn Joo finally acknowledges to the reader that a good portion of her childhood was spent imagining the good mother she longed
for, the narrative shifts focus to her relationship with her father, sus-
pending a mother-daughter story in which the mother purportedly
remains unchanged and unruly, while the daughter continues to discipline and reinvent herself. Ahn Joo never fully returns to the story of
her mother, and the mother appears excluded from or denied the narrative of transformation centralized in NMD. In addition, in the final
pages of the novel, Ahn Joo recounts the preparations she made to leave
her father and the moment when she learned that she was adopted.
Recalling the Freudian family romance that fantasizes liberation from

the constraints of the family through an interrogation of origins and imagining the self as orphan, this narrative twist supplies easy closure for Ahn Joo and the book, as it releases Ahn Joo from what she sees as her mother's inadequacies and refusal to transform (Hirsch 9). The diasporic mother Ahn Joo blamed, the absent mother Ahn Joo mourned throughout her childhood, and the ideal, self-sacrificing mother Ahn Joo nostalgically longed for and reinvented in her poetry and fiction, were not her mother, either in a wholly satisfying emotional sense or in a technical, biological sense. Read in this way, the ending suggests that despite so many efforts to subject her mother to the discursive technologies of neoliberal citizenship, or perhaps because of those efforts, Ahn Joo's relationship with her was entirely fictive, which seems to release the daughter.

Laden with the family plot as allegory for social belonging, *A Cab Called Reliable*'s closing more convincingly suggests that despite the promise of higher education for Ahn Joo, the neoliberal American Dream in the late twentieth century is a fantasy of transformation. In the end, the book finally recounts how familial ties are strained or even severed in striving to adhere to or adapt dominant scripts of belonging.[37] Ahn Joo clarifies that while her father's small business provided enough income for them to move to the suburbs, she remembers a childhood of working alongside her father in the evenings, on weekends, and in the summer, when she witnessed how he was repeatedly humiliated and the business vandalized. Contrary to what she reported to her mother in the unsent letters, immigrant entrepreneurship as a successful route to the American Dream is rigorously challenged by Ahn Joo's own story, particularly when she recalls her response to the burglary of her father's store when she was in high school:

> I wanted to tell him the robbery and the urine were absolute injustices, we were wronged, and the guilty would eventually have to pay their karma debt. All of them. For stabbing Angela's father, for holding Yoo Jin's mother at gunpoint underneath the toilet, for shooting off Mr. Hong's ear for a couple of hundred dollars and a bag of chips, for calling Mrs. Kim a stingy money-hungry chink because she refused to give her customers cleaning for free or because she charged extra for boxed shirts, for making me write badly to save myself from being accused of copying out of a book, for telling me to go back to where I came from (how can I return to my mother's womb?), for stretching their large, long, curly-lashed

eyes at me while singing about my being Chinese and Japanese, for making me want to look, walk, eat, sleep, talk like them, for expecting me to sit quietly in the back of the classroom, for making me repeat my question two or three times because no one could hear my voice squeezed out of a throat that always had clay caught in the center except when it was speaking to Father. (P. Kim 124–25)

This private list of grievances is a long and important one, but it omits both the labor and the injustice that Ahn Joo's mother endured and again illustrates the repressed narrative of maternal labor in Ahn Joo's story. The narrative resurfaces, however, because the list alludes to a much longer one that the young Maxine in *The Woman Warrior* tried to tell her mother one day in their family laundry business (Kingston 198–200). Maxine's painful litany of over two hundred items also details injustice for Asian immigrants in the United States. What is unbearable from Maxine's perspective is that it had gone unspoken, which Maxine believed created emotional distance from her mother.

Kim's allusion to *The Woman Warrior* suggests that Ahn Joo's list of grievances also separates the daughter and mother in *A Cab Called Reliable*.[38] The list is problematic to their relationship not so much because it remains unspoken but more precisely because of what it excludes or represses, which is any recognition of the mother—not her labor, not her mistreatment or suffering, not even her departure and supposed refusal to mother. In this context, Ahn Joo's comment about writing "badly" may be read as an unconscious but nevertheless pedagogical statement about how the culturally adaptive practices that she learned and displayed in her juvenilia nearly displaced her mother entirely, not only in the writing that was publically rewarded but even more so in her own psyche. Implicitly commenting on the relationship between genre and genealogy, Kim's allusion acknowledges Kingston as a "literary mother" and also remarks upon shifts in historical and material conditions under which the genre is remade by authors in the 1990s in Kim's generation, including Cao. Indeed, both authors wrote their novels after neoliberalism had become hegemonic and in the specific historical moment in which immigrant mothers receiving welfare were demonized as irresponsible and then removed from the rosters of public support or assistance. Finally, in Ahn Joo's comment I read Kim's ironic stance toward the authorship of mother-daughter narratives as a route to cultural belonging and toward the model of neoliberal female citizenship that centralizes bourgeois motherhood.

As with *The Woman Warrior, A Cab Called Reliable* features a narrator-daughter on the verge of an educational rite of passage, typically understood as empowering and fundamental to the American Dream of upward mobility; however, it registers intense anxiety about precarious family life, immigrant exploitation in ethnic enclaves and family businesses, and costly efforts to participate in mainstream US consumer culture. While *A Cab Called Reliable* suspends the narrative of transformative femininity for a diasporic Korean mother through a narrator-daughter who both compulsively projects and represses her mother's story, the daughter's belonging is also questioned by an uncertain narrative futurity. The novel cautions readers that, for Asian American female subjects, contributing to the narrative of the American Dream by managing the match between ideal motherhood and neoliberalism or through reproducing the gendered racial figure of the maternal model minority may still leave them simultaneously excluded and retained but now through their own "badly" written stories.

Empowering Entrepreneurs in *Monkey Bridge*

One of the first published fictional narratives about refugee Vietnamese in the United States written by a Vietnamese American, *Monkey Bridge* is often described by reviewers and critics as a story about the traumatic losses of war, about the futility of trying to repress or to forget a traumatic past, or about how the effects of wartime trauma further complicate immigration and acculturation. It is acknowledged as mother-daughter writing only to the extent that the mother-daughter story provides a vehicle for healing or resolving the effects of the war, especially the fragmentation of family, which operates as an allegory for the healing of the nation, always understood as the United States. In short, it has been read as an "authentic representation" of Viet Nam as an inevitably tragic but now resolved episode in the static past of *American* history, a form of representation that absolves the United States of its responsibility as an imperial, invading power (Janette 50–51). Read in this way, *Monkey Bridge* is a disturbing narrative.

My analysis takes as its point of departure, however, Michele Janette's contention that Cao "deploys irony to disrupt understandings and expectations of sincere, authentic, or sentimental narratives of Vietnam" and "leaves readers with the uncanny feeling of knowing that their knowledge is a problem, is partial, and comes to them pre-scripted" (50, 51). While the book jacket advertises "Vietnamese lore, history, and dreams," the epigraph from T. S. Eliot's *The Waste Land* presents a caveat that, once inside the narrative, readers will not find a "mirror of their expectations, but instead 'fear in a handful of dust'" (Pelaud 86). In fact, all of the characters echo Mai's statement, "The Vietnam delivered to America had truly passed beyond reclamation" (Cao 128). Rather than being concerned with readers' knowledge of refugee Vietnamese, Viet Nam, or even the American war, I contend that *Monkey Bridge* is instead more about readers' knowledge of the ideological components of the American Dream, especially the contemporary model of Americanness for female subjects that is defined by transformative femininity and the mandate to manage family and fertility through neoliberal cultural values.[39] While Mai's recollection of her childhood is similar to Ahn Joo's in its critique of American Orientalism and racism, Mai's story even more closely resembles Ahn Joo's in its portrayal of her teenage engagement with mainstream culture and her deep disappointment in a mother who failed to conform to bourgeois motherhood. But the narrator-daughter in *Monkey Bridge* ironically reflects on her youthful embrace of transformation and the ways in which she attempted to reform her mother into a maternal model minority, undermining her own authority as she narrates a mother-daughter story. I begin with Mai's relationship to transformative femininity and then focus on the suspension of the mother-daughter relationship.

Sprinkling the initial chapters of *Monkey Bridge* with familiar storytelling conventions such as "once upon a time," Mai recalls her initial astonishment at the ideological power of American transformation narratives and her wonderment at how "those numerous Chinatowns and Little Italys sustain the will to maintain a distance, the desire to inhabit the edge and margin of American life. . . . A mere eight weeks into Farmington [Connecticut], and the American Dream was exerting a sly but seductive pull" (Cao 37). As aware as she was, at this early point she already perceived belonging and exclusion in privatized terms, with individual free will, choice, and desire determining the immigrant relationship to national scripts and cultural myths. Mai remembers too that the entire Vietnamese community "was preoccupied with . . . revisions" in which "[n]ot only could we become anything we wanted to be in America, we could change what we had once been in Vietnam. Rebirthing the past, we called it" (40). Rebirthing the past was "the Vietnamese version of the American Dream; a new spin, the Vietnam spin, to the old immigrant faith in the future" (40). Mai describes herself, after she and Thanh moved to Falls Church, as an immigrant who explored the American Dream and quickly embraced the tenet of transformation. She also recalls with fondness that her new best friend Bobbie "opened up America" by teaching her the late-twentieth-century lexicon of US consumer culture and how to be a discerning consumer. Bobbie took Mai to the public park, the movie theater, and the local upscale mall, where Bobbie knew the products and the brand names, and discussed them all with Mai as if she too "had grown up with such gadgets, and wizardry" (27).

At the beginning of the neoliberal era of responsible citizenship, Mai read in the newspaper "that refugees were a burden to the economy" and learned that to belong in the United States she must become a striving individual, invest in reinvention, and participate in consumer culture (Cao 15).[40] She recounts how she enthusiastically embraced the imperatives and, despite limited material resources, used the marketplace as a tool to accomplish and display her cultural transformation. Mai's story in *Monkey Bridge* is preoccupied, however, with her profound disappointment that Thanh did not do the same.

On her second day in Connecticut, before Thanh arrived, Mai bought groceries with Aunt Mary and studied the American "science of shopping" with its formulas of coupons and numbered aisles. Mai initially found a parallel between Mary's "genius" in negotiating the choices and "temptations of dazzling packaging" at the Farmington A&P and her mother's "slick bargaining skills" in the randomly organized outdoor markets of Saigon (Cao 32–33). But once Thanh arrived, Mai lamented that her mother "did not appreciate the exacting orderliness" and "could not give in to the precision of previously weighed and packaged food" (33). Mai explains this revelation as a "defining moment" for them, one in which the demands of contemporary consumer capitalism irrevocably changed the terms of their relationship and required a shift:

> Now, a mere three and half years or so after her last call to the sky market, the dreadful truth was simply this: we were going through life in reverse, and I was the one who would help my mother through the hard scrutiny of ordinary suburban life. I would have to forgo the luxury of adolescent experiments and temper tantrums, so that I could scoop my mother out of harm's way and give her sanctuary. Now, when we stepped into the exterior world, I was the one who told my mother what was acceptable or unacceptable behavior. (35)

While the premature adulthood that Mai describes has never been unusual for children of immigrant parents, her emphasis on the skills needed to function safely and successfully in the marketplace links motherhood and consumer culture. With the pedagogical purpose of helping Thanh become a sophisticated consumer of material goods and services and thus a "good" mother and citizen, as defined by neoliberalism, Mai takes on the role of expert advisor. Thanh must switch roles with her daughter, who serves both as ideological guide through US consumer culture in general and as translator of popular culture more specifically.

Mai's ability to parse mainstream American culture had quickly given her new powers over her mother, and Mai schooled Thanh in bourgeois motherhood and the methods of intensive mothering that are the standards for neoliberal cultural citizenship (Cao 38). In "translating and more" the ending of an episode of Thanh's favorite television show, *The Bionic Woman*, for example, Mai omitted the moral to obey and listen to one's mother and replaced it with one in which the bionic woman (Jaime Sommers) praises a daughter for her strength and heroism (38). Although inserting an independently powerful daughter as the heroine in this version upstages Sommers's more masculinist central character, Mai's "spin" was less a feminist reading against the grain than it was a lesson in the child-centered ideology of intensive mothering. The show cautions that not listening to your mother can result in danger, but rather than the human mother, it is the cyborg who saves the drowning girl. Like the original script, Mai's revision displaces the mother's agency, but Mai's version additionally omits the moral and displaces the mother's authority. As televisual narratives of NMD, both versions tacitly instruct viewers that the good mother defers to her children and to experts who can aid the mother in child rearing.

In transferring the authority of mothers to "experts," the methods of intensive mothering not only undermine the trust in ordinary women to mother, but also lend themselves to a consumer-based model of mothering or the commodification of motherhood.[41] Hays argues that intensive mothering should be understood specifically as a capitalist ideology that is consumer driven and relies on a fundamental material contradiction in advanced capitalism, since in the contemporary United States most women are required to work in the paid labor force to economically support families and therefore cannot devote themselves wholly to nurturing motherhood and unpaid maternal labor (9–10). At the same time, women must purchase products and services to conform to the disciplinary model, which makes them even more dependent on low-wage gendered and racialized employment. In the scene described above, which focuses on the decidedly postmodern act of television viewing,

Monkey Bridge emphasizes the central role of mainstream popular culture in national subject formation. It also illustrates more specifically through its focus on Mai's translation skills how the media operates as a cultural apparatus or technology of citizenship through which neoliberalism governs at a distance, "translating," as Rose has put it, dominant ideology or "the goals of authorities into choices and commitments of individuals" (quoted in Ouellette 226).

Mai came to rely heavily on participation in consumer culture to claim and prove Americanness, specifically vigilant subscriptions to the offerings of the self-help, pharmaceutical, and education industries. In one "New World trick," Mai practiced popular psychology, which she astutely characterized as the new American religion. She used it, in fact, to establish their new home, adapting the language of well-rounded "balance" and irrational "phobias" to convince their apartment manager to let them move to a different unit where her mother would feel more comfortable. Here Mai picks up one of neoliberalism's more important cultural tools, for self-help or self-improvement culture aids in privatizing governance, transferring the responsibility for addressing social needs, such as housing and social services for low-income immigrants, to the individual. Barbara Cruikshank asserts that self-help culture wages "a social revolution, not against capitalism, racism and inequality, but against the order of the self and the way we govern the self" (231).[42]

Similarly, Mai used over-the-counter medications—now one of the most identifiably American cultural products on offer in US consumer culture—to cope with post-traumatic stress disorder:

> My philosophy was simply this: if I didn't see it at night, in night-mares or otherwise, it never happened. I had my routines: constant vigilance, my antidote to the sin of sleeping and the undomesticated world of dreams. I reached for the pills, my kind of comfort—verifiable peace in every hundred-milligram pellet of reliable, synthetic caffeine. (Cao 11)

According to this passage, NoDoz did more for Mai than help her avoid the traumatic memories that appeared in dreams and flashbacks, for it entirely displaced the history of the "undomesticated" or foreign world of the war that haunted her and provided peace. However, when she did not self-medicate, Mai would wake from a nightmare at three in the morning with the feeling that "one wrong move, one minor mistake, and the world, unhinged, could explode like a fantasy coddled much too long" (202). Clearly, NoDoz is a strategy for dealing with psychological suffering and the body in pain (Scarry 11).

Mai's use of NoDoz additionally helped contain a personal history that threatened "to parade an unpleasant American experience in America" (Cao 42). Within the prevailing Orientalism that rendered refugee Vietnamese both "permanent guests" and representatives of "a national scar," "invisible and at the same time awfully conspicuous," Mai recalls carefully managing her identity and devising an acceptable calculus of difference that would not offend the mainstream. She realized that the requisite "shape-shifting" for belonging in the United States meant that her community would "have to relinquish not just the little truths—the year of our birth, where we once worked and went to school—but also the bigger picture as well.... We would have to make ourselves innocuous and present to the outside world a mild, freeze-dried version of history" (42). As Marita Sturken argues, various practices of late-twentieth-century consumer culture depoliticize the loss, grief, and fear associated with traumatic events to help maintain the notion that the United States is *un*implicated in global strife (4, emphasis added). Allowing politically naïve responses, masking US imperialist policies, and positioning Americans as "tourists of history," memorial culture—everything from reenactments to snow globes and teddy bears—currently operates as consumer culture has operated in the United States throughout its history, generating therapeutic narratives of healing that allow *individuals* to come to terms with the past and render them "capable of reinvention" (105, 14).[43] Consumer products and practices that even more thoroughly foreclose memories or discourage remembering forcefully participate in the governing technology of reinvention.

One of the primary strategies of reinvention in the contemporary United States, psychopharmacology has also developed, according to Toby Miller, as a popular response to the cultural and economic changes accompanying four decades of neoliberalism, specifically diverse and complex immigration and a national decline in economic mobility (*Makeover Nation* 10). "Pill popping" both invests in transformation through consumption and comes with specific claims of transformation—claims of social adjustment to the conditions of neoliberal economic life—that are "reshaping" the mythology and experience of the downwardly mobile American Dream. Similar to self-help products, self-medication functions as a technology of governance and citizenship in which subjects take care of themselves, reconciling and remodeling the self in the wake of diminished public resources and social welfare programs.

Mai's embrace of consumer culture as a route to reinvention and belonging is nowhere more apparent than in her desire for an elite education, a commodity associated with conspicuous consumption and the accumulation of cultural capital, or a direct path to upward mobility. As Mai makes clear, her quest to attend Mount Holyoke College was the most pressing motivation behind her efforts to help rehabilitate her mother. Indeed, the dilemma of Thanh's health frames the novel, for her healing and independence are necessary for Mai to begin her "own new life" in Massachusetts (Cao 17). We might understand Mai's motivation for choosing an elite school such as Mount Holyoke as an effort to establish her mother's belonging as much as it was an effort to establish her own, given that prestigious education reflects well on parents' success as Americans, particularly for Asian immigrants (L. Park 5). Rather than repaying her mother, however, Mai confides that she was actually looking for what her mother failed to provide, fleeing what she experienced as "a phantom world that could no longer offer comfort or sanctuary" (Cao 17, 32). Indeed, it is more accurate to understand Mai's conspicuous consumption as a substitute for her mother and the promise of the women's liberal arts college in the sanctuarial terms of intensive mothering.

Monkey Bridge directly engages the discourse of healing, since its occasion is Thanh's stroke and rehabilitation, and since the narrator highlights her use of the therapeutic properties of consumer culture. But it also denies the healing claims of US consumer culture by ending with the suicide of Thanh and a severed mother-daughter relationship. More accurately, in this novel consumption cannot fully contain or repress trauma; depoliticize loss, grief, and fear; nor generate narratives of healing that allow for reinvention. Consumption is instead represented as a hierarchical, "political act based upon social relationships that reinforce class and race boundaries," and that render the American Dream "a fictive, disciplinary measure that keeps in place normative, unequal social structures" (L. Park 9, 8). At times, Mai seemed quite aware, at least as she recollects her past, of the cost and fiction of transformation, as in her memory of the night before her Mount Holyoke interview: "I could feel a tiny tear dislodge itself from my eye and descend invisibly within me. Tonight, more than any other night, I could see in myself the ability, honed since America, to apply make-up, to conceal and disguise" (Cao 91). Much of the scholarship on recent makeover culture explores the now familiar process of producing the "after body" and its final display in the "big reveal" of popular culture's spectacular transformations (Weber 5, 14). In contextualizing contemporary makeover television in the history of American Dream narratives, however, Lynn Spigel cautions that makeovers and the national cultural imaginary of self-transformation "have historically been used to whiten-up ethnic features, objectify female bodies, and demarcate sexual norms.... [F]rom this point of view, the myth of the 'Great American Makeover' is always also a national cover-up for more deadly historical trends" (237). As Dana Heller puts it, makeover narratives are backward-glancing as well as forward-looking (3).

In hindsight, Mai the narrator critically recognizes the constraints of consumer culture, and she regretfully presents her teenage exuberance for transformation as a mistaken overinvestment in the ideology of the American Dream, perhaps even a contributing factor in her mother's death. Mai shamefully confesses, in fact, that Thanh died in her mind in their first year in the United States, long before her stroke, while they watched an episode of *I Dream of Jeannie* together on a cool autumn evening. After witnessing Thanh struggle to comprehend both cooler weather and mainstream popular culture, Mai concluded that her mother was "imperfect and unable to adjust" (Cao 70). Thanh's tenuous connection to her new environment held several meanings for Mai, but chiefly that Thanh could not take care of herself and that she could not take care of her daughter. Mai remembers how she hastily concluded that Thanh's "ability to navigate and decipher simply became undone," and led her to "relinquish motherhood" (34). As narrator, Mai implicates herself in her mother's suicide, in the beginning of her narrative as she recounts the power she exerted over her mother in their early years, and throughout the narrative as she glosses the increasing emotional distance between Thanh and herself during what she supposed was Thanh's rehabilitation process. Finally, Mai's critical self-assessment is confirmed when she admits that she mistook Thanh's ritual preparations for death as an entrepreneurial reinvention. Mai finally asks herself (and the reader), "Would it have been different had I been more perceptive? Could I have understood a week-long four burner feast to be a death mask or funeral arrangement, a happy face to be a face of despair, a double lifeline to be a single line of imminent death?" (256).

The recuperation that Mai believed she witnessed in Thanh was the apparent palliative effect of the traditional medicine of Thanh's friend, Mrs. Bay, and the group of Little Saigon friends who came to the Nguyen apartment every week to provide community and include Thanh in "a plan that needs tinkering" (Cao 140). Mai mistook the plan for a *hui* or community loan club, which she understood as "an immigrant strategy for economic survival that was taking on great possibilities" for her mother's recovery (140). Relieved, Mai embraced the possibility that Thanh "could be seduced into the American Dream," and thought she saw her mother and Mrs. Bay creating a new reality, which Mai imagined as "a courtly entrepreneurial future . . . in the here and now of America" (144, 166). Given her desire for Thanh's healthy independence, this would have been a comforting prospect for Mai. As Lisa Park explains, the Asian immigrant entrepreneur is "an important symbolic representation for Asian America" since as an American ideology that renders difference consumable, it offers "a more palatable version of U.S. history" in its confirmation of the model minority, and here the maternal model minority (14).

Mai's teenage optimism flew in the face of Thanh's explicit resistance to mainstream neoliberal cultural values. While Thanh observed "You can lose a country. But no one, no war can take away your education," when Mai left for her interview at Mount Holyoke, Thanh rolled her eyes at the idea that eighteen-year-olds who leave their families to attend college become their own person, and she ridiculed Mai's conspicuous consumption, repeating with a sneer Mai's first impression of America as "the great brand-new?" (Cao 31, 60). In her diary, which Mai reads while Thanh is recovering in the hospital, Thanh wrote critically of the entrepreneurial reinvention that figures so prominently within neoliberalism and that Mai embraced:

> Mai is under an illusion of freedom. Unless you create your own
> circumstances, make your own luck, determine your own fate,
> forge your own path through uncharted territory, you're not free
> in her eyes. That is why she wants to leave home to go to college. So
> she can have a new beginning unrestricted by a past life. There, her
> eyes will always be glued to the far horizon. (169)

Thanh objects as well to the advanced-capitalist model of child-centered parenting that Mai accepts, "In Vietnam, the saying used to be 'Parents point, children sit.' In this country, it's become 'Children point, parents sit'" (60). Nor does she yield to a belief in the wisdom of the innocence and purity of the child. In her direct criticism of Manifest Destiny and the American preoccupation with winners and losers, and perhaps in an indirect criticism of her daughter, Thanh takes a swipe at both American political culture and intensive mothering, commenting, "It must be the American sense of invincibility, like a child's sense that nothing she does can possibly have real consequences" (55). Rather than the individual transformation, naïve political optimism, and historical amnesia of the American Dream, Thanh believed that connections to the past cannot be denied, and that it is one's relationship to ancestors that guides the future.

In her final letter to Mai, Thanh describes an entirely different approach in her experience of motherhood, however. Thanh confesses that the family narrative that she had always told Mai, and even her recent letters detailing her own childhood, had been "fictional reimaginings," alternative versions of her life, and part of a new world that she created in an attempt to leave Mai a different legacy (Cao 229). This final letter, which is reproduced in the novel, explains that in order to save her family during desperate poverty, Mama Tuyet, Thanh's mother, became a concubine to Uncle Kahn, and that he, rather than Baba Quan, was her father and Mai's grandfather.[44] She reveals other family transgressions and secrets, including that she was not able to give her mother a proper funeral, that she witnessed Baba Quan murder Uncle Kahn in jealous revenge, and that she herself was a victim of napalm attacks.

Thanh then goes on to describe the five miscarriages she endured during the war years before giving birth to Mai. But rather than the familial sins or even the traumatic events of war that she has finally acknowledged, Thanh attributed the miscarriages to her individual unhappiness and inclination to expel her fetus. At the center of this letter is Than's transformation narrative, when she describes Mai as a "miracle baby," confirms that love "inhabits a mother's heart completely," and declares that "my primary concern became your well-being and your safety" (Cao 237). In this new narrative in which Thanh represents her suicide as an act of sacrifice that would shield Mai from a history of family misfortune and sin, Thanh suddenly takes the role of intensive mother and borrows generously from NMD, which she trusts will provide Mai with a way to understand the suicide:

> In that way, motherhood is the same in every language. It touches
> you, exaggerates your capacity to love, and makes you do things
> that are wholly unordinary. It calls for a suspension of the self in
> a way that is almost religious, spiritual. The true division in this
> world, I believe, is not the division found between tribe, nationality,

or religion, but the division between those of us who are mothers and those who aren't. (252–53)

But with Mai's revelation that the Nguyen family history that she thought she knew was untrue, all versions of Thanh's mother-daughter narrative became unreliable. Rather than a genuine transformation to the all-consuming, sacrificial, and emotional embrace of motherhood, Thanh's final sentimental claim of maternal sacrifice is read by Mai as a mere narrative performance, and she is ultimately deeply skeptical of the "brand-new slate" that her mother had "supposedly" bequeathed as a gift (257).

As with *A Cab Called Reliable*, the promise of an educational rite of passage and the disentangling trope of adoption appear at the end of *Monkey Bridge*, when Mai learns that, just before she left Viet Nam for the United States, and in the chaos of evacuation, Thanh signed papers to give Uncle Michael custody of her daughter.[45] Rather than triggering a release, this only adds weight to Mai's profound disillusionment, so transformation and belonging again seem less certain for the narrator-daughter in the context of a suspended mother-daughter relationship. At the end of this novel, both the premise of transformative femininity in female belonging and the authorship of mother-daughter narratives are ironically questioned by the narrator who has exuberantly displayed them in her youth and in her storytelling. More than Ahn Joo, Mai was a "good subject" while growing up, and she herself even took on the mantle of the good mother. But Cao's narrative also refuses the formulaic happy identification between generations, the healing that would symbolize social reconciliation, or even the abjection of the diasporic Asian mother that enables the American subjectivity of the daughter. This novel closes with a daughter's singular realization that she completely misrecognized as an entrepreneurial healing process her mother's ritual preparations for death.

Going Public with Maternal Romance

Perhaps, in our eager search for shelter and love, we children invest our faith too elaborately in parents who can never humanly meet our exorbitant expectations. Perhaps the sheer distance between what we want of our parents and what we can actually receive can never be truly reconciled.

—LAN CAO, *MONKEY BRIDGE*

The past that nostalgia seeks, Susan Stewart argues, "has never existed except as narrative and hence, always absent, that past continually threatens to reproduce itself as a felt lack" (23).[46] If *A Cab Called Reliable* and *Monkey Bridge* are nostalgic for a past that has only existed in narrative, and I contend that mother-daughter narratives are typically nostalgic by virtue of their retrospective temporality, then the narrative they strive for is the maternal romance, a fantasy of desire about all that the mother can provide as well as her devotion to fulfill that desire. The nostalgic, fictive past that never existed is the past when every need and desire was met unconditionally and immediately by mothers. Further, in mother-daughter narratives this nonexistent past of unlimited maternal care and self-sacrifice threatens to reproduce itself and the feeling of absence or "lack" that comes with it.[47]

A Cab Called Reliable and *Monkey Bridge* disclose that mother-daughter narrative may revive national mythologies and update them to align with neoliberalism for the normative reproduction of the nation. In authoring maternal romances, however, Kim and Cao contribute ironic allegories to NMD and cautionary tales to the repertoire of Asian American mother-daughter narrative. For even if their versions attempt to produce maternal model minorities, they do not fit the paradigm of "model minority discourse" with its sentimental family plot of healing the racial and gender wounds of marginalization for disciplined participation in advanced-capitalist production. Moreover, while the maternal romance figures desire for belonging through a fantasy about the mother-daughter relationship in a plot similar to the "mother-daughter romance" that Patricia Chu has identified, in these maternal romances the mother is not fully recuperated, the daughters' subjectivity is stilted, and the mother-daughter relationship and thus belonging are suspended, caught in the narrative between exclusion and retention. Indeed, the mothers in these novels cannot access the role of the maternal model minority that aligns neoliberal marketplace demands and motherhood in a reconfiguration of the American

Dream, one that relies upon new forms of gendered racial labor, consumption, and subjectivity.

The fantasy of the maternal romance, in which all desires can and will be met, is uncannily similar to the fantasy of neoclassical economics. The economic narrative does not describe most people's actual relationship to the market but one that neoliberalism frenzily circulates in US consumer culture, through sites such as NMD, to promote a consumption-driven form of commodity capitalism (Feiner 195). The dominant economic narrative of neoliberalism posits a nostalgic, fictive past in which market capitalism was free of the regulation and intervention of the welfare state. At the same time, neoliberalism promises a global economic future in which the possibilities for participation and thus belonging will be limitless, so long as individuals strive for privatization, entrepreneurial reinvention, and consumption. And those are, we are constantly told, the terms of the contemporary marketplace in which the inadequate individual must take responsibility for herself, or more accurately, take responsibility for her family and nation, to transform the social order. Glancing backward, looking forward, but evading present realities, US neoliberalism has become, as "an ideological mandate that mutates," a metonym of American reinvention (Weber 52).

While the maternal romance or perfect mother fantasy echoes the perfect market fantasy of the dominant neoliberal economic narrative, they both tacitly threaten regulation, scarcity, and crisis as they proclaim access, abundance, and security. Affectively and symptomatically, the stories these narratives tell about familial and market relationships express unresolved contradictions and deep anxieties. As Susan Feiner observes, "the prospect that markets may fail us tends to awaken our earliest horrors and fears of abandonment" (195). In the fears they draw upon and reproduce, the fantasy narratives of perfect relationships also allegorize material realities. Representing the beginning of the neoliberal economic era in the 1970s and addressing the model of female citizenship that became hegemonic by the time these texts were published in the mid-1990s, *A Cab Called Reliable* and *Monkey Bridge* portray how cultural citizenship practices of Asian American women contend with aspiring white, middle-class motherhood and participation in consumer culture as transformative routes to belonging. Akin to Chua's *Battle Hymn of the Tiger Mother* but declining to provide successful examples of the maternal model minority, they nonetheless indicate where and how Asian American women are imagined to manage shifting versions of the American Dream, as the old fear of abandonment in the Freudian family romance overlaps with and is updated by anxiety about consumer capitalism and economic life under neoliberalism. *A Cab Called Reliable* and *Monkey Bridge* communicate that the limits of cultural citizenship for Asian American women are closely linked to the repronormative labors required for transformative femininity, and as much as they caution against subjecting one's story entirely to this dominant script, they also represent the negotiating power of subjects who are able to fantasize about belonging.

3 / Romancing the Self and Negotiating Postfeminist Consumer Citizenship in Asian American Women's Labor Lit

There's no real strategy to finding the right path to life and success. Anyone who's ever played to win knows that working hard is the best way.

—MICHELLE YU AND BLOSSOM KAN,
"THOUGHTS TO WYN," *CHINA DOLLS*

Given the association of chick lit with popular entertainment, conspicuous consumption, and the "bubble culture" of the 1990s and early 2000s, some imagined that this popular literary phenomenon would play itself out in the current global economic crisis (C. H. Smith 274). There were pronouncements about "the death of chick lit," sighs of relief that the stream of snarky diminutives such as "bridezilla lit" or "hen lit" would finally dry up, and promises that booksellers would no longer market all books written by women as some form of "chick lit" (Bilston). With barely a pause and only slightly diminished sales, however, "recession lit" was born, brandishing such titles as *The Recessionistas* by Alexandra Lebanthal and *The Penny Pincher's Club* by Sarah Strohmeyer and reassuring readers that they were not alone as they faced the uncertainties of change on social and personal levels. Even the filmic adaptation of Sophie Kinsella's novels could be modified with an ending reshoot for the early 2009 release of *Confessions of a Shopaholic.*

The enduring popularity of chick lit in print and on screen should not be surprising if we recognize first that the genre leverages the fantasies of both consumer culture and romantic discourse, primarily but not exclusively heterosexual, and second that it chronicles a contemporary period of intense change in which the reconfiguration of political subjectivity or citizenship with increased demands for women's consumption and labor figures prominently. Even as female subjects must demonstrate a normative femininity that is nonthreatening to dominant conceptions of Americanness, the "new sexual contract" of neoliberal citizenship urges women "to make good use of the opportunity to work, to gain qualifications, to control fertility, and to earn enough money to participate in consumer culture" (McRobbie, *Aftermath of Feminism* 54). Thus, although they typically disrupt the script of marriage or the code of heterosexual mating as satisfying life goals, chick lit narratives—similar to weddings—seem "recession-proof" since they call on and adapt the story of romance, simultaneously providing a "secure meta-narrative" during unsettled times and a site for reimagining both personal relationships and social belonging.[1] In short, the genre of chick lit offers a seemingly endless and dynamic engagement with the fantasies and realities of neoliberalism.

The two novels I analyze in this chapter, Michelle Yu and Blossom Kan's *China Dolls* (2007) and Sonia Singh's *Goddess for Hire* (2004), recombine fantasies and realities to represent Asian American heroines who hope to find in professional careers respect, reward, and recognition as fully entitled and contributing members of US society. These texts thus revise romance, I contend, in relation to employment and a specifically neoliberal work ethic. In search of meaningful work, the heroines must negotiate a neoliberal marketplace in which production and consumption are intertwined, and "good" citizens must continually cultivate and reinvent the self through acquiring and demonstrating that most important qualification: marketplace expertise. In other words, in addition to the qualifications specific to occupations, successful workers in a globalizing US economy must display "romantic consumerism," or highly cultivated taste distinctions about the ever-expanding range of commodities available under neoliberalism, including material goods, culture, and even personal relationships, as my analysis of mother-daughter narratives in chapter 2 suggests (J. Collins 186). Romantic consumerism is linked to the mandates of neoliberal cultural citizenship "to prove and claim Americanness" through publicity or the imperative to display alignment with neoliberal values via participation in mainstream culture (S. J. Lim 10). It not only requires understanding and participation in normative processes of the marketplace but also demands their creative application to the self in a decidedly romantic conception of individual "authorship." As authors of their own success, workers who re-create and display themselves as marketplace experts confirm, in the model of neoliberal consumer citizenship, postfeminist and postracial ideologies or updated versions of American bootstrap ideology.

Through melodrama, specifically repetition in *China Dolls* and satire in *Goddess for Hire*, the novels comment on the model of the citizen as a romantic consumer and disclose that for Asian American women in particular it requires prodigious material and affective labor. More specifically, to produce and display re-creative selves who possess the marketplace qualifications needed for successful employment in the neoliberal economy, Asian American women must negotiate the exclusionary processes of conspicuous consumption, objectification, and capital accumulation. Further, the romance with the laboring self fits squarely within an American Dream ideology that relegates Asian immigrants, who have limited access to social mobility and are still considered perpetual foreigners, to contingent belonging (L. Park). Perhaps even more true now as in the predownturn economy, chick lit "greets the novel's closet skeletons in a new marketplace" (Harzewski, "Tradition" 43). The Asian American "labor lit" I analyze underscores, in fact, how the genre registers not only the gender, commercial, and domestic concerns of the novel's roots but also contemporary concerns, including the labor of consumer citizenship for gendered racial subjects. I begin by contextualizing chick lit as a postfeminist cultural text and by discussing postfeminism as a popular neoliberal discourse of gendered consumer citizenship. The next section theorizes the importance of rewriting to the genre and elaborates the subgenre I am calling "labor lit." Finally, I consider the ways in which *China Dolls* and *Goddess for Hire* illuminate the negotiation by Asian American female characters of the labor required in neoliberal consumer citizenship.

Chick Lit, Neoliberalism, and Postfeminism

> *Arguably, what readers enjoy about the chick lit genre is not so much an escape from feminism's dictates but rather the humorous ways in which women negotiate what it is to be female in an allegedly postfeminist, insufficiently feminist world.*
>
> —JENNIFER SCANLON, "MAKING SHOPPING SAFE
> FOR THE REST OF US"

Expressly targeting young women readers who work, and humorously chronicling contemporary consumer culture, chick lit may be considered a characteristically neoliberal cultural form: as a commodity it illustrates the energetic production and consumption cycles that animate advanced capitalism, and as a cultural narrative its major concerns of labor, consumption, and romance not only reflect but also lend themselves to the continual reinvention of the self that the reigning model of neoliberal subjectivity compels for a worker-insecure and consumption-led capitalism. Neoliberalism in the United States may be seen as a broadening and intensification of earlier forms of consumer culture, further dissolving the boundaries among commercial, cultural, and political practices and remaking citizens. For some scholars, "the distinction between consumerism and citizenship is spurious from the ground-up—in the United States there is no citizenship outside consumption, and part of the pleasure of consuming is that the act itself constitutes one as a citizen, someone who 'matters' in this particular body politic and historical moment" (Banet-Weiser 212–13). At the same time, labor is fundamental to neoliberal citizenship, and neoliberal governmentality now "*requires* populations to be free, self-managing, and self-enterprising individuals" or "entrepreneurs of the self" (Ong 14, emphasis added).[2] Indeed, neoliberalism has also blurred the boundaries between consumption and production, a phenomenon clearly registered in most chick lit though not always recognized by critics and reviewers.

In feminist media studies scholarship, contemporary popular texts that centralize female subject formation, such as chick lit, and especially forms featuring an obvious makeover narrative structure, such as reality TV, are analyzed as technologies of citizenship in which neoliberalism governs at a distance and communicates to citizen-subjects how to transform, discipline, and take care of themselves for appropriate consumption and labor participation in the global economy (Ouellette 226). In literary studies as well, chick lit is closely tied to the neoliberal marketplace, but literary critics have devoted far less serious attention to understanding the cultural work the genre may be doing with regard to the reformulation of subjectivity and particularly citizenship. Except for the few scholars who focus on the differences among subgenres or the few who consider the reception of chick lit part of "a long tradition of discounting both women writers and their readers" in Anglo-American literary studies (Wells 48), much commentary seems to fall in line, if more subtly, with mainstream media critics or reviewers who regularly chastise authors and readers alike for their interest in consumer capitalism, characterizing chick lit as a "middlebrow" genre that crassly focuses on superficial pleasures defined in material and individualist terms.[3] Such treatment suggests that "enlightened" readers find pleasure in texts that somehow lie outside the concerns of consumer culture, often relies upon a simplistic understanding of consumption as "the act of purchase and the reproduction of consumer capitalism," and may be (often is) mired in conventional gender, class, and racial ideology (Hollows and Moseley 11).

Across the spectrum of cultural authority, chick lit novels are similarly and roundly recognized as a form of postfeminist culture. I too contextualize *China Dolls* and *Goddess for Hire* within postfeminism, a discourse within which the fantasies and realities, desires and anxieties about women's market participation in the neoliberal global economy—both as consumers and as producers—are registered, reproduced, and negotiated.[4] Postfeminism is often conceptualized as simply another antifeminist backlash, a temporal repudiation of liberal feminism, or a coherent ideology in lockstep alignment with neoliberalism. These definitions may be attributed to scholarly intentions to excavate the vast cultural expanse of neoliberalism, define it, and understand how it undermines political agency and collectivity. The resulting dynamic, however, has been an impoverishment of approach in studies of postfeminist culture, including chick lit, with critical practice at times mirroring the reductive terms identified in the postfeminist text under consideration. In short, there has been a tendency toward the description of postfeminist popular culture in relation to a seamless neoliberalism. Although there is certainly a relationship, neoliberalism and postfeminism should not be considered coterminous. Totalizing categorization of chick lit and definitions of postfeminism as neoliberal may well disregard the polysemic nature of cultural texts, how subgenres rewrite chick lit, and the multiplicity of feminisms at play within postfeminist discourse, which may indicate "an inability to recognize difference not only in the genre, but between different feminisms as well" (Butler and Desai 4). Moreover, since neoliberalism is not without contradictions and is a mutating ideology that adapts to specific locations and other rationalities, analysis of postfeminist discourse and its cultural manifestations requires a repertoire of reading practices or approaches, rather than a recital of the neoliberal rubric.

This analysis builds on an understanding of postfeminism as a "complexification" of the backlash concept and a popular discourse that responds to and "deploys a variety of positions with respect to feminism," particularly in relation to neoliberalism.[5] I approach the subgenre of labor lit in texts written by Asian American women with questions about gendered racial labor, immigration, and political economy that emerge from Asian American, transnational, and materialist feminisms. Here, postfeminism is treated as a popular discourse of neoliberal consumer citizenship in which consumer practices are commonly addressed although not always accepted as the primary component of political subjectivity. Consumption may be conceptualized as a political right that enables abundant opportunity for labor, unlimited individual consumer choice, and empowering, satisfying personal and social relationships for all women, but it may also be represented in constrained relation to widespread sexism, racism, and economic injustice.[6] In addition, postfeminism customarily posits the paradox of the deficient yet fully self-reliant female subject whose happiness and success, often figured in relation to the marketplace, have been compromised, presumably because of the individual's less than judicious "choices," but she must strive nonetheless for a better life. Finally, as Ralina Joseph argues, just as "discourses of post-race are undeniably gendered . . . discourses of post-feminism are undeniably raced," so critique must engage these discourses in tandem (239).

A decade after "postfeminism" first appeared as a term in mainstream US news media in the early 1980s (McRobbie, *Aftermath of Feminism* 31), its themes exploded in popular culture, as expectations and fears over change brought about by feminism and other political movements mounted and met with the hegemony of neoliberalism; cultural forms such as chick lit, Hollywood romantic comedies, and female-centered prime-time TV dramas, as well as advertisements, music, magazines, political rhetoric, and material commodity culture, addressed a female subject and aggressively targeted female consumers to an unprecedented degree (Negra 5). Crucially, postfeminist cultural texts customarily feature an ambivalent narrative structure that registers dilemmas, uncertainty, or dissatisfaction about options and social problems. But texts regularly decline to directly address contradictions and treat the problems they chronicle through deflective humor, as the epigraph to this section suggests, or superficially and fantastically resolve them through "evasion, escape, or retreat" (7). The narratives on offer in postfeminist culture are markedly patterned, enough so that Rosalind Gill describes postfeminist culture as a "distinctive sensibility" with interrelated themes that hew toward individual "choice," improvement (makeover), and empowerment, rather than social critique or change (147).

In fact, while postfeminism as a discourse "'works on' some of the most intractable problems in American life" (Negra 7), postfeminist cultures in the United States and the United Kingdom incorporate feminism in selective ways that overlap with other post ideologies (post–civil rights and postracial discourses), "posting" the need for or positing the "pastness" of social justice movements with assumptions that they have successfully accomplished their political goals. Moreover, the empowered consumer threatens to displace the political subject, and consumption becomes a strategy "for the production of the self" (Tasker and Negra 2). Taking their cues from the neoliberal marketplace, postfeminist narratives may proceed through a fetishization of female desire, a rhetoric of individual female empowerment, or a notion of "female success" primarily based on conspicuous consumption (Negra 4). Even when texts are overtly critical of consumer citizenship or consumerism, and this chapter emphasizes that chick lit does engage the contradictory nature of advanced capitalism, postfeminism consistently makes evident that "good" citizenship for women in the United States now mandates a variety of market-based activities. In sum, consumption consistently plays an important role in the neoliberal forms of female subjectivity that are represented in postfeminist discourse, which links them to residual (and resurgent) ideologies that define womanhood in the United States through middle-class status, native-born whiteness and motherhood, and social inequalities and structures of exclusionary otherness.

While recognizing that uncertainties and dissatisfactions are regularly articulated in postfeminist discourse, numerous critics have lamented what they consider the apolitical nature of female subjectivity in postfeminist texts. Citing popular representations of the redundancy of feminism as a political movement and the displacement of political subjects, Angela McRobbie has suggested that the female subject in postfeminist popular culture declines social analysis since she is, "despite her freedom, called upon to be silent, to withhold critique, to count as a modern sophisticated girl" (*Aftermath of Feminism*, 18). More specifically, Diane Negra suggests, postfeminism presents "diagnostics of femininity that take the place of [feminist] analyses of political or economic culture" through privileging matrimonial and maternalist models of female subjectivity (5). Still others find slightly more of a blend of modes of female subjectivity where an emphasis on "freedom" and "choice" sutures feminism and femininity through a grammar of individualism, and a subjectification of women as "active desiring sexual subjects" invested in pleasing themselves, rather than participating in collective political agency.[7] Consistently, the terms of subjectification are noticeably downgraded and "reflect a shift from liberal concerns with state-ensured rights to a neoliberal politics understood through the notion of choice," especially consumer choice and marketplace freedom or participation (Butler and Desai 8).

I similarly aim to highlight limitations in the model of political subjectivity within neoliberal consumer citizenship, although specifically for Asian American women. It seems crucial, however, not to use as a standard a model that is unlikely to surface in contemporary popular culture. Few chick lit characters will transform themselves into radical activists who thwart the structural adjustment policies of the International Monetary Fund, camp out with Occupy Wall Street, or create immigrant rights organizations that fight against the feminization of migration. While this is a deliberate exaggeration of the search for explicit commitment to political change in cultural production, such as that depicted in Choi's *American Woman*, I wonder what space scholars' desires leave for feminism in cultural production? What kinds of fictional texts would be sufficiently political, and would they reaffirm the oppositional political consciousness of earlier identity politics? Would they reinstate a political culture with conventional notions of the public sphere and a literary culture with aesthetic values that privilege psychological interiority, complex character development, or figurative language (Farr 210)? A more useful critical practice involves wrestling with the lexical and grammatical frames of neoliberalism as it rearticulates with feminist discourse and locating space in its cultural manifestations where we may recognize or imagine new visions of individual agency and collective change within the constraints of contemporary models of political subjectivity. As Sarah Banet-Weiser has asserted in her study of the televisual production of consumer citizenship:

> Reimagining citizenship is . . . called for, but not as a nostalgic longing for a past vibrant political culture and a yearning for those identities that apparently inhabited that culture, and not based upon a naïve assumption that commercial culture is the only site for social change and political identity making. Rather, a reimagining of citizenship is required that situates citizenship as residing and taking on meaning within these contradictions. To imagine citizenship as existing outside the commercial world is not only unrealistic but, more importantly, it is limiting. (212)

As part of postfeminist discourse and the "re-negotiation" of contemporary feminist and antifeminist thought in the age of neoliberal capitalism, chick lit is concerned with consumer citizenship and the romance with the self or the model of political subjectivity it extends to women, but we need to read through the language of the marketplace—the contemporary lingua franca (Gerhard 41).

Asian American Labor Lit and Rewriting Chick Lit

Although work typically loses the competition with consumption and romance for attention and disappears into the more mundane background of chick lit, analysis of *China Dolls* and *Goddess for Hire* elaborates how the subgenre of labor lit foregrounds employment and chronicles dissatisfaction with the neoliberal workplace, particularly the necessary qualification of marketplace expertise and the kinds of transactions this expertise demands.[8] Recognition of this reformulation builds from Suzanne Ferriss and Mallory Young's description that chick lit "features single women in their twenties and thirties 'navigating their generations' challenges of balancing demanding careers with personal relationships'" (3). It also acknowledges connections to nineteenth-century tales of working women in Anglo-American literature, especially in their negotiation of definitions of womanhood and the necessity of wage labor.[9] Finally, my analysis of Asian American labor lit follows Christine So's suggestion that scholars look more closely at how Asian Americans authors appropriate normative forms and ideologies (8). Similar to the genre as a whole, labor lit's occasion is the neoliberal demand for women's flexible labor, and its dramatic comedy is work-based (Van Slooten 237). Chick lit heroines are characteristically committed to the idea of a career, while often "portrayed as dissatisfied and struggling in their jobs" in the "dead end" service sector (Gill and Herdieckerhoff 495). Unlike much of the genre, labor lit highlights the demands of work, romance, and consumption under neoliberalism in more equal measure; or, work and personal relationships are closely linked, and consumption appears to take a backseat, sometimes becoming the antagonist of the narrative, as in Emma McLaughlin and Nicola Krauss's *The Nanny Diaries* (2002), or even satirized, as in Kinsella's "Shopaholic" series. Even as labor lit shifts narrative weight toward the rewards and disappointments of employment, it necessarily addresses consumer citizenship, since neoliberalism's demands for employment are about ensuring participation in consumer culture and thereby taking responsibility for one's self. As I will show in analysis of *China Dolls* and *Goddess for Hire*, labor lit also serves a pedagogical function, providing insight into how the contemporary marketplace operates and offering guidance on how to negotiate the demands of labor, consumption, and subjectivity under neoliberalism.

Labor lit includes narratives about women struggling to establish careers in less than living wage occupations in "assistant lit" and "nanny lit"; in "working girl lit" or "cheque lit" about female professionals who are conventionally successful but who are frustrated with conditions that contradict the promise of full citizenship for neoliberal feminine subjects; and more recently in "recession lit" about involuntary retreatism, the "new" gender division of labor, and redemptive austerity.[10] In addition to a focus on literal employment and specific occupations, labor lit includes those versions of chick lit that give narrative priority to the labor involved in gaining marketplace advantage and becoming an entrepreneur of the self, or the work of "self-care," defined as the ability to provide for one's own needs and service one's own ambitions (Brown 6–7). Finally, labor lit may focus on unpaid reproductive labor, especially when it is directly parlayed into successful or lucrative market employment, as in Julie Powell's *Julie and Julia: 365 Days, 524 Recipes, 1 Tiny Apartment Kitchen* (2005). Labor lit may, like other chick lit that ambivalently registers neoliberal ideals circulating in postfeminist discourse, fantastically or reductively resolve the untenable contradictions and inequitable conditions of women's market employment. At times, however, texts point to contemporary conditions in which women now make up the majority of the US workforce while employment rates for women of color and single mothers are decreasing, wage discrimination and occupational segregation stubbornly persist or are even increasing, and gainful employment requires continual acquisition of new qualifications and entrepreneurial self-improvement (Newman).

Despite the popular perception that chick lit is a formulaic brand, semiotically identifiable by its "packaging in pink" and a conventionally comforting heterosexual mating plot that features large doses of commodity fetishism, I contend that the genre is utterly devoted to rewriting and variation, and not only to sell itself. Certainly, chick lit subgenres use conventions to communicate their generic category and to create structural stability, providing easy entry into narratives and points of recognition for readers. The commercial tropes of chick lit, especially the upscale accessories of "statement handbags" and designer shoes, are an important extension of the genre's conventions or trademark indicia that signify the brand "chick lit." The tropes address or interpellate readers as subjects with similar desires and loyalties to specific commercial products. Tropes may also be read more broadly as metonyms for the "brand culture" of neoliberalism, or as signifiers of the market fundamentalism in advertising and marketing strategies that naturalize purchases as cultural practices, assigning vast populations to classifications that are linked to economic status in a reductive typology of lifestyle identifications. Far more than substituting commodities for human relationships, "[i]n the contemporary capitalist context, where commercial culture does not simply infuse every aspect of our life but is constitutive of every feature of our lives, the brand takes on added significance in terms of its importance in the formation of identities, notions of entitlement, and feelings of belonging" (Banet-Weiser 22). If we read chick lit with this sort of understanding, when subgenres deploy the commercial tropes of the genre, their rewriting may critically point to ideologically rigid foundations and what remains *inflexible* in neoliberalism, despite declarations of novelty.

Chick lit's strong emphasis on rewriting is, at the same time, easily understood as one of the ways it is a characteristically neoliberal genre, ideally suited to chronicle rapid change under current conditions. Subgeneric revisions are part of and reflect a context that is reformulating subjectivity and citizenship, demanding new forms and levels of consumption and labor, and blurring distinctions between cultural, political, and commercial practices. This interpretation of rewriting is consistent with the idea that all popular genres must be dynamic enough to reflect changes in or "track" dominant social knowledge to remain popular. My analysis of Asian American labor lit also builds on scholarship that recognizes subgenres as important variations and one of the ways in which chick lit may critically comment on conditions, processes, or contradictions under neoliberalism. As Pamela Butler and Jigna Desai suggest, "rather than reading . . . expansion as simply more of the same, we might ask why issues such as immigration and race ('Bollywood' and 'black' chick lit), labor ('nanny lit'), and consumption ('shopping lit') are such popular topics in contemporary women's genre fiction" (2). If critical reception has largely focused on the earliest and most popular articulations of the genre to establish a prototype or to identify and describe the neoliberal rationality of postfeminism, the permutations and divergences within chick lit subgenres, such as labor lit, are more instructive, for they throw the conventions that are taken for granted into relief and subject their own signification to question. Or, as Wenche Ommundsen observes about the ways in which global chick lit remakes Bushnell's *Sex and the City*, "By claiming similarity, they emphasize difference" (110). Most often, the unmistakable branding of the genre in mainstream versions has diverted attention away from the more nuanced ways it engages neoliberalism and rearticulates with feminisms. In this sense, branding may be understood to provide very effective cover for less familiar concerns and require more innovative reading practices. At any rate, generic conventions, including commercial indicia, should not be taken at simple face value, since, as Jacques Derrida reminds us, generic classification, or the social contract of expectation with the reader, and the book as material object are always as much indicators of the ways that texts transgress genre as they are statements of convention. While the branding of chick lit—the visual, narrative, and commercial framing of the genre—certainly operates hegemonically, signifying dominant values of the age and promoting the print mode as a commodity, it also opens space, I assert, for authorial and reader negotiation of neoliberal ideologies and specifically consumer citizenship.

This analysis of the ways in which Asian American labor lit engages the discourse of postfeminist consumer citizenship draws from approaches that understand the branding or generic trademarks of chick lit metonymically, symptomatically, and deconstructively.[11] Rebecca Traister comments that the genre's branding, and specifically its commodity fetishism, should not be trivialized, and she indicates a pedagogical as well as documentary function for chick lit:

> For the first time in Western history, a population of (privileged, urban) adult women is single by choice; they live alone; they can have sex with whomever they want when they want; they have incomes with which to buy overpriced footwear and stupid cocktails. Sometimes a cosmo is just a cosmo; in chick lit it may be shorthand for an independence and selfishness that is a revolution of its own. Chick lit chronicles exactly what the sensationalist gothic and sentimentalists could not: the young female experience of professional, sexual, and economic power. (*Salon*)

Traister is careful not to claim that chick lit's trademark conventions and commercial signifiers chronicle a *progressive* revolution or are representative of most women's lives, and she rightly acknowledges that shifting material conditions produce different cultural forms that document social realities in both direct and symbolic, clarifying and occluding, ways. Additionally, then, we need to recognize how chick lit metonymically chronicles, although far more opaquely, the realities of low-wage working women. For those workers who make shoes and serve cocktails, exploitation and limited access to the pleasures of commodity fetishism far more accurately characterize the gendered racial labor demanded by the particular moment in Western history associated with the New Economy.

In a more symptomatic approach that foregrounds the dissatisfactions characteristically narrated in chick lit, Tania Modleski contends that chick lit novels are less novels of female success than novels of female disillusionment, with both capitalism and heteropatriarchal romance, so "[w]omen are still writing novels that point to their discontents, some of them explicit . . . some of them implicit" (xxvii).

> Richard Dyer argues that mass culture is utopian insofar as it promises what capitalism (and we might add patriarchy) has always promised to deliver but often does not or cannot. Hence, a fair number of chick lit novels have protagonists who live in a land of relative plenty (or shop as if they do), and who are faced with a cornucopia of "choices" that a postfeminist society claims have been bestowed upon them. To the extent that their exists a gap between the relatively privileged life of these chick-lit protagonists and life as the majority of women live it (shopping for Payless shoes, not Manola Blahnik's), there is room for a feminist politics to insert itself. (xxvii)

Beyond compensatory pleasure, chick lit may be seen as the current form of antiromantic romance that parodies the deficiencies of heteropatriarchal romance and the romantic fantasies of the marketplace (xxiv). Although she also emphasizes the context of neoliberal consumer culture and reads against the grain of chick lit as a chronicle of "female success," Caroline Smith counters the view that reading chick lit amounts primarily to wish fulfillment that provides vicarious and temporary pleasure. Instead, chick lit dialogues with consumer culture and other neoliberal cultural forms that address women, responding specifically to popular advice manuals, such as women's magazines, self-help books, and romantic comedies, to problematize their ideology of "consume and achieve" and to offer alternative instruction in helping female readers become discerning consumers (6).

In addition to suggestions that chick lit is an "antigenre" (generic parody) or an "outlaw genre" (generic deconstruction), I theorize that chick lit is a "hypergenre" (generic revision) that invites us to read for its emphasis on rewriting and the neoliberal capitalist preoccupation with reinvention.[12] Rewriting is fundamental to the genre in its very conception as it recycles established literary traditions, including popular romance, the bildungsroman, and the novel of manners; as it converges with other popular media such as television and Hollywood film; and as it documents and participates in the reformulation of subjectivity and belonging for women in relation to work and consumption, or the remix of neoliberal fantasies and realities in its narrative content.

In many estimations, chick lit emerged most directly from a recasting of popular romance fiction, simultaneously indicating changes in intimate relationships and "the tenacity of notions of heterosexual romance given cultural and demographic changes including divorce, increase in single person households, and diversification of family forms" (Gill and Herdieckerhoff 490).[13] So, rather than the escapism for which romance is known, chick lit novels "hover between fantasy and reality," a provocative positioning that *China Dolls* and *Goddess for Hire* exploit in their negotiated address of consumer citizenship (Van Slooten 237). Realism, and specifically the female bildungsroman, is important to the genre, especially for how it addresses young women's recognition of and struggle with increased expectations for consumption and labor. Instead of depictions that are representative of the material realities of most women, however, chick lit often delivers to postfeminist discourse descriptions of or fantasies about the desired ideal, according to neoliberal ideology, and in various ways provides advice and information about how women might improve themselves to attain it. In this sense, the novel of manners is clearly discernible in chick lit and has been perhaps the genre's most explicit literary predecessor, with some of the most famous renditions, such as Helen Fielding's *Bridget Jones's Diary* (1996), McLaughlin and Krauss's *The Nanny Diaries*, and Candace Bushnell's *Trading Up* (2003), making use of the canonical figures and fictions of Jane Austen, Charlotte Brontë, and Edith Wharton, respectively. Stephanie Harzewski's view that "chick lit presents a new novel of manners not as an exaggerated version of its codes but as a synthesis of diverse popular and literary forms" comes closest to my theorization of chick lit as a hypergenre ("Tradition" 41).

Much of the popularity of chick lit clearly has to do with the fact that even before and certainly since the commercial phenoms of *Bridget Jones's Diary* and *Sex and the City* emerged in the 1990s, different versions of those white, middle-class, professional "singleton" and heterosexual-focused narratives recombine and rewrite "the dailiness of women's lives" (Ferriss and Young 5). The focus shifts in various ways in women of color subgenres, such as "chica lit" or "sistah lit"; life cycle subgenres, such as "hen lit"; other social identifications, as in "mom lit" (which does double duty in neoliberal maternal discourse as discussed in the previous chapter); and through further hybridization, including chick lit mystery and detective fiction, such as Lynn Harris's satirical *Death by Chick Lit*. Diana Szu, the editor at St. Martin's Press who acquired Michelle Yu and Blossom Kan's *China Dolls*, believes the genre lends itself to enough adaptation that it will continue evolving to appeal to an increasingly diversified consumer market or female readership (Yang).[14] As suggested earlier, even after the Great Recession began and brought a downturn, sales for women's fiction in the United States, which includes all genres of fiction that are marketed to women, remained strong and have even witnessed new sales records with the "abstinence porn" of the *Twilight* franchise (by 2010 over 116 million copies worldwide) and the "mommy porn" of *Fifty Shades of Grey* fame (the fastest-selling paperback of all time).[15]

While the marketing of humorous, women-centered narratives as "chick lit" has generated a veritable arcade of subgenres, arguably rebranding various forms of women's writing, ethnic women's literature, and canonical women's literature, the genre's hyperactivity also extends to product placement, author tours, websites, blogs, and material culture spin-offs that link novels horizontally to a range of cultural media, entertainment platforms, and users or consumers. Chick lit best sellers are routinely adapted into films, and chick lit has been remediated, most popularly in HBO's series *Sex and the City* (1998–2004), which combined the television sitcom and glossy women's magazines with chick lit to reach a near-global viewership (Arthurs 83). The importance to chick lit of "remediation," or the process by which new media arise as each medium "responds to, re-deploys, competes with and reforms other media," cannot be underestimated (Bolter and Grusin 35). The genre's narrative style is, it seems, able to incorporate or be adapted to just about any media form that uses an identification-based first-person perspective, from epistolary newspaper columns to confessional blogging, as well as many forms that employ other narrative perspectives, such as the myriad self-help media that hail women through second-person imperatives to "Live your best life!" as in *The Oprah Winfrey Show* and *O, The Oprah Magazine* (Sanders and Barnes-Brown 30). The growth of chick lit into a popular cultural phenomenon has had much to do with the rise of global media conglomerates that savvily began in the 1990s to place superstore bookstores both physically and virtually in the center of a sophisticated, media-driven consumer culture in which various textual forms of "writing" spectacularly converge.

As much as it is a reflection of a particular (advanced) moment of consumer capitalism, the rewriting in chick lit participates in blurring the boundaries among political culture, commercial culture, and literary culture. In a double gesture, "chick lit" announces itself as a form of literature while also deploying the idiom of the vernacular, which provocatively draws attention to the conventional dichotomies between mass and high culture (Harzewski, "Tradition" 33). One critic observes that "the persistent appearance of literary women authors' names—particularly, though not solely, Austen's—in discussions of, and judgments about, chick lit suggests that many readers and reviewers wish to case the genre as the descendant of literary, not popular, fiction" (Wells 64). Such framing may indeed be an attempt to recuperate chick lit from its frequent dismissal as popular frivolity, but it may also signify a challenge to literary culture and a refusal of aesthetic theories of value that would (and do) exclude chick lit and indeed most popular forms. Echoing in part Caroline Smith's assertion that chick lit engages in dialogue with popular media or advice manuals to help readers negotiate consumerism, Jim Collins contends that the most popular literary forms of chick lit, the versions often considered benchmarks for the genre, maintain an ambivalent relationship to contemporary "Serious Fiction," which offers "no help at all in negotiating the complexities of contemporary desire" within consumer culture (188). Instead, they make extensive use of canonical literature to "self-consciously reinvent the novel of manners for contemporary audiences" (187). Such "postliterary novels" as *Bridget Jones's Diary* and *Trading Up* recycle canonical works to provide guidance in romantic consumerism, with lessons in self-cultivation or the informed and normative, modern consumption of love, culture, and material goods (186–87). In turn, subgenres that remake postliterary chick lit provide additional insight into neoliberal consumer citizenship, with labor lit focusing intently on the various kinds of labor involved in romantic consumerism, and Asian American labor lit disclosing the gendered racial meanings of this form of belonging.

Romancing the Self in *China Dolls* and *Goddess for Hire*

China Dolls and *Goddess for Hire* illustrate another round of revision for chick lit as the new novel of manners and provide illuminating variations of the genre's standard bearers with heroines who negotiate romantic consumerism and neoliberal mandates to reinvent the self according to the normative values of the marketplace. Searching for careers that will provide respect, reward, and recognition as fully entitled and contributing members of the United States, the heroines of *China Dolls* and *Goddess for Hire* must contend with a decidedly romantic work ethic, one some consider characteristically American since it promises social mobility and belonging in exchange for diligence.[16] I argue that to a great extent romantic relationships in these novels are displaced by the neoliberal romance with the laboring self. In this way and others, the novels chronicle that the romantic work ethic has become even more entrenched in the United States under neoliberalism, since it requires that citizen-subjects improve and reinvent the self or be entrepreneurs of the self. As Jim Collins's understanding of chick lit emphasizes, however, the romantic recreation of the self in contemporary life is both a productive process and firmly rooted in consumption, or, as I contend, consumer citizenship. It underwrites the phenomenon of the belabored self, as discussed in chapter 1, in which workers are required to continually work on themselves through consumer culture, specifically self-help and makeover culture, to remain employable and active consumers and thus legible as citizens (McGee 12). Rather than the "giddy infatuation with brand names," chick lit centralizes the romantic recreation of the self through informed consumerism and instructs readers in what now counts as currencies of value and commodities worth trading for in the neoliberal marketplace, as well as the more subtle transactions between cultural and financial capital that secure belonging (J. Collins 189). As the characters of *China Dolls* and *Goddess for Hire* strive to re-create themselves in the terms of the neoliberal marketplace, the novels confirm that for Asian American women this labor comes with added burdens and constraints, both material and emotional. More specifically, as protagonists seek to demonstrate the marketplace qualifications or informed consumerism that is deemed necessary for the re-creation of the self and professional employment in the neoliberal economy, they must negotiate the exclusionary processes of conspicuous consumption, objectification, and capital accumulation that simultaneously betray Asian immigrant and working-class women who struggle at the margins of the marketplace.

Through authoring *China Dolls* and *Goddess for Hire,* or versions of the mainstream form of chick lit, Yu, Kan, and Singh gain a public visibility and level of recognition as cultural citizens that few other genres or types of writing could provide, save perhaps mother-daughter narrative. Further, in writing chick lit the authors participate in postfeminism, a popular discourse that addresses gendered neoliberal consumer citizenship. Yu, Kan, and Singh rewrite fantasy and reality in labor lit to chronicle contemporary conditions under neoliberalism, including Asian American women's dissatisfactions or frustrations with employment and the particular qualifications that they are compelled to gain and demonstrate for success. The focus on employment in *China Dolls* and *Goddess for Hire* is not primarily about obtaining the means for the "more important concern of shopping" (Hale 107).[17] Nor is it about valorizing good neoliberal offspring of professional Asian immigrants who fit remarkably well "into the ideal of mainstream American life" (Song 354). Refusing the invitation of certain postfeminist and postracial aesthetics, these novels openly address race, ethnicity, immigration, and gender in the anxieties and grievances about employment that they narrate. Even more specifically than the "underling lit" and "assistant lit" that detail characters' struggles with establishing careers and "women's working conditions as demeaning and ultimately destructive," *China Dolls* and *Goddess for Hire* assert that the professional world is "the ultimate chick challenge" (Ferriss and Young 7) with particularly distressing obstacles for Asian American women.[18]

The struggles of the characters in *China Dolls* and *Goddess for Hire* have to do with the difference between expectations and experiences. They largely subscribe to the romantic notion, perhaps even fantasy, that diligence is the primary and most effective route to success, but they are confronted with a different reality. Certainly, hard work is still required, but the novels cameo characters who discover that labor is now fundamentally defined through consumption, which reveals disturbing problems for Asian American female subjects. Even in *Goddess for Hire*, in which the protagonist effectively rejects the romantic model of hard work as the route to success and social belonging, the novel highlights through satire that the qualifications needed for consumer citizenship are alienating, as well as pleasurable. As Elizabeth Hale suggests, "the cause of much of the pain" in narratives about the professional workplace "may be the gap between the heroine's expectations (and fantasies) about her working life and the reality of work" (105). In the remainder of this chapter, I first provide summaries of *Goddess for Hire* and *China Dolls* and discuss evident ways they participate in the genre's trademark themes. I then analyze how the novels chronicle and address the qualifications Asian American women must demonstrate as workers for belonging in the model of neoliberal consumer citizenship.

Through magical realism Sonia Singh splendidly recombines the neoliberal fantasies and realities of chick lit in *Goddess for Hire* to address the search for meaningful labor. In this novel, the unemployed thirty-year-old protagonist Maya Mehra of Newport Beach, California, learns that she is the incarnation of the Hindu goddess Kali. Unenthusiastic about any of her physician parents' ideas about a career in medicine and marriage to "a nice Indian guy," Maya takes on the work of social justice through fighting evil and dispensing Karmic retribution upon greedy cheats and country club elites. In this fantasy, the development of goddess power in the service of "taking care of the world" overrides both consumption and conventional romance, and it is also a satiric stand-in for the romantic model of labor required in consumer citizenship. As Maya says in her typically banal tone, "I believed in the tangible, like credit cards. But, here I was, trying to summon up cosmic energy from my fallopian tubes" (Singh 49).

Although it does not use magical elements, *China Dolls* also rewrites fantasy and reality, most obviously through an exploration of the Orientalist fantasy and central metaphor of its title. The novel is emphatic in its retelling, providing not one but three intertwined stories of Asian American women in male-dominated occupations who are relentlessly subjected to the exoticizing fantasies of American Orientalism. Structured like a combination of Amy Tan's *The Joy Luck Club* and Bushnell's *Sex and the City*, *China Dolls* is divided into three sections, one for each of the trio of second-generation Chinese American friends who are the main characters: M. J. Wyn, a sportswriter for *Sporting Life* magazine with aspirations to become a sportscaster; Alex Kwan, a successful attorney who "wouldn't admit to wanting a partner"; and Lin Cho, a risk-taking stock broker who traces her interest in finance to mahjong (Yu and Kan 109).

China Dolls conforms to several narrative conventions of chick lit. The novel is set in New York City, *the* global city of urban consumer lifestyle; all three characters are single, twentysomething, middle-class heterosexual working women; much of the development of the characters occurs in the frequent meetings at various clubs, restaurants, and parties where "the girls" process family dynamics, workplace challenges, and the difficulties of dating and meeting men; and the authors incorporate diverse forms of writing or "documents from real life," such as M. J.'s sports column "Thoughts to Wyn" and Lin's "Hot Stocks" bulletin titled "What's Moving the Cho Show." Despite its suburban Newport Beach setting, *Goddess for Hire* conforms even more strictly to narrative conventions of the genre in at least two ways since it focuses on a single heroine in a first-person direct address of the reader and provides a reluctant heterosexual love interest, Tahir, who does not threaten to dominate the narrative but hovers just below the surface in a subplot.

China Dolls and *Goddess for Hire* shift attention toward work, but Yu, Kan, and Singh take full advantage of the lexicon of consumer culture to create legibility for a broad readership and to emphasize connections between consumerism and labor. The authors adorn their texts with the same commodity tropes—Kate Spade bags and Jimmy Choo shoes—that function as recognizable emblems of normative femininity and signify the commercial publishing brand "chick lit" to construct familiar touchstones and easy entry into the narratives (Gill and Herdieckerhoff 489). *Goddess for Hire* firmly grounds Maya in the material affluence of her Hummer SUV, Starbucks lattes, and Dolce & Gabbana ready-to-wear, and her parents bankroll her Southern California lifestyle. *China Dolls* actually boasts "sponsorship" by Ling Skincare Spa and Salon (where readers might purchase a China Doll collection of self-care products), the White Rabbit Lounge, and the Rickshaw Dumpling Bar, all Asian-inspired entrepreneurial ventures in New York City that appear as embedded advertising and provide upscale settings to emphasize the marketplace practices and in particular the conspicuous consumption of the main characters. Both books created commercial splashes when they were published: a cross-country publicity tour and the buzz of a possible movie deal for *China Dolls*, according to Annabelle Udo (12), and the launch of a new ethnic chick lit line by Avon Trade Paperbacks with the publication of *Goddess for Hire* (Fredriksen 40). Yu and Kan were explicit in their desire for a "wider audience" and even mass popularity, and they marketed their book aggressively because they wanted to "inspire more Asian American women to dive into writing commercial fiction" (Yang, "Asian Pop"). Certainly not wholesale condemnations of consumer culture, these novels nevertheless make important observations about the qualifications for the reinvention of the self that are demanded in a contemporary workplace, emphasizing connections between consumption and production and highlighting conspicuous consumption, objectification, and capital accumulation.

The prologue for *China Dolls* opens with a scene in New York City's Chinatown and introduces the three main characters as successful professionals and good consumer citizens. More specifically, the scene emphasizes both their conspicuous consumption of fashionable or brand-name attire and their occupational status. Just as "Alex stood out from the crowd in her crisply tailored black linen suit," her two best friends "were quite the odd couple":

> Lin, with her perfectly coifed hair, pashmina wrap, and expensive
> silk sheath—and M. J. with her ponytail, layered Billabong T-shirts,
> and cargo pants. A stockbroker and a sportswriter, respectively,
> they occupied opposite ends of the spectrum in both appearance

and personality. Alex was so busy grinning at the contrast that she almost didn't notice their companion: Lin's diminutive mother, Kim. (Yu and Kan 1)

This description establishes a range of subjectivities for Asian American, and more specifically Chinese American, women since it highlights how different the main characters are from one another. In consumer culture, as Sharon Zukin observes, "Once we have developed a fine eye for differences among goods, we can make distinctions among the people who use them" (41). But the "spectrum" Alex uses is limited to the taste distinctions that signify professional employment, so their contrast to one another is eclipsed by their shared difference from the residents of Chinatown—immigrant shopkeepers and "sewing ladies"—who are described as a mass of barking merchants and "bustling Asian grandmothers" (including Lin's immigrant mother) that notably disappears into a background "sea of strange faces" (Yu and Kan 1). In many ways the opening scene depicts characters from the perspective of a neoliberal marketplace that distinguishes Asian American women who have the qualifications to participate in mainstream consumer culture from those who are segregated by foreigner racialization and gendered exploitation in the immigrant labor markets of ethnic enclaves or ghettos.

As the scene unfolds the taste distinctions signified by upscale clothing are conflated with careers, and the characters' salient differences from those who work, live, and shop in Chinatown are emphatically occupational. In fact, the women meet in Chinatown to visit a fortune-teller or *tai-sheung* who reads their faces to reveal their professional fates— that Alex "wasn't going to end up selling herself on Forty-second Street" but rather have a "prosperous old age to look forward to," and "whether M. J. will achieve her dream of becoming an on-air sportscaster" (Yu and Kan 3). Although conspicuous consumption is supposed to ensure belonging under neoliberalism, *China Dolls* begins by illustrating how it also creates otherness and alienation for Asian American women, a point I return to shortly in a discussion of high-status careers and capitalist accumulation. Moreover, in beginning with this scene, *China Dolls* joins other labor lit in exposing the feminized low-wage manufacturing and service-sector labor that most women in industrializing and postindustrial economies perform within a logic of capitalist accumulation or global neoliberalism that constructs feminine belonging through commodities and services requiring considerably larger incomes (Gill and Herdieckerhoff 495).

Certainly, the main characters in *China Dolls* joyfully participate in a conventional culture of femininity that centralizes the pleasures of consumer culture. However, all three increasingly struggle with the acquisition and display of luxury brand-name goods and services as a way to illustrate their marketplace expertise and self-cultivation, undermining the assertion that such purchases offer "a means of creating identity and achieving success in both personal and professional spheres" (Van Slooten 220). Especially in M. J.'s first section, the novel is saturated with an insistence that "she didn't care about designer labels or girly beauty products or sleazy brokers on the make," with declarations that she was "beginning to question the importance of clothes and looks and labels," and with questions from her friend such as, "When are you going to realize that there's more to a person than their appearance?" (Yu and Kan 68, 80, 59).

Singh takes a different approach in *Goddess for Hire* and satirizes Maya's conspicuous consumption, exaggerating in order to deconstruct her heroine's extensive marketplace expertise. Actually, it is Maya who narrates her informed consumerism through cataloguing purchases and incessantly dropping brand names, from the opening scene in which she describes her thirtieth-birthday eight-bag shopping spree to the final pages in which she contemplates registering at Nordstrom to make giving easier for her worshippers. Moreover, Maya maintains her preoccupation despite the celestial importance of the work for which the universe has chosen her and despite a sardonic disparagement of the worldly importance of consumption.[19] In fact, the material rewards just keep getting more extravagant, including diamonds and a condo by the end of the novel, when Maya has finally learned how to deliberately apply her goddess powers. Of course, this is humorous because the reader understands that social change work and spiritual devotion are rarely accompanied by such material rewards. Singh suggests, however, that the world of consumer capitalism would be far more ethical if they were. Although Maya remains a material girl like her idol Madonna, *Goddess for Hire* offers an alternative system in which acts of social justice are a currency of value that can be acquired, displayed, and exchanged for both material products and symbolic commodities, such as adulation, to cultivate the self. As satire, Singh's narrative practice in some ways resembles Kinsella's in the Shopaholic series, which ironically comments on heroine Becky Bloomwood's compulsive shopping, despite crippling debt (Caroline Smith 14).[20] Similar to Becky, Maya thoroughly recognizes that consumption is the idiom through which contemporary life is understood. At times, however, Maya's perception is not limited to the conventional wisdom of consumer culture, and she is able to discern its compensatory limitations and its usefulness outside the mandates of neoliberal consumer citizenship. When she wavers in the face of her new goddess responsibility to save the world from the forces of evil, for example, Maya quips, "Life wasn't a 50-percent-off sale. But if it were, I was having the most critical case of buyer's remorse ever" (Singh 67). Ultimately, she rejects the notion that consumption is the only or most important process for producing subjectivity or signifying success. Instead of unequivocally endorsing the gendered consumer citizenship that postfeminist discourse often represents as empowering and fulfilling, *Goddess for Hire* recognizes the influential role of conspicuous consumption and offers a character who negotiates "the temporary illusion of decadently and stylishly 'having it all'" (Van Slooten 220).

In addition to conspicuous consumption, *Goddess for Hire* and *China Dolls* address marketplace objectification and commodification, remarking on the fetishization of Asian women in consumer cultures generally and in American Orientalism more specifically. Clearly, the titles of the novels reference objectifying processes by foregrounding infantilized and hyperfeminized representations of Asian women. The titular figures seem to be added to the bevy of commercial tropes or branding associated with chick lit, which can be understood as metonoymic chronicles of neoliberalism, symbolic excesses of consumer culture, or symptomatic fantasies of capitalism that cannot be delivered. Pointing to the latter, the titles may actually draw attention to the specious claims of consumer citizenship as universally available, since these all-too-familiar cultural stereotypes signify exotic female otherness far more than national belonging. Butler and Desai argue that Singh's use of magical realism not only subverts the realist imperatives of chick lit that may conflate author and protagonist but also "refuses to allow authenticity to be read in any simple way" (20). It also refuses, I argue, the title's promise of a "real" spiritual goddess narrative. Although Maya is a worshiped goddess in the novel, she is reluctant and signifies the opposite of nearly every aspect of the spiritual stereotype, given her valley girl materialism, her irreverence toward family and heritage, and her rather mercenary relation to retributive goddess work. Similarly, Yu and Kan dismantle any expectations readers may have for passive Chinese playthings. M. J., Alex, and Lin are all far more devoted to their jobs and one another than to men, and their strong personalities challenge the exoticizing interpellations they regularly encounter. Similar to *Goddess for Hire*, the title of

China Dolls is undercut through heroines who provide counterexamples of the stereotype, and their concerns for the fantasies of consumer culture displace the preoccupying fantasies of heterosexual romance.

The fetishization of Asian women is more than a title in *China Dolls* since it is a recurring problem that all three characters encounter in flash backs to failed relationships and the ephemeral meetings of speed dating, in service arenas such as restaurants and spas and, of course, in advertising. Nearly everywhere they encounter stereotypes, of the sexually submissive or the sexually aggressive version, and they understand them as part of consumer culture. M. J. characterizes racialized sexualization by white men as shopping for a particular kind of "Chinese ware," while Alex readily sees a client's offer to be his "escort" for dinner as "yet another man trying to cultivate me as his own oriental delicacy" (Yu and Kan 83, 110). *China Dolls* teems, in fact, with parodic white men who wear Jet Li T-shirts, sport Chinese-character tattoos, and think all Asian women look alike.

In *China Dolls* the characters link the spectacular objectification and fetishization of Asian women in consumer culture to the production of the self in the workplace. A specific workplace incident, when a white professional basketball player recalls a previous meeting with M. J., is the eponymous scene: "I knew I'd remember a sweet china doll like you. There aren't that many in the business, ya know?" (Yu and Kan 51). This kind of encounter is basically repeated in all three workplace environments with increasingly dramatic consequences, almost ending Lin's career at Merrill Lynch when her ambitious colleague and lover Drew publicly announces to their entire office that "no one does a *meeting* like" Lin (238, emphasis in original). A clear reference to the numerous gender discrimination lawsuits brought against brokerage firms just a few years prior to the novel's publication, this incident is obviously not limited to a particular firm, or, as suggested by similar treatment of the other characters, a particular industry. Although Lin has the resources to salvage her career, these representations may be read as metonyms for a racially and sexually stratified global economy, recounting who pays the price, at least on one end of the occupational spectrum, for the Orientalist fantasies that circulate in the marketplace.

While *Goddess for Hire* and *China Dolls* protest the processes of objectification and exoticization of Asian women in consumer culture, their respective heroines also demonstrate the informed consumption of the same objectified cultural images. Maya is so susceptible to reproducing stereotypical images of South Asian women, as when she flippantly mentions "bride burnings in India where mothers-in-law shoved their daughters-in-law into the oven after dutifully collecting their dowries," that she must use on herself the "Goddess Gaze" or mind control that she has developed to help fight immigrant-hating thugs and machine-gun packing socialites (Singh 9). While the evocation of dowry murder could be read as self-Orientalizing, I suggest that Singh both mocks such static cultural representations of "oppressed Indian women" and acknowledges that South Asian American women are compelled to adopt normative marketplace values and circulate them under consumer capitalism. When neoliberal technologies of subjection and subject-making construct female citizens as agents through the display and expression of romantic consumerism, empowerment is defined through their control of the gaze in the marketplace (Weber 52). At times *Goddess for Hire* itself succumbs to the "ethnographic imperative," as Yoonmee Chang refers to the pressure to provide "insider" cultural information, with Maya relaying basic information on the partition of India, for example, or that Dharma means "life purpose" in Sanskrit, and somewhat more detailed information on Kali, clearly not an image of an oppressed Indian woman, either as a deity or as incarnated in Maya (Chang 27). Still, the instruction is usually balanced by comic relief provided through Maya's irreverence for her cultural heritage and a dubious attitude toward her newfound powers. Singh's narrative practice calls attention to these moments by presenting them as self-conscious or constructed cultural images, as when Maya confides, "I felt like a character in a bad movie who suddenly remembers incredibly vital information she somehow coincidentally forgot, until prodded," or when Maya refers to one crime-fighting episode as a film titled *Country Club Carnage* (Singh 23, 102). Maya produces these images through adopting the colonial gaze of the neoliberal marketplace but then presents them as commercial spectacles and inauthentic fantasies.

In *China Dolls,* Yu and Kan's characters cycle through a series of relationships with white men who are mostly interested in fulfilling the Orientalist fantasies cultivated in consumer culture. The characters are well aware of and negotiate their lovers' interpellations and leverage their "sexual capital," a form of cultural capital. Susan Koshy theorizes sexual capital as the shifting value encoded in images of Asian American femininity within the United States and as the "aggregate of attributes that index desirability within the field of romantic or marital relationships in a given culture and thereby influence the life-chances and opportunities of an individual" (15).[21] The athletic M. J. recalls that she began to present herself as a "girlie girl" in the sixth grade when classmates "were convinced that she was a lesbian," and saw her as "the tall girl with the Kmart clothes and the weird Chinese lunches, the girl who never got a passing glance from any of the boys except when they were facing off against her in gym class" (Yu and Kan 45, 68). She deliberately masters the important consumer practices of shopping, following fashion trends, and dressing seductively. In one club scene, for example, M. J. draws a group of men into a game of sports trivia because "there was nothing sweeter to her than toying with a bunch of Neanderthals" (15). When one man asks, "Did anyone ever tell you that you look like Lucy Liu," M. J. smiles and says, "I can definitely kick some ass—when the situation calls for it," at once demonstrating and commenting on her willingness to trade in the currency of one version of Asian American femininity that circulates widely (15). She then wins the next round of drinks. In addition, when M. J. and old flame "golden boy" Kevin attend *Dunk* magazine's twenty-fifth-anniversary gala at Manhattan's exclusive 40/40 Club, she frames their coupledom through the spectacles of consumer culture: "As they glided into the room, M. J. caught a glimpse of their reflection in a passing mirror. They looked beautiful—not quite Ken and Barbie, but at least Ken and Suzie Wong. Walking next to Kevin, M. J. felt like she was born to frequent such places" (49). Such transactions between sexual capital and the financial capital of her profession display the informed consumerism of a neoliberal marketplace that objectifies, commodifies, and fetishizes M. J.'s image, and the exchanges help her achieve social status and a feeling of heteronormative belonging.

The commercial tropes that brand the genre as a whole also polka dot the narratives of *China Dolls* and *Goddess for Hire*. The novels seem at first to reinscribe the American Dream and the myth of meritocracy in which the cultural values of competitive hard work and striving individualism are rewarded with upward economic mobility into the middle class and social inclusion in the nation. Children of immigrant parents, the characters enjoy affluent lifestyles, replete with frequent evenings out at hip clubs and restaurants, invitations to art openings, and prestigious addresses in either Manhattan or Orange County. The novels also emphasize that the characters have been promised material success and urged to pursue lucrative, high-status careers as a route to belonging, both by the larger social order and by their families. However, just as *China Dolls* and *Goddess for Hire* challenge the more obvious forms of conspicuous consumption, their characters become frustrated with careers that promise upward mobility through accumulation of cultural, social, and financial capital. Rather than universal access and reward for any rational economic agent willing to work hard, they discover that the American Dream "is a capitalistic, free market ideology in which only those who can pay the price of admission may enter," and that "achievements are made despite the barriers in occupational structure and racial/gender/class discrimination imposed by U.S. society" (L. Park 7). Alex in *China Dolls* faces this realization in a moment of self-examination:

> What had she spent the past decade doing? The answer was easy: she'd spent the last ten years chasing career success—racking up the billables at her firm and slaving through all nighters. Being Asian and a woman in the predominantly white, male world of law meant having to go the extra mile and having to outwork everyone else just to keep pace. (Yu and Kan 107)

To varying degrees, the young female characters in these novels come to understand that their professional careers are linked to designer handbags and spa treatments. They function as evidence of marketplace expertise through which conformity to normative neoliberal ideologies is displayed and exclusionary claims to belonging are communicated. As McRobbie observes, wage-earning capacity functions symbolically "as a mark of respectability, citizenship, and entitlement" (*Aftermath of Feminism,* 2).

Both *China Dolls* and *Goddess for Hire* reveal the most unsavory aspects of consumer citizenship and accumulation, specifically for Asian Americans. In Lisa Park's theorization of consumer citizenship, Asian Americans in particular are compelled to subscribe to an American Dream ideology in which the conspicuous consumption of status symbols, in the form of cars, clothes, and careers, demonstrates belonging because Asian Americans continue to be seen as perpetual foreigners in the United States; capital accumulation or class status becomes a crucial route to display social citizenship and make claims to full citizenship, particularly for children of immigrant entrepreneurs who often consider it a way to repay the familial sacrifice of parents who have toiled under adverse conditions (5–7). Conspicuous consumption becomes "the primary evidence of their parents' successful or unsuccessful incorporation to the United States" (L. Park 5). Belief in the promise of the American Dream or at least participation in its mandates of acquisition and conspicuous consumption are the "test" and "proof" of Asian American social belonging or citizenship in the racial ideology of US capitalism. However, the evidence of belonging is established at a substantially higher cost than for white Americans since that cost includes the exclusion of immigrant parents and family whose social mobility is prevented by racialized barriers to occupational access and other forms of discrimination (7).

All three of the main characters in *China Dolls* increasingly struggle with the contradictions of this route to belonging. While none of the characters in *China Dolls* entirely rejects the citizenship test of economic success defined by the accumulation of financial capital, and only one chooses a profession—sports reporting—that would probably not allow her to pass it, they share the contradictions of working within an unjust social order, and difficult questions about rewards in relation to costs complicate M. J.'s, Lin's, and Alex's different careers. M. J. explicitly recognizes the problems with this model of belonging and confronts the paradox of a differential politics of citizenship in the United States that largely excludes her parents, qualifies her own participation, and enlists them all in the violent hierarchies of the racial order. In M. J.'s view, her family was "the classic Chinese immigrant family," since it was "overzealous" in pursuing the promise of the American Dream:

> The only things her family ever seemed to care about were who went to what school, who was in what career, and who made how much money. In the first category, it was all about the Ivy Leagues. In the second category, there were the doctors, the lawyers, and maybe a stockbroker or two. As for the last category, the answer was obvious. (Yu and Kan 41)

M. J. is an "outsider" in her family, since she was not one of the "perfect" offspring "with family approved professions and six-figure salaries" (41). While the marginalization is painful and she yearns for the approval that lucrative employment would bring from her family and society, M. J.'s resolve is crystallized through an episode in which she connects her family's antiblack racism to her boyfriend's anti-Asian racism. After numerous rejections by Kevin and his wealthy white family, including at that iconic site of exclusion, the country club, M. J. realizes that her own family's investments in white privilege have everything to do with her desire for Kevin, as well as her experience of exclusion on both the familial and the social level. Once M. J. makes these connections, she fully commits to a career as a sportscaster.

Similar to M. J., Maya in *Goddess for Hire* declines the citizenship test of financial success and capital accumulation, and this novel suggests that the pressure to become a physician in order to maintain family cohesion and to demonstrate social membership is symbolically so strong that only magic or divine intervention can counter its extraordinary force and justify Maya's refusal. While social justice work seems to choose Maya in a fantastic "goddess-napping," even before she learns of her spiritual powers Maya humorously but emphatically condemns the lucrative career as one of several problematic currencies of value carrying unrealistic demands for South Asian Indian women in the United States:

> In traditional Indian culture, a woman is supposed to get married and have children—strictly in that order—by the time she's twenty-five. My female cousins and I, having been born and raised in America, have it considerably harder, not easier. We're supposed to get married, have children, and be either a doctor, lawyer, or engineer, all by the time we're twenty-five. (Singh 3)

Maya seems proud, in fact, that "of all the ninety-seven adult members of the Mehra clan spread throughout the United States, ninety-six are doctors, the sole exception being yours truly" (4). The coercions of the American Dream take many forms, but as Maya's comments imply, in the neoliberal period they are deeply connected to labor market demands and preference categories in post-1965 immigration policy. More subtly perhaps, Maya's reluctance also points out that this manifestation of the American Dream depends on the privileges of English-speaking, middle- and upper-class Indian immigrants who could access visas designed for certain workers who were seen as appropriate, such as the H-1B visa, as Inderpal Grewal has observed (5).

Maya's insight into the exclusionary terms of the American Dream is integral to her higher calling. In one of her most important providential works Maya thwarts Gwen Danner, the murderous "socialite extraordinaire," literally saving hundreds of innocents from the destructive forces of commodity-defined and displayed social status at a country club. Maya summons her powers against this crime because, as she tells the reader, "I hated country clubs. I despised their homogenous membership, their backward, narrow-minded thinking, and their superior air. But mostly I resented not being a member. My parents were in the right tax bracket but didn't exactly hang with the 'right' crowd" (Singh 99). Through humorous marketplace melodrama, *Goddess for Hire* conveys its narrator's (and perhaps its author's) anger at the clear limits to belonging for South Asian Americans, even when they conform to the mandate of accumulation in consumer citizenship. In this and other scenes in which Maya confronts economic injustice and her feelings about it, the labor lit novel provides "a measure of vengeance" against the contradictions of neoliberal capitalism (Hale 105).

In fact, if initial reader identification with characters in *China Dolls* and *Goddess for Hire* may be around normative femininity as defined through conspicuous consumption, recognition is also produced through the contradictions, especially for Asian American female subjects, of working to belong in an exclusive social order and through the understanding that the "free market" in which the characters' labor is a fantasy, far from rational and far from liberating. M. J. feels the alienation most acutely:

> I guess I never felt like I really belonged anywhere. Not with my family, who thinks I should be a good little Asian daughter and get a real job that pays real money. Not at the country club where they let me play tennis but won't let me into the membership. And certainly not in the sports world, where being a woman and Chinese means that I couldn't possibly know anything about sports. (Yu and Kan 90)

The novels of Yu and Kan and Singh indicate that chick lit is quite capable of reflecting the increasing social cleavage, financial instability, and geopolitical conflict that have become identifiable contours of neoliberalism.

Postfeminist culture typically treats women in the workforce with deep ambivalence, and "the importance of finding suitable, lucrative, and relevant labor" often recedes as women are reminded of "all the personal and romantic goals their laboring might put in jeopardy" (Leonard 103–4). Although this trope is discernible in *Goddess for Hire* and *China Dolls* in the various romantic interests that shadow the main characters' professional interests, as well as in the chronicle of unfulfilled promises and dissatisfactions with working conditions, the characters do not find sanctuary in either heterosexual romance or normative, heteropatriarchal family. In fact, the "retreatist paradigm" of denouncing professional or occupational ambition that Negra identifies in contemporary postfeminist culture (especially chick flicks) does not hold for these examples of the subgenre of labor lit (89). The romantic re-creative consumer-worker maintains a place of privilege in the narratives.

Goddess for Hire and *China Dolls* highlight characters who discover that romantic consumerism is a necessary qualification and central to the success of the laboring female citizen. One must become a "flex subject," a worker who is valuable for her understanding and expertise in market rationalities or "maximizing the reach and frequency of market transactions" by extending them to the cultivation of the self (Harvey 3). Further, Asian American female readers are schooled that gaining this qualification is a challenge: they must either ideologically deny structural hierarchies in the labor market that present barriers to full belonging, or dissemble to affectively negotiate the dissonance that results from the gap between what they are promised in neoliberal ideology and what they encounter in the workplace. These novels may be read as cautionary tales, but they also provide guidance in the negotiation of the re-creation of the self in gendered consumer citizenship and seem to prepare readers for the work of authorship they are expected to perform in the neoliberal economy. However, instead of functioning as coherent templates or efficient technologies of neoliberal citizenship, *China Dolls* and *Goddess for Hire* complicate the romance with the self, decline fantastic resolutions to marketplace contradictions, and disclose the disingenuity of "free-market" claims. Indeed, these novels question the neoliberal American Dream that promises meritocratic reward for diligence by revealing that working hard is not enough and not necessarily the "best way" to succeed in life. While postfeminist culture often responds to the disingenuity of neoliberalism with similarly disingenuous resolutions that evade, escape, or retreat from the realities of social conditions, *China Dolls* and *Goddess for Hire* illustrate that such resolutions fail to contain the contradictions of contemporary capitalism.[22]

In this analysis of Asian American labor lit, I have aimed to complicate perceptions that chick lit novels are only simple, escapist, and superficial consumer fantasies that render its female readers even more vulnerable or amenable to neoliberal capitalism. In fact, the recombination of fantasy and reality in *China Dolls* and *Goddess for Hire* does not give up entirely on the fantasies of neoliberal consumer culture but recombines them for complex and provocative outcomes that acknowledge the fluidity of identification within cultural fantasies. That chick lit trades in the currency of fantasy as it mixes with reality is to a great extent what makes it popular at this particular historical juncture. As Stephen Duncombe argues, "Fantasy and spectacle have become the *lingua franca* of our time," and the crafted fantasies in consumer culture speak to "something deep and real within us" (9, 16).[23] Moreover, we need to dispose of the deeply gendered ideas about the ideological and aesthetic dangers of fantasy and "make peace with the less-than-rational nature of politics" (10). Or, as Jane Park has recently reminded us, "Imagination is the politics of dreams," so instead of condemning the language of commercial fantasy, "which is spoken predominantly by younger media audiences and producers, we need to develop more sophisticated critical ways to examine the relationship between the formal terms of this language and its ideological messages, especially with regard to representations of race and ethnicity" (200).[24] As a reinvention of chick lit that rewrites the genre's blend of realism and fantasy, the Asian American labor lit discussed in this chapter addresses the mandate of marketplace expertise for gendered racial subjects in consumer citizenship and acknowledges that people have dreams and desires for change within this material and ideological context of constraints.

4 /   Neoliberal Detective Work: Uncovering
Cosmopolitan Corruption in the New Economy

The revival of popular interest in the figure of Charlie Chan has been confirmed by Yunte Huang's "biography" *Charlie Chan: The Untold Story of the Honorable Detective and His Rendezvous with American History*, which quickly became a national best seller after its publication in 2010, won or was nominated for several prestigious awards, and is, at the time of this writing, being considered for adaptation to the big screen. For many, this revival is a failure, a regression, and a cause for concern, since Chan represents, as Huang asserts, "an American stereotype" as "the country's first beloved Chinaman," one that stands in contrast to but is oppositionally dependent on the yellow peril figure of Dr. Fu Manchu (xix, xviii). Indeed, the iconic Chan "has become a persistent thorn in Asian Americans' side, an instrument of assimilationism that relentlessly reminds Asian Americans of the model minority imperatives by which they are to abide" (Betsy Huang 53). Given such deep investments in the racialization of Asian Americans, with the Orientalist image of the inscrutable and dangerous doctor on the one hand, and the stereotype of the deferential good subject of Chan on the other, the detective novel is not historically well established in Asian American literature, and one can easily imagine why authors seem to have been cautious in taking up crime fiction of any description.

For some, however, renewed popular interest in the detective novel offers an opportunity to address persistent racism in US institutions, specifically the law, policing, and citizenship, as well as the range of anxieties about American social identity and belonging that the images in the Charlie Chan archive reflect, whether in the context of modernity or postmodernity. This is particularly true for cultural studies scholars but also for the numerous Asian American authors who have enthusiastically and successfully taken up crime fiction, whether of the mystery or detective variety, since the 1980s. While Chang-rae Lee's *Native Speaker* (1995) and Susan Choi's *American Woman* (2003) make use of crime fiction conventions, Leonard Chang, Henry Chang, Dale Furutani, and Naomi Hirahara have all produced series with Asian American sleuths, and Gus Lee, Lisa See, and Amitav Gosh have written popular thrillers. Furutani, author of the Ken Tanaka series, has commented that, because Charlie Chan and the other fictional Asian detectives he encountered did not "talk, think or act like any real Asians," he was motivated "to write about Asian Americans as we feel, think, are" (quoted in M. Reddy, *Traces, Codes, and Clues* 49).

Rather than aiming for authentic representations, it may be necessary, Betsy Huang suggests, to return to the subgenres of crime fiction as influential sources of the racially abject Chan and the sinister Chinatown to "diffuse" their iconic power (59). In her estimation, at least some contemporary authors are using crime fiction "to unsettle its power to sustain Orientalist binaries that have shaped Asian American subjecthood in popular and legal discourses" (50). In light of the current ideological and market preference for a postracial literary aesthetic, which "suggests that race is immaterial, that race is obsolete as an organizing— and damaging—structure of social life," the American detective novel with an unmistakably racialized figure firmly established in its genealogy may well provide a viable alternative for those who cannot ignore or who wish to explore the persistent injustices of social life for Asian Americans (Chang 202).

Undoubtedly, resurgent popular interest in Chan is connected to China's increasingly elevated status on the global stage of the neoliberal economy, and indeed this link highlights the ways in which detective fiction serves as a register for anxieties about and a site for interpreting the dynamic social conditions of capitalism as well as the enduring structures of inequality in modern life. We must understand the current Chan phenomenon, then, in the context of the tremendously broad popularity of detective fiction and the various ways in which it has been recast in the past forty years to chronicle the contemporary social order that is associated with neoliberal economic globalization. Moreover, observers must be careful not to let the recent focus on "the Chinaman" obscure the central role that female detectives and women writers have played in the detective novel's reimagination. In fact, it is imperative that we attend to the gendered dimensions of what might be called the "re-Orientalization" of the detective novel, and indeed the gendered racial operations of US neoliberalism writ large that contemporary detective fiction chronicles, especially if we wish to address the idealization or "success" of the Asian American female as neoliberal citizen-subject.

I consider Asian American women's detective fiction in relation not only to the specific history of what Charles Rzepka refers to as "Chinatown Regionalism" and Asian American reworkings of it, but also in relation to the revision of the American hardboiled detective novel in the past three decades by women writers, including feminists and women of color broadly. As Linda Mizejewski noted in 2004, "The number of female-investigator novels published in the United States has tripled every five years since 1985" (19). I observe as well the popularity of women's detective fiction on a cosmopolitan scale that includes the neoliberal states of the United States, the United Kingdom, and Japan. To be sure, the timing of a "boom" in popular fiction characterized by a pool of professional female detectives corresponds to the cycle of economic "booms" and "bubbles" associated with the neoliberal global economy and its demands upon women as laborers and as consumers. In short, the business of female detective fiction is booming, and it invites serious investigation on a number of levels.[1]

Second only to romance in the US market share of book sales, detective fiction has similarly witnessed both a commercial renaissance and a generic revision under neoliberal conditions that have spawned a proliferation of media forms addressed to and consumed by women.[2] Just as I argued in chapter 3 that chick lit is mobilized by Asian American women writers in ways that help us understand the labor skills necessary for consumer citizenship—centralizing the mandates of marketplace expertise and the re-creation of the self, declining fantastic resolutions to marketplace inadequacies, and complicating the romantic consumerism necessary for belonging—I argue here that the mobilization of detective fiction by Sujata Massey and Suki Kim provides insight into cosmopolitan citizenship and the specific demands upon women's labor within a global US economy.

Similarly positioned as cosmopolitan books, both *Girl in a Box* and *The Interpreter* have been translated into several languages, and Massey and Kim are award-winning, internationally known writers, though to different degrees, given the much longer publication record of Massey.[3] The self-conscious generic play of these detective novels also exhibits the international sophistication and decidedly postmodern sensibility that are associated with contemporary cosmopolitanism, so they provide a historical snapshot of the cultural moment of the bubble economy of the United States at the turn of the century, and just a few years before the economic downturn of the Great Recession in late 2007. Published in 2006, Massey's *Girl in a Box* includes a nod to the chick lit phenomenon at its height, since Rei's undercover employment is in an upscale store in Ginza, the fashion mecca of cosmopolitan Tokyo. While I would not go as far as reviewer Ruth Jordan, who described the novel as "Chick Lit with a lot of Ludlum," or consider *Girl in a Box* "mystery lit," the book is described on Massey's website as "Espionage, fashion and romance galore in [an] upbeat continuation of the series."[4] *The Interpreter* (2003) is somewhat further removed in tone from the chick lit that has so effectively capitalized on the cosmopolitan conditions of the genre's typical New York setting, but neither can it resist recycling the commercial tropes of that feminizing genre, such as heels from Prada, fragrance from Chanel, and diamonds from Tiffany & Co.

In the following pages I explore how, given the Orientalist and masculinist investments of detective fiction, Massey and Kim are able to use this subgenre to comment on contemporary United States belonging for Asian American women who labor in a global economy. *Girl in a Box* and *The Interpreter* contribute to the contemporary reworking of the hardboiled detective novel, I contend, by investigating the operational terms of the "New Economy," a popular discourse of neoliberal cosmopolitan citizenship in the United States that demands culturally skilled workers be mobile and mutable in a knowledge-based, information-driven global capitalism. Borrowing from the American hardboiled novel and "metaphysical detective stories," *Girl in a Box* and *The Interpreter* revise generic codes to reveal that the ethically ennobled discourse of neoliberal cosmopolitanism rather crudely appropriates difference, particularly the cultural knowledge of Asian American female subjects who migrate for work in the global economy and who are often considered ideal neoliberal subjects for their flexibility and mutability.[5] More startling, the protagonists uncover cosmopolitan corruption on a massive scale and learn about the lethal dimensions of the New Economy, including the insidious dangers of the circulation of the neoliberal American Dream.

The first section of this chapter situates texts written by Asian American women within the vast landscape of detective fiction, at the crossroads of American hardboiled fiction and the metaphysical detective story, and it describes the contours of the cultural work these generic variations perform. I discuss contemporary permutations of detective fiction with specific attention to the treatment of racism and the emergence of the professional female detective in popular literature and media culture. The second part of the chapter provides broader context by discussing how detective fiction chronicles the New Economy, which emerged in the early 1980s as a discourse and is now ubiquitous. In the third section, I analyze *Girl in a Box* and *The Interpreter* for how they mobilize detective fiction to comment upon cosmopolitan citizenship and its mandate that workers collect and interpret knowledge in alignment with a globalizing US neoliberalism.

The Subgenre of Detective Fiction

More than any other popular form of literature, detective fiction has received serous attention from literary critics and cultural theorists, especially in the past forty years. Rather than a formula that simply reflects and resolves dominant ideological tensions and discursively produces conformity, critics now acknowledge the complexity of detective fiction, its engagement with questions of subjectivity, its capacity to interrogate received knowledge, and its tendency to survey social structures. Understood as part of the larger category of crime fiction, detective fiction is formally diverse, drawing from and revising realistic and romantic modes, modernist and postmodernist conventions, and experimental and hybrid narrative practices.[6] While most genealogies, including this one, link today's popular variations and subgenres in some way to the Anglo-American tradition, especially the influential works of Edgar Allen Poe or Sir Arthur Conan Doyle, detective fiction has flourished the world over, adapting to local concerns and addressing contemporary conditions, from Australia to France, Argentina to Japan, India to the Ghana.[7] Nels Pearson and Marc Singer remind us that "the detective genre has been intrinsically engaged with epistemological formations that are not simply those of 'society' in the abstract—that is, dominant cultural groups and their hegemonic discourse—but those produced in encounters between nations, between races and cultures, and especially between imperial powers and their colonial territories" (3). They also point out that the genre has evolved "from seeing transgressions of national and racial boundaries as preconditions for crime to seeing them as keys to its detection and resolution, especially where such solutions include indictments of broader social and political conditions" (7). I extend this observation to underscore that contemporary detective fiction quite often addresses the ethical claims of new formations, such as cosmopolitanism and transnationalism, which aspire or purport to transcend boundaries of identity and to reformulate belonging.

Similar to detective fiction broadly and indeed the whole range of crime fiction, the more specific subgenre of American hardboiled detective fiction has always been concerned with power and the social categories of identity, including race, ethnicity, gender, sexuality, and social class, that have been used to rationalize violence and inequality for the Others of dominant, white Americanness.[8] The hardboiled detective story that emerged in the 1920s in the United States positioned itself against elitism and the "racialist fantasies of imperialism and imperial adventure fiction" that relied on exotic settings or isolated mansions and were associated with the more genteel English classic detective tradition and the contemporaneous "golden age" mysteries (Pearson and Singer 5). The hardboiled aimed to document the harsh realities of an urban world, in particular the "mean streets" of the industrial US city, which was represented as "a place of violence and illegitimate power" (McCann 53). There was a palpable connection to social life in the United States, and like earlier subgenres of American crime fiction, hardboiled fiction was initially produced and consumed in the context of a "crime wave" or sensationalized public concern around social disorder, policing, and the law, this time following World War I and during the rise of organized crime, Prohibition, and intense vigilante (white) racial violence (McCann 42–43).[9] Rather than a factual document of corruption and social conflict, however, in practice the hardboiled story functioned as a popular cultural fantasy that customarily tapped into white anxieties about the Other and desires for bringing the "savage world under control" (44). In fact, early hardboiled fiction resembled the classical detective fiction of the 1920s and 1930s that dominated best-seller lists in both England and the United States in that it was typically marred by racial stereotypes and the xenophobia that held widespread currency at that time (Rzepka 1464).

Moreover, although the figure of the hardboiled detective may have been designed for "rule subversion" and writers sought to create an expectation in readers for the violation of the generic code of the detective, the hardboiled detective did not unequivocally challenge the social problems he revealed.[10] If more closely associated with the English genteel tradition of detective fiction than the American hardboiled, Charlie Chan nonetheless provides an instructive lesson in the limitations of rule subversion. As the first detective of color, one who initially appeared in the pages of the popular *Saturday Evening Post* in 1925 in Earl Derr Biggers's serialized novel *The House Without a Key*, Chan was created with the explicit intention of contesting the yellow peril discourse and the threatening evil of the Orientalist figure of Dr. Fu Manchu that appeared so often in public discourse of the period. In addition, Biggers removed Chan from the purported evils of the setting of Chinatown. But Chan's subservience reduced him to a racially abject role and his accented English reinforced stereotypes of Asians as "immutably foreign." Just as Biggers's attempt at rule subversion backfired, so too did the contemporaneous writers of hardboiled fiction fall short, for while their heroes demonstrated "bravado, physical prowess, and street smarts," the hardboiled detective crystallized as an individual, ordinary man with "limited abilities to redress . . . injustice" (McCann 46, 56). Hardboiled fiction symbolically left in tact the disordered status quo, "consistently reinscrib[ing] a conventional racial order" (M. Reddy, "Race and American Crime Fiction" 137).

The hardboiled subgenre of detective fiction was thus built on moral and subjective ambiguity as well as formal conflict and tension that extend beyond the ending of any given text for further reflection, as well as serialization and adaptation. The slippery and open-ended examination of the social in relation to the individual in hardboiled fiction is in large part what makes it not only popular but also "endlessly available for variation" (McCann 42). As John Scaggs summarizes, the attempts of the hardboiled "to contain various threatening 'others' ultimately deconstruct it, and the general tendency of hardboiled fiction to replicate, explore, and even interrogate its own conventions allows the entire subgenre to be appropriated for a variety of ideological, formal, and generic purposes" (78). This "writerly" quality of the hardboiled has lent the subgenre to the postcolonial, transnational, and cosmopolitan concerns of contemporary authors, and, not surprisingly, this is the subgenre of detective fiction in the United States that has been most successfully adapted by feminists, women writers, and writers of color for sleuths whom they imagined might detect the postindustrial world differently. In short, the "traditional positioning of the detective as an 'outsider witness whose very marginality reveals the compromised honor of those in power, socially, politically, and/or economically'" is one convention of the subgenre that is readily available for complex revision, particularly within emergent literatures (M. Reddy, "Race and American Crime Fiction" 144). To be sure, the detective in contemporary popular hardboiled fiction is no longer always a white, heterosexual male.

Even if, or perhaps because, women writers and the woman detective "have as long a history in crime fiction as do their male counterparts," with Agatha Christie and Dorothy Sayers holding venerated positions in the golden age of the genre, detective fiction in the American hardboiled vein is a decidedly masculinized genre (M. Reddy, "Women Detectives" 191). The early hardboiled novel was arguably gendered as thoroughly as popular romance but with far more attention to the other end of the gender binary through, Maureen Reddy explains, a mutually reinforcing combination of aesthetic, cultural, and marketplace forces:

> Among other things, the hardboiled represents an intensifica-
> tion of the crime novel's commitment to a particular variety of
> realism that depends heavily on a tough, uncompromising sur-
> face verisimilitude. At the time, women were debarred from most
> law enforcement positions and were unlikely to be found work-
> ing as private detectives; they thus are also barred from the world
> of the fictional private eye. The intense masculinity of the hard-
> boiled, its centralization of an alienated male consciousness and
> its positioning of women as either dangerous, seductive villains or
> nurturing but essentially insignificant helpmates simultaneously
> reproduce and explain the very same cultural myths that made
> female professional private eyes unlikely outside the novel as well.
> (193)[11]

Once it became illegal for public law enforcement in the United States to openly discriminate against females in hiring in the early 1970s, the female detective was finally represented in fiction as a *professional* woman, rather than the adventurous girl, "the curious old lady, the spunky spinster, or someone's girlfriend" (Mizejewski 17–18). As the professional female sleuth began to appear in series in the 1980s, she transformed the publishing market in a new golden age of detective fic-tion reinhabited by women authors, characters, and fans; by the end of the century, US bookstores carried "more than a hundred crime series featuring heroines who were private investigators, cops, sheriffs, forensic experts, constables, or federal agents" (19). This development was fueled by and part of the heightened address of women and the concomitant explosion of media forms, as outlined in chapter 1, which began to aggressively target female audiences once neoliberal media capitalism recognized their huge market potential.

While Mizejewski argues that the "female dick" "asks us to re-imag-ine sex, bodies, and gender" by disrupting the genre's hypermasculinity,

I will show that the female detective presented in both *Girl in a Box* and *The Interpreter* actually relies upon hardboiled masculinity to distinguish herself in a relational construction of gender identity, so she shares to some degree the appropriative dimensions of this form of American subjectivity (15). Appropriation is not specific, of course, to the hardboiled version of hegemonic masculinity, and scholarship on contemporary masculinity documents the ways in which different popular culture forms across media platforms register ongoing adjustments in gender ideology or "affirmative reactions" in an effort to maintain white masculine privilege (Carroll 7). Several critics contend that the white, heterosexual masculinity in hardboiled fiction, a historically specific form of hegemonic masculinity, was itself a reaction against particular constructions of white manhood. Some characterize the hardboiled detective as a "backlash to the intellectual, sometimes effete detective exemplified in Wimsey or Poirot [or the golden age English detectives]. The new American detective was smart, but more important, street-smart, a tough action hero" (Mizejewski 17). For others, the hardboiled figure reflected a social "crisis" in male identity, a reaction to threats against hegemonic masculinity from shifting gender roles, and, especially in film noir versions after World War II, to material threats posed by the increased participation of women in the labor force (Breu 3–5).

Christopher Breu resists the "crisis thesis" that depends so much on the gender binary and that appears so often in masculinity studies, persuasively arguing that "hard-boiled masculinity" was both a reaction against and an adaptation to changes in US capitalism, specifically the advent of monopoly or corporate capitalism. This sort of masculinity, Breu explains, "represents an aggressive reformulation of male hegemony as much as a defensive reaction to what might have been perceived as a set of economic and social threats to this hegemony" (5). In this insightful reading, "white, hard-boiled masculinity borrows in disavowed ways from the iconography of black masculinity [as vitally and violently primitive] in order to define itself against both older forms of Victorian manhood [as a middle-class, internal moral quality] and the larger social order [corporate capitalism] of which it is a part" (15). It also borrows from the figure of the femme fatale forms of connection or intimacy that it both desires and repudiates. Importantly, hardboiled masculinity, a twentieth-century form of "national manhood" that inscribed a gender and racial hierarchy in order to manage the destabilizing and exploitative effects of capitalism, was a cultural and collective

fantasy, an iconic conception of male identity that "found approxima-
tions in both fiction and life" but that remained a site of unresolved
contradictions (2).

If the reformulation, negotiation, and maintenance of white hegemonic masculinity are evident in early to mid-twentieth-century popular fiction by such writer heavyweights as Dashiell Hammett, Ernest
Hemingway, and William Faulkner, the subjective dimensions of the
genre are just as discernible in popular versions of hardboiled fiction in
the late twentieth and early twenty-first century as US capitalism again
creates new demands and gendered racial models of political subjectivity
or belonging under neoliberalism.[12] *Girl in a Box* and *The Interpreter* join
those recent texts that "chart the transformation of the postwar city as
its contours and its social geography have been reshaped by the decline
of American industrialism and the rise of the postindustrial economy,"
and with particular respect to gendered racial political subjectivity or
belonging for Asian American women as they navigate the global economy (McCann 56).

Certainly, the extent to which the hardboiled world has been dis-
lodged ideologically is a matter of debate in readings of specific texts, but
scholars tend to agree that the feminist counter-tradition of American
crime fiction in the 1980s that challenged masculinity as a requirement
for detectives was expanded by a critical mass of African American writers who challenged "the centrality of whiteness" and the construction of
white masculinity in the hardboiled and other subgenres of crime fiction in the 1990s (M. Reddy, "Race and American Crime Fiction" 142).[13]
Reddy contends that the most radical revision came with black women
writers who began in that same decade to author crossover fiction, which
addressed and interpellated black women as their primary audience and
white women as a secondary audience (145). The complexity of this genre
revision is magnified by "the fluidity of fantasy," which, as feminist film
theory has established, is not necessarily linear or consistent since it is
characterized by multiple or conflicting desires and fears (Mizejewski 8).
Simply put, fantasy does not work through the reader's (or viewer's) strict
identification with one character, but rather fluctuates among several,
and, as suggested above, may extend beyond the text, plot, and characters. Fantasy may also involve disidentification, as Breu suggests when
he observes that readers and fans did not necessarily accept or enact the
hardboiled masculinity offered in the heyday of the genre's popularity.
Such fluidity helps us understand the crossover appeal of popular genres
in general and specific texts, such as *Girl in a Box* and *The Interpreter,*

that are popular with audiences across gender, sexual, racial, social class, and national identifications.

Recognizing the complexity of genre revision and the fluidity of fantasy acknowledges the sophisticated register of contemporary hardboiled fiction and takes us a long way toward understanding why it is such a popular imaginative vehicle for expressing cultural fantasies, assumptions, and anxieties about the shifting sands of citizenship within neoliberalism. The postmodernist detective story, also known as the contemporary metaphysical detective story, is a particularly effective form for this endeavor, since it parodies or subverts traditional detective story conventions to pursue questions about "mysteries of being and knowing which transcend the mere machinations of the mystery plot" (Merivale and Sweeney 2). That is, the metaphysical detective story self-consciously questions the nature of reality, including the nature of the world, the self or identity, and knowing itself. While it typically concludes that reality is unknowable, "or at least ineffable," constructions and beliefs are revealed to be just that (4). With origins in Poe's self-reflexive and philosophical stories but not named as a narrative pattern until 1941, the metaphysical detective story also has a decidedly cosmopolitan genealogy—from Poe to Jorge Luis Borges, to Alain Robbe-Grillet, to Kobo Abe and back again to American postmodernists (4–5). More than many other detective story forms, the metaphysical detective story centralizes the subjective dimensions—self-knowledge and the subject's search for meaning—of detection, especially in the figure of the detective, so it is unsurprising that it makes a robust popular appearance within contemporary neoliberalism, an ideology devoted to reshaping the citizen-subject, as much as to reshaping society.

When blended self-consciously with the hardboiled, the metaphysical detective story not only focuses intently on the private eye, sometimes at the apparent expense of investigating the details of criminal activity, but it also maintains "a shortage of solutions, and thus a distinct lack of narrative closure," which leads the reader back to the hero rather than the plot of the story (Merivale 102). I argue that *Girl in a Box* and *The Interpreter* combine the hardboiled detective novel and the metaphysical detective story to create a revised form that negotiates neoliberal cosmopolitan citizenship through investigating its imperative for labor, specifically culturally sophisticated knowledge work in the New Economy. Hardboiled subjectivity offers, in fact, a ready vehicle for investigating social demands for neoliberal work from the cosmopolitan citizen—its material as well as its subjective dimensions—since by convention "the private eye is a professional investigator who works for a living, and, more significantly, who works for him- or herself, " answering "to nobody but him- or herself" (Scaggs 60). With strong roots in the figure of the hardboiled detective, but also available for rule subversion, the emphasis on work or labor is compellingly adapted in contemporary metaphysical detective stories, which encompass both employment for survival and the philosophical work of understanding identity and one's place in the world.

The New Economy and Cosmopolitanism

In the United States, the demands of the neoliberal global economy first became widely established in public discourse during the recession of the early 1980s. Recession rhetoric at the time clearly registered the economic orthodoxy that soon after guided all US policy and the cultural values of neoliberalism that became hegemonic as a social philosophy in the 1990s, as illustrated by the May 30, 1983, cover story of *Time* magazine titled "The New Economy." On the illustrated cover, a robot with a torso fashioned from a computer monitor pushes a wheelbarrow loaded with a miniature factory toward the bottom right-hand corner of the cover, signifying that the industrial age is being cast off, dumped over the edge, by the postindustrial era of information technology and global economy. A bulleted list promises to address "Where the Jobs Will Be," "Industry Winners and Losers," and the "Menace of Protectionism." Outlining the effects of the 1981–82 recession, Charles Alexander's story rewrites the script for the US economy, laying out a plan for success under the altered conditions of neoliberalism, though that term would not be widely used for at least another decade.[14] The New Economy is characterized as two-tiered, with dying "smokestack industries reeling from foreign competition" and burgeoning high-technology companies "leading the world in innovation" (C. Alexander 62). Beginning with a redemption tale about a woolen mill in Massachusetts that reinvented itself, first from the production of carpets to blankets and then again to computer manufacturing, the tone is decidedly optimistic. No less than pedigreed industrialist Delaware governor Pierre du Pont IV is quoted as saying, "The transformation of our jobs, the movement of our people, the improvement in our skills over the first 80 years of this century have been stunning. But is entirely likely that those changes will be matched and exceeded during the final 20 years of the century" (62). As an example of the fabulous fortunes to be made for those able to make the transition to the New Economy, the author cites what is now a global brand but what was then a phenom in the "winner" industry of information technology: "[I]n six years Apple, a leading manufacturer in personal computers, has evolved from a two-man operation in a garage to a corporation employing more than 4,000 people. Last year it ranked 411 on the Fortune 500; no company had ever gone from a start-up to the Fortune list in so short a period" (62).

As emphasized by a photograph of a technician working on a blueprint for a circuit board, *Time*'s story reads like a blueprint for neoliberal policy, highlighting "free" trade and the importance of expanding export markets globally through deregulation; the necessity of retraining, flexibility, and mobility with regard to labor as "a permanent part of American business and society"; and the driving force of the private entrepreneurial spirit of the individual American citizen. The article concludes with its most emphatic claim to a future of US prosperity, appealing to a modified version of the national cultural fantasy of the American Dream: "The roots of American economic success have been in individualism and entrepreneurship. The dream of making a fortune by launching a new company runs deep in American society and has been the source of great business strength. In addition, the United States has by far the largest pool of private venture capital available to back risky, new businesses" (C. Alexander 68). As a discourse, the New Economy, a phrase now synonymous with "the global economy," also delineates that the work required of individual citizens is mutable and mobile or labile, so the New Economy operates as a discourse of neoliberal cosmopolitan citizenship.[15] Further, to achieve social belonging in the United States as well as to circulate the American Dream internationally in the service of preserving the preeminence of the United States globally, individual citizens must perform entrepreneurial labor in which they collect and interpret knowledge and take on the risks of a deregulated global workplace.

Responding to the framing of neoliberal globalization or global economic restructuring as a new form of cosmopolitanism, progressive thinkers soon began to wrestle with this cosmopolitan discourse, pointing critically to a history of European cosmopolitanism deeply implicated in Western cultural imperialism. In this genealogy, cosmopolitanism, or world citizenship, was revealed to be a rather blinding enlightened universalism, constructed as an unbiased perspective or consciousness but one reserved for elite Western subjects of a traveled and educated intellectual class who possess cultural capital and the means to appropriate the local cultural knowledge they encounter (Black 227).[16] Critics pointed out that goods, capital, people, knowledge, and culture travel through violent displacements as well as altruistic circuits and networks. Influentially, James Clifford's recognition of "discrepant cosmopolitanisms" acknowledged that cosmopolitanism is not a Western invention and that there are multiple forms of cosmopolitanism, linked to the hybrid identities, knowledge, cultural practices, and expressions of postcolonial migrants, exiles, refugees, and diasporic subjects (108). In fact, "the notion that there are many, different, cosmopolitan practices with their own historicities and distinctive worldviews, all coexisting in late modernity, has led to an exploration of marginal cosmopolitanisms" (Werbner 112).[17]

For those who advocate a global sense of interconnectedness and responsibility that goes beyond more particularistic or local affinities of national, ethnic, or religious community without subsuming them, certain versions of cosmopolitanism offer a "provisionally viable way of conceptualizing and forming communities across borders" (Black 228). Seeking "an ethics for globalization," cosmopolitan analytics emerged as part of "the turn toward ethics" in contemporary social theory as scholars across the disciplines found themselves contending with structural change on a global scale (Calhoun 429). Cosmopolitan analytics and ethical theory more broadly have become major concerns in literary studies in the United States, gaining urgency after the events of 9/11.[18] In an essay on the importance of remembering the American war in Viet Nam through literature written by Asian Americans and Latinos, Viet Nguyen argues, for example, that "literature, with its ability to offer other stories besides the ones that justify war, plays a key role in cosmopolitanism's efforts to imagine peace and cope with war's enduring aftermath, its long after-life in memory" ("Remembering War" 151). For Nguyen, cosmopolitanism is "the endeavor to create citizens of the world who would strive for conversations and human contact across all kinds of borders," "connect individual feelings to shared social feelings through compassion," and use those shared feelings to enact progressive change (151). He asserts that, "just as warfare needs patriotism, the struggle for peace needs cosmopolitanism to provide the imagination for a utopian future" (162).

Literature can play a significant role in imagining and creating a structure of feeling for a different world, including one that defends peace instead of war. My analysis of neoliberal cosmopolitan citizenship also cautions that feelings easily take the place of concrete political action in the context of neoliberal forms of governance that aggressively manage subjects through culture. As Berlant suggests, the substitution of private feelings for public politics may well be the hallmark of neoliberal citizenship. Adoption of a cosmopolitan aesthetic or even worldview does not axiomatically constitute a progressive or even an explicit politics, and cosmopolitanism may be a substitute for nationalism.[19] In *Time's* 1983 article, for instance, cosmopolitanism and patriotic nationalism are closely linked in its claim about the US capacity to lead the neoliberal global economy, which depends upon repackaging the American Dream as individual entrepreneurialism in the service of global capital advantage for the United States. Similarly, in the 1990s, nationalist claims in Great Britain foregrounded its sophisticated, metropolitan, and multicultural appeal to consumers and transnational businesses: "'Cool Britannia,' or the rebranding of Britain itself," illustrates the commercial cosmopolitanism that can flourish as part of economic and statist projects (Calhoun 432). As Craig Calhoun argues, "Cosmopolitanism signals direct connection between the individual and the world as a whole. But if this is sometimes given ethical emphasis, equally often the world appears simply as an object of consumption" (433). Nguyen acknowledges that past cosmopolitanisms may be retailored for a new age, one "much better suited for culturally sensitive capitalists in the service of dominating nations like the US and global entities like the World Trade Organization and the International Monetary Fund" ("Remembering War" 162).[20] This is precisely the issue, for rather than transcending belonging, cosmopolitanism is enabled by social institutions, "produced and reinforced by belonging to transitional networks and to a community of fellow cosmopolitans. There are different such communities—academic and corporate and NGO, religious and secular. One may participate in multiple such networks, but it is an illusion—an ideological illusion—to imagine citizenship of the world as simply freedom from belonging to more sectional groupings" (Calhoun 442). Neoliberalism's disarticulation and rearticulation with various ethical regimes as a technique to remake the social and citizen-subject requires that we remain vigilant about its ethical claims to cosmopolitanism.

Girl in a Box and *The Interpreter*

Girl in a Box is ninth in the ten-book series that Sujata Massey began in 1997 and completed in 2007. In it, thirty-year-old biracial Japanese American Rei Shimura works in contemporary Tokyo as a "special informer," a type of undercover US government agent.[21] However, Rei's employment with the Organization of Cultural Intelligence (OCI), an alphabet agency linked to the CIA, is recent, beginning in book eight on a contingency basis when she helped recover stolen antiquities in war-torn Iraq. Employed by OCI on a permanent basis in *Girl in a Box*, the job is Rei's first truly professional gig for the "supersecret spy agency" (Massey 2). This opportunity is contrasted not only with Rei's previous occupations, or what the book jacket refers to as her "chronic under-employment," but also with her cover occupation as a temporary sales clerk at Mitsutan, a major Japanese department store. Rei's assignment is to use her cultural knowledge, as well as her aplomb with electronic devices such as cell phones and computer systems, to gather and inter-pret information about the financial practices of Mitsutan, which the US Treasury Department suspects is fixing its books, perhaps to avoid a buyout by US investors. After a course in cultural deception at the Defense Language Institute, and armed with a false résumé highlight-ing a Japanese father's occupation as an investment banker, a foreign education in the United States, and language abilities in English, Japa-nese, and Spanish, Rei is hired by the department store to work with international customers on the "K team," a small group of *kokusaijin,* or cosmopolitan Japanese who are comfortable with foreigners. She uncovers corruption among international investment banking, con-nections to organized crime in a particular branch of *yakuza* (Japanese organized crime), and money laundering. Two deaths, a listening device in a diamond navel ring, and a high-speed chase through the labyrin-thine streets of Toyko later, Rei's boss Michael Hendricks steps in, only to be saved himself by the newly initiated but expert cultural poseur and translator, Rei Shimura.

Suki Kim's first and only novel, *The Interpreter,* features a twenty-nine-year-old Korean American immigrant, Suzy Park, who lives in New York City and works as a criminal court interpreter. Although the novel foregrounds the global consumer culture of its setting and continually reminds the reader that this is a cosmopolitan story, *The Interpreter* is a far darker fiction about detection than is *Girl in a Box,* since the protago-nist's parents have been murdered in their small Harlem grocery store. Further, Suzy is compelled to pursue the mystery of that traumatic crime when she is confronted with undeniable clues while interpreting in court. Despite Suzy's bilingual and bicultural knowledge and her promising occupation as an interpreter, she is largely isolated and struggles both financially and psychologically, particularly to recover from her parents' death. Suzy has few friends, spends much of her time alone in her Upper

East Side apartment, and has been alienated from her family for most of her adult life, which she understands as a consequence of leaving Columbia University in her senior year to live with forty-nine-year-old married professor Damien Brisco. As the novel opens in 2000, Suzy is in another relationship with a married man, Michael, an international businessman in whom she has little interest. When Suzy uncovers a possible link to her parents' murder, she tries to locate her estranged sister Grace to learn more about what happened. But Grace is missing, and as Suzy becomes invested in finding her, she follows clues about an immigrant family and community she actually knows very little about. Suzy discovers that her parents had provided the Immigration and Naturalization Service (INS) with information about undocumented Korean immigrants in exchange for citizenship and a livelihood, and that Grace had acted as interpreter in the process.

In her suggestive reading of the novel as a metaphysical detective story, Soo Yeon Kim argues that, "insofar as Suzy's interpreting skills and multicultural knowledge leave her utterly vacuous rather than enriching her life with a better understanding of both cultures, Suzy remains a 'loser' in a global city rather than becoming a cosmopolitan hybrid" (199). I fully agree that the novel makes use of the metaphysical subgenre to comment on the production of cosmopolitan subjectivity, but rather than lamenting Suzy's failure to fulfill the mandate for culturally sophisticated knowledge work, I suggest that *The Interpreter* takes aim at the work cosmopolitan subjects are compelled to do on behalf of the US global economy in order to be considered good or successful neoliberal citizens. Operating in complex relation to the contemporary hardboiled novel and the metaphysical detective story, *Girl in a Box* and *The Interpreter* address and remark upon a model of American subjectivity that is characteristically associated with the hardboiled novel and identifiably reformulated in neoliberal cosmopolitan citizenship. Adopting and revising the generic codes and conventions of American detective fiction, the novels reveal the appropriation of the labile cultural labor of Asian American women in the figure of the adventuring detective hero who contends with the powerful and corrupt forces of the global economy.[22] I focus on the highly recognizable tropes of "the mean streets," "the Purloined Letter," and "the Continental Op," which combine to help Massey and Kim uncover the operations of neoliberal cosmopolitan citizenship and their gendered racial meaning for the Asian American female protagonists who are figured as ideal neoliberal workers in a globalizing US economy.

THE MEAN STREETS

Not unlike the hardboiled's interests in the modern capitalist landscape of the industrial United States, *Girl in a Box* and *The Interpreter* are primarily concerned with assaying and surveilling the neoliberal landscape of the postindustrial United States, weighing its characteristics and watching over its physical, political, and social geography. While much of the interest in the geographical landscape extends from the occupations of the female protagonists, who in different ways participate in the institutions of authority that police neoliberal citizens, their labor eventually turns in on itself to disclose the criminality and corruption of those institutions and neoliberalism writ large. As is well understood, the "mean streets" trope was central to the development of hardboiled fiction from John Daly through Dashiell Hammett and then Raymond Chandler, who understood the historical significance of setting and its modern relevance to the figure of the private investigator as a "hard-boiled, pig-headed" hero, "neither tarnished, nor afraid" (Hammett and Chandler quoted in Scaggs 55–56). As Scaggs explains, Hammett's Continental Op, who first appeared in the pulp magazine *Black Mask* in 1924, was a descendent of the Western adventure hero, that wildly popular protagonist of both the nineteenth-century American dime novel and later of short fiction. Although the dime novel anticipated the adventurer's migration, Hammett is generally credited with "relocating the frontier hero of the Western into an urban environment" (56). With the new setting came the translation of the romantic, rugged individualism of the Western frontier hero into the honorable detective living in a modern but hostile city. So the physical geography or location once again echoed the social ideology of the protagonist: "The hard-boiled private eye is a private 'I', a loner, an alienated individual who exists outside or beyond the socioeconomic order of family, friends, work, or home" (58).

The protoyptical hardboiled detective desires to save the world from the evil-entangled mean streets, but often has difficulty locating the cause of evil and thus redressing injustice. In hardboiled fiction, the mean streets are typically figured in terms of gangdom and the underworld, as well as a corrupt social order and the inability of institutions to protect ordinary people from the ruling powers. Carl Malmgren has argued that a decentered world distinguishes detective fiction from mystery fiction, "which has a center, an anchor, a ground; a centered world is one in which effects can be connected to causes, where external signs can be linked to internal conditions" (13). In hardboiled detective fiction, then, searching (and often getting lost in) the maze of the mean streets and mapping or reading them for clues is one of the first methods of detection. As part of this procedure, the detective becomes a denizen of the mean streets and even complicit in the criminality that resides there.

The impossibility of escaping the corrupt social order is perhaps where the metaphysical detective story most clearly overlaps with hardboiled detective fiction, which emphasizes setting to explore the various levels of meaning linked to the mean streets. In a metaphysical hybrid of the hardboiled that she calls the "metaphysical gumshoe story" or "Gumshoe Gothic," Patricia Merivale convincingly argues that Poe's "The Man of the Crowd" (1840) is an early manifestation of the hardboiled, or at least has affinities with it (104). In this story, "a man shod in 'caoutchouc over-shoes' (that is, rubber galoshes ca. 1840), 'tying a handkerchief about [his] mouth,' inaudibly and obsessively pursues another man—seemingly the 'type and genius of deep crime,' whose secret he, detective like, wishes to discover—through the mean streets of a labyrinthine modern city" (106). When the detective finally catches up to the man, the detective process comes to a halt, because "it becomes apparent that the narrator has projected his sense of his own (literally) un-utterable wickedness upon the Man of the Crowd, who, for any evidence we are given about him, may be no more than the quite innocent and wholly terrified victim of the narrator's sinisterly silent, masked, seemingly motiveless pursuit" (106–7). Where Poe's "The Man of the Crowd" shrouds its main point about complicity, the contemporary or postmodern metaphysical detective story, such as Massey's or Kim's, "flaunts its lack of closure, the failure of the detective process, and makes explicit the synonymity of detective, criminal, and even victim which is always at least potential in the hard-boiled detective story, if not the detective story as a whole" (107).

Whether implicit or explicit in the narrative, the detective's ability to see the world and the conditions of social life for what they are highlights the genre's interests in looking, and "the detective is classically the character who sees what others miss and even sees what's missing" (Mizejewski 7). In fact, the hardboiled investigation of the mean streets operates as a kind of ethnographic method for detection and provides a controlling gaze for the detective-narrator, lending structure to the narrative and interpellating readers as voyeurs. Nowhere is this structuring trope more apparent than in the Orientalist detective novels that focus on Chinatown. As Betsy Huang points out, the classic opposition between the sinister Chinatown and the idealized hardboiled detective, particularly the figure of Charlie Chan, operates within the binary constraints of the racialization of Asian Americans (50). Yunte Huang argues that in the Cold War period of anti-Chinese hysteria, the opposition collapsed; "Chinatown" and indeed anything associated with China, came to symbolize a villainous underworld and "stained the archetypal Chinaman, Charlie Chan" (269). The paranoia about communism combined with the older form of anti-Chinese racism and became embodied in a newly destructive figure of Charlie Chan in yet another round of yellow peril discourse in the United States (Y. Huang 269–75).

In our current neoliberal era, the primarily political threat of communism that anything coded "Chinese" symbolized in popular culture has been eclipsed by a more generalized and mobile economic threat emanating from a variety of Asian countries, including especially Japan in the 1980s; the "Asian Tigers" (Hong Kong, Taiwan, Singapore, and South Korea) in the 1990s; and India, the Middle East, and China (once again) in the 2000s. If Chinatown operated metonymically and served as "a symbol for the crime-ridden dark side of the City of Angels" or immutably "foreign" threats from within the popular culture of the Cold War era, threats to US power in the New Economy or global economic restructuring may be represented by a number of sites and settings, both internal and external, signifying multiple forms or sources of Asian capital (Y. Huang 276). Moreover, in the context of market fundamentalism and the idealization of Asian immigrants and Asian Americans as neoliberal workers, the detective of the revived Oriental detective story does not easily collapse to a stable or unambiguous symbol of threatening Asian capital. In *The Interpreter*, for example, at the beginning of the millennium when Suzy is about to turn thirty, she remarks the confidence of Korean American youth, since "[b]eing Asian is no longer embarrassing. Being Asian no longer suggests a high-school chess team. Being Asian might even be hip, trendy, cool" (S. Kim 199). Here Suzy observes the function of late 1990s liberal multiculturalism that produces Asian immigrants and minority ethnic subjects as valuable cosmopolitan subjects and thus ideal workers. Most importantly, if the detective is closely association with the criminal and both are ambiguous registers of the social order in recent detective fiction, so too is the "victim," understood to be the United States, complexly implicated in the threatening elements of the New Economy, as the detective, criminal, and victim come together.[23]

In Massey's and Kim's mobilization of detective fiction, *Girl in a Box* and *The Interpreter* do not represent the mean streets or the physical landscape of US criminality in terms of the "ethnic enclave" or ghetto and its purportedly evil underground activities. Instead, the mean streets extend into Japanese and Korean locales, and spaces (still) inhabited by immutably "foreign" figures are scattered both within and outside US domestic or national borders, suggesting not so much their dissolution or a deterritorialization but rather their expansion as the United States reorganizes its political reach beyond formal, physical territories. That is, US social hierarchies persist in the cosmopolitan spaces represented in these novels, with race, gender, class, and national ideologies, including American exceptionalism and the American Dream, structuring institutions and relationships hegemonically. The adventurous and independent frontier hero who is invested in taming criminal or vigilante elements in order to expand (or reinstall) social order is thus relocated and translated once more in the cosmopolitan female detective figure in Massey's and Kim's novels. Surveying and assaying this broader and dynamic landscape of criminality in its complex physical, political, and social dimensions demands the labor of equally labile subjects (Scaggs 56–58).

Similar to their predecessors, the detective heroines of *Girl in a Box* and *The Interpreter* recognize the corruption of the US postindustrial capitalist landscape, including the illegitimacy of legal authority, particularly in relation to the appropriation of their respective cultural knowledge as Japanese American and Korean American cosmopolitan subjects, in the global expansion of market fundamentalism. The cosmopolitan protagonists in *Girl in a Box* and *The Interpreter* work for neoliberal institutions and gather mounting evidence that those institutions which purport to protect global citizens or citizens of the world are technologies of governance that maintain US hegemony. In fact, as Rei and Suzy interpret information for US (state) institutions, they discover the ways in which the neoliberal global economy is manifestly criminal but also how it operates outside democratic regulation or extralegally. Finally, they come to see their cosmopolitan labor as complicit in a US system that circulates globally, importing and exporting a corrupt neoliberal American Dream that secures hegemonic political subjectivity or citizenship instead of a level playing field in which anyone can succeed and then belong through hard work. To highlight the cosmopolitan knowledge of their sleuths, Massey and Kim modify the tradition of hardboiled writers who "reached back to the example of the once widely popular dime-novel detectives ... adventure heroes who were distinguished ... for their ability to call on cunning and disguise to navigate the farthest reaches of the city" (McCann 44).

Girl in a Box begins in Monterey, California, where Rei is attending the Defense Language Institute, shifts to Washington, DC, as the home base of her employer, the US government, and then settles in Tokyo, with most of its action taking place in that global city or crucial hub in the network of the global economic system. Indeed, the mean streets of Tokyo are clearly connected to those of the United States. As a runner, Rei traverses the terrain of Monterey and DC quickly, knowing exactly where she is going, and this capacity is amplified in her ability to expertly navigate the Tokyo subway system; her ease and comfort moving around and exploring cosmopolitan spaces, both physically and socially, are components of her "street smart" creativity or cultural lability, the primary reason she is hired as a special informant for the US government (Massey, *Girl in a Box* 234). The streets of the global city, including the vehicles that careen through the narrow streets of Tokyo, are also literally the site of the most dramatic criminal activity in the novel, with scenes involving a victim's dead body in an abandoned van, a high-speed chase in which Japanese organized crime or *yakuza* pursue Rei in a taxi, and the attempted murder of Michael, who is stuffed in the trunk of a car and left to die in Mitsutan's parking garage.

The gangster underworld and neoliberal institutions, particularly as they operate within the global political geography of the New Economy, are similarly under surveillance as sites of criminality in *Girl in a Box*. From the start of Rei's assignment to covertly gather information about Mitsutan's financial practices, she vacillates between believing that the Japanese concern is corrupt, in league with organized crime, and similarly suspecting that the US government and OCI as its representative are attempting to unlawfully intervene in Japanese business and aid the global expansion of US commercial interests. Michael contends that American banker Warren Kravitz is "worried for our country. He sees Japanese companies engaged in unscrupulous business practices that take over so many markets that once were ours—cars, cameras, televisions, videos. Now with China on the rise, Japan is more desperate" (Massey, *Girl in a Box* 224). But Rei is far more dubious than her boss about Kravitz's "patriotic" complaint to the US Treasury Department that the finances of the Japanese department store are a matter of national security. Rei continues to collect evidence that Mitsutan is inflating reported profits to hide the cash flow of Nozumi-gumi, a *yakuza* group, but simultaneously pursues her suspicions about Kravitz. Ultimately, the clearest source of criminality in *Girl in a Box* is located on Wall Street or in the heart of the political economy of the United States, since Kravitz, who is vice president of the Tokyo branch of the US bank Winston Brothers, is deeply implicated in funneling drug money from a rival *yakuza* group that wants to shut down Nozumi-gumi. Rei understands that Kravitz's role "means that gangster money is coming into a major American bank, which means that our economy is already tainted" (256). Furthermore, Kravitz is responsible for the murder of Ravindra Shah (Ravi), a recently hired investment banker at Winston Brothers who tries to expose the laundering. Rei closes her assignment only partly satisfied, because the corrupt US player in the global financial market will be held accountable for his role in the murder of Shah but not for his duplicity in claiming to operate within a system of "free trade" and then attempting to game it. The manifest criminality of unregulated banking and the corruption of commerce seem to be accepted as an inevitable fact of neoliberal cosmopolitanism. The Organization of Cultural Intelligence and Rei do not remain unscathed in the novel, however, since although OCI disrupts and reveals the identities of individuals or entities that operate extralegally, it operates similarly as a surreptitious government agency that does not officially exist. As Emily Davis observes, "By taking the detection process into the 'mean streets,' the detective novel demonstrates that crime is not an isolated phenomenon associated with disturbed individuals but is part of a larger field of social disorder and inequality" (17).

The social geography depicted in *Girl in a Box* is equally complex since it both places a Japanese American female in the detecting driver's seat and demands that she conform to some of the most conventional gender and racial hierarchies in Japan in order to do her job. A far cry from the history of gendered racial exclusion of Asian immigrant women from the United States or even the history of foreigner racialization that rationalized the expropriation of land from Rei's ancestors in the name of World War II national security, Massey's novel presents a Japanese American woman who is hired by the US government for her professional-level cosmopolitan knowledge and to gather information to safeguard the nation's economic interests.[24] Her work is limited, however, by the necessity that she pose as "an excessively protected, well brought up" young Japanese woman or "girl in a box," and in the final scene she is a literally contained in a hotel room, becoming the figure of the novel's title, before she decides to defy orders and rescue Michael from being killed by Kravitz and his *yakuza* partners (114). In several ways, the novel reproduces an Orientalist East/West divide, representing Japan as culturally sophisticated but socially backward as well as destructive, with sexism and homophobia more prevalent in Japan than in the United States.

Rei is replacing, after all, the murdered OCI agent Farraday, an American spy who was operating undercover as a gay model. However, as in hardboiled crime fiction, *Girl in a Box* largely adapts the conventional hero of the Western as a liminal figure who straddles legal authority and the criminal underworld of the urban frontier (McCann 44–45). In this sense, the central conflict between gangdom and society is revealed to be a simplistic binary, since both are powerful forces with which Rei struggles. Just as the physical geography is relocated and expanded, the social geography of *Girl in a Box* is changed but remains familiar, especially in terms of the positioning of the protagonist, a knowing detective who surveys the mean streets and links them to the political economy and social order of the United States.

The mean streets of *The Interpreter,* similar to those of *Girl in a Box,* are explicitly located in a global city, but here in *the* global city, New York. In Kim's novel, however, the cosmopolitan detective is unfamiliar with the complex physical geography of the mean streets, which are obscured, fragmented, or entangled by the postindustrial rearrangement of manufacturing centers, ethnic enclaves, and outlying suburbs. Once more, most dramatic action and serious detection literally take place in the streets, or in that arbiter of the streets, the courtroom, and again crime is presented as global gang activity. The mean streets of *The Interpreter* flow, in fact, through the mobile networks of Korean gangs that traffic through adoption fraud that brings South Korean children to New York as orphans destined for American homes, but then keeps them as child laborers and grooms them to become gang members, as Suzy discovers was the case with Johnny/DJ. But before Suzy can investigate any clues, she must search for the mean streets, so she heads to the many neighborhoods where her family lived while she was growing up and visits the Korean-owned markets, bars, pizza joints, and pool halls that her sister frequented in high school in the South Bronx. She finds little information and broadens her investigation to a variety of locations and some very unlikely sites, such as at the Fort Lee New Joy Fellowship Church in the "ethnoburbs" of New Jersey, where her missing sister Grace is a member, or the pretty coastal village of Montauk, Long Island, where Grace scattered the ashes of their parents. Eventually, Suzy finds Grace's only friend, Maria Sutpen, and figures out that Grace likely drowned her now ex-gang-member boyfriend Johnny/DJ in Montauk for his role in their parents' murder. While Suzy is clearly in the cosmopolitan knowledge business, taking her translation skills out of the courtroom and into the mean streets leads to unfamiliar sites of criminality where she makes unwelcome discoveries about the political landscape of the global city.

As in *Girl in a Box*, both informal and formal neoliberal institutions are under surveillance in *The Interpreter*, with the third-person narrative offering Suzy's perspective as she links them. Yet Suzy has a far more troubled relationship to the underworld and the legal authorities than does Rei, first because she witnesses the poor treatment of immigrants in the courtrooms and the failure of public institutions to protect and serve, and second because she experiences firsthand the authorities' refusal of social responsibility. Suzy is deeply disturbed by the dropped investigation of her parents' murder, but she is thoroughly disillusioned when she learns that the "lazy Bronx detective" Lester knew all along that her parents were murdered by Fearsome Four gang members but refused to investigate, calling it a "random killing" and apparently preferring to let Korean immigrants kill each other. With the guys who "work for Uncle Sam," Suzy observes, "you can never be sure which side they are on" (S. Kim 177). Similar to Rei's recognition of a corrupt American Dream in the streets of Tokyo, Suzy assays the mean streets, from Jackson Heights, where Koreans are half the population, to the classrooms of Columbia University, where the majority of students are privileged whites. Suzy sees not the land of opportunity, where hard work pays off with belonging for immigrants, but a segregated political landscape where immigrants are the object of state surveillance as "aliens" and "forever guilty before the customers, the policemen, the inspectors, the district attorneys, the IRS agents, and the INS agents" (263, 238). While the novel emphatically returns the gaze of Orientalist surveillance, Suzy's occupation as a court reporter is implicated in it, and her investigation into her parents' murder reproduces similar dynamics of presumptive guilt, so the novel simultaneously polices Korean immigrants. Instead of Wall Street, *The Interpreter* represents 26 Federal Plaza, where the INS is located and from which it controls the flow of workers into the United States for the New Economy, as "the scene of the crime" (264).

As *The Interpreter* represents the social geography of neoliberal cosmopolitan America, Korean immigrants are played off African Americans in the racial hierarchy, especially as Suzy describes the negative effects of the 1992 Los Angeles riots on Korean-owned businesses in New York City. Toward the end of the novel, after Suzy interprets an INS hearing in which a Korean woman is deported for assaulting a sixteen-year-old African American girl who called her a "fucking chink" and stole a six-pack of beer from her store, Suzy concludes, "Immigrants are not

Americans. Permanent residency is never permanent" (S. Kim 274). At the same time, in the criminal court where Suzy usually interprets, she observes that no one else is Asian, and almost everyone, except the white attorneys and judges, is black. For Suzy, "[t]he power structure is pretty clear. Between those who get locked up and those who do the locking is a colored matter. There are no two ways about it" (87). Arguably, Kim uses the cosmopolitan knowledge that Suzy interprets and collects from the mean streets to provide a social context, though not an alibi, for the Parks' "viscous and immoral act" of reporting illegal immigrants in exchange for legal citizenship for themselves and their two daughters (240). To be sure, Suzy does not consider her parents innocent victims, and she condemns her father's conservative patriarchal ideology, with strict "Korean girl" rules and nothing American "allowed" (53). For both novels, the mean streets of the contemporary metaphysical-hardboiled hybrid stretch back to Poe and implicate the subject, who searches for the social ill health that lurks within them.

THE PURLOINED LETTER

As in so much other detective fiction that uses the classic trope of the purloined letter, the detectives in *Girl in a Box* and *The Interpreter* search for a text or for information that is hidden, misappropriated, and/ or missing from the neoliberal landscape, particularly, I suggest, on the terrain of its social geography. Because both epistemological and onto-logical questions may be explored through the trope of the purloined letter, it is especially useful for investigations into how the material conditions and concerns of contemporary capitalism may alter the meaning of social life. Perhaps one of the most important tropes of detective fiction given the genre's concern for the value of knowledge, the purloined letter emphasizes the unreliable status of knowledge.

The trope of the purloined letter comes, of course, from the 1844 Edgar Allen Poe story of the same name, the third and last of his Dupin stories, featuring the genius armchair (amateur) detective C. Auguste Dupin.[25] To briefly review, the story is told by an unnamed narrator-friend in Dupin's Paris home, and concerns the theft by Minister D— of a letter containing compromising information from "the royal *boudoir*" (the queen of France's private chambers). The minister took the letter that was in plain sight, replaced it with a meaningless one, and is blackmailing the queen (and the letter's author). The prefect of the Paris police, or "G—," has come to Dupin, who has recently solved two murder crimes, for help in finding the letter. Unlike G—, Dupin suspects that the letter has not been elaborately hidden, and he finds the letter by returning to the minister's apartment and simply looking, as if through the minister's eyes. Again, the letter is in plain sight but is disguised, since it has been refolded and sealed with the minister's own seal. Dupin leaves his snuffbox so that he can come back the next day with a duplicate letter about the minister. Dupin switches the letters in hopes that the minister will try to use the duplicate and then expose himself. Importantly, the content of the original letter is never revealed to the reader. For most "'The Purloined Letter' is treated as a pretext, which is to say, read as a parable of the act of analysis" and focuses on detection (Irwin 29). In this story, recovering the missing text requires the detective's ability to think and see as the criminal does, which, similar to the detective-denizen of the mean streets, has become a convention that positions the detective in close association with the criminal and with the authorities who were either corrupt or inept. Indeed, while the Paris police look in all of the wrong places and cannot see what is in front of them, Dupin extends the minister's logic of duplicates and inconspicuous replacements, so the structure of the story "involves doubling an opponent's thought processes in order to turn his own methods against him" (33). Further, because the reader is also interpellated into the detective's subject position, all are focused intently on the criminal's analytics as well as on finding the missing text. The structure is complemented then by metatextual commentary about narrative itself, in particular its influence in the construction of meaning, its close relation to valuable or powerful knowledge, and its susceptibility to corruption.

While central elements of "The Purloined Letter"—the missing and misappropriated text, the value of its mysterious content, and the analytics of recovering the text—quickly became generic conventions, the crime fiction of the later industrial era required a corpse as the evidenciary minimum for the murderous crimes it customarily focused on, and as the twentieth century advanced, the text and corpse increasingly merged.[26] The recent metaphysical detective story often replaces the "corpse-as-signifier," however, with the missing person, so instead of reading the dead body as the text, the unknown, missing, or absent person (literally or psychically) becomes the text to be interpreted and a key to understanding the crime (Merivale 101). The reader may encounter, then, a variety of missing texts; along with the purloined letter, Merivale and Sweeney cite "the embedded text, *mise en abyme* [text within a text], textual constraint, or text as object" as common variations on the theme (8). They also note that "letters, words, and documents no longer reliably denote the objects that they are meant to represent; instead these texts become impenetrable objects in their own right" (9).

The purloined letter is used classically in *Girl in a Box* and *The Interpreter,* with both featuring literal texts that are misappropriated or hidden in various ways. In *Girl in a Box,* the financial accounts of Mitsutan are a hidden text, and the misappropriated currency from Nozumi-gumi is a text that must be located and traced or read for clues. Of course, money is that most special text, a medium of exchange or a "bank note" that has historically represented other commodities (gold, silver, and so on), and is understood as an especially revealing one. Reading or tracing money, also known as forensic accounting, is a specialized form of detection in high demand in contemporary neoliberalism (as is suggested by efforts to "follow the dark money" of Super PAC donations in US presidential politics following the *Citizens United* Supreme Court decision).[27] In several scenes, Rei observes Kravitz or Melanie Kravitz, his wife, use envelopes of cash to make expensive purchases at the department store, so when Ravi tells Rei that he's seen similar envelopes at the bank, she begins to suspect some kind of money-laundering operation. Similar to Dupin's identification of Minister D—'s disguised letter, in one of the final scenes of Massey's novel, Rei and Michael identify the seal on an envelope as that of the *yakuza* group they suspect.

In *The Interpreter,* a letter written by Grace to her friend Maria also surfaces at the end of the novel. After Grace arranges for a substitute for her classroom at Fort Lee High School and "disappears" with Johnny/DJ, ostensibly to get married, she sends the letter to Maria, directing her to open a second, enclosed letter only if she doesn't hear again from Grace by her birthday, approximately two weeks away. The second letter, a text within a text within a text (the novel), is not unlike the purloined letter Minister D— disguises by folding it in on itself. It is Grace's will, in which she bequeaths everything to Maria, except a small grocery store that Grace wills to Suzy. By demanding that Maria open the second letter before Grace's birthday, Suzy learns that Grace planned a boating accident off the coast of Montauk, which a newspaper article confirms, reporting that an unidentified Asian male in his thirties did not survive the accident. Although *yakuza* cash in Massey's novel provides clues that help Rei reveal global financial crimes, as well as solve several murders, the letter in Kim's novel is more open-ended, since although it points clearly to ex-global gang member Johnny/DJ as the murderer of Mr. and Mrs. Park, it also implicates Grace in murderous revenge. And the novel ends with Grace still missing.

Central to my reading is that texts must also be translated and interpreted by Asian American female detectives in these novels, and this labor both draws on and modifies the figure of the cultural informant that has been so prevalent in Asian American literature.[28] Suzy's profession as an interpreter emphasizes the importance of reading codes and managing the flow of information in the New Economy. The translation of texts is Rei's primary form of collecting evidence in her assignment. Most of these are texts stolen by Rei using high-tech listening devices she plants in various places, including shoes and telephones; Rei returns to her apartment, listens to recorded conversations, and then reports translated findings to Michael and OCI. Soon after Rei begins working at Mitsutan, her bosses discover her navel ring in a revealing scene at an *onsen,* or hotspring. Mr. Yoshino, director of accessories, then seeks her advice on a new line of navel rings for the store, and insists she try on several at a bar where they meet so he can see how they look. As payment for her employee loyalty, Yoshino gives Rei a diamond navel ring, which turns out to have a tiny listening device in it. Although Michael quickly destroys the ring, from this point on, surveillance is ubiquitous and stolen texts that demand interpretation multiply.

The purloined letter or the missing text is just as surely figured as the missing or unknown identity, a thematic that operates in *Girl in a Box* and *The Interpreter* in the unknown identities of criminals but more interestingly in the unknown identities of the female sleuths. While one conventional way of reading unknown or missing identities in Asian American literature has been as an "identity crisis" in which a character is torn between allegiances to an ancestral homeland and the United States, such a reading is not fully supportable in either novel. Whereas Rei feels at home both in the United States and in Japan, Suzy feels as if she's never had a home, with no memory of Korea and no sense of belonging in the United States. Another way to read the missing or unknown identity in Asian American literature, more critically and with a basis in social history, has been to read it in terms of the invisibility of the Asian American as citizen-subject. This pertains in several ways to *The Interpreter* because Suzy feels no sense of connection to the United States and also holds no passport. When she asks her lover Michael to use his connections to look into it, he finds out that she is a naturalized US citizen, but her INS record is "blank," suggesting a special pardon, amnesty, or a National Interest Waiver, none of which makes sense, until Suzy figures out the agreement her parents made with the INS (S. Kim 216). Still, both Rei and Suzy work for the

US government, so at least partial citizenship is acknowledged in that association.

The most persuasive reading of the missing text as the missing or unknown identity both in *Girl in a Box* and *The Interpreter* recognizes the status of Rei and Suzy as preferred subjects of the US global economy—cosmopolitan subjects who work within or for the New Economy but who are otherwise unknown or illegible as subjects. Indeed, as Helen Heran Jun writes, while Asian Americans and especially Asian immigrants are simultaneously targeted for new forms of exclusion, they are now often discursively produced "as idealized subjects of a neoliberal world order," particularly in terms of the perception that they are disciplined and valuable workers (9). Several feminist scholars have critiqued the ways in which the Asian female worker is positioned as the ideal or even "natural" transnational worker in the neoliberal global economy.[29] Echoing this problematic construction, the paratext of the Rei Shimura series and much of the narrative itself in *Girl in a Box* suggest that Rei becomes a full citizen-subject by working for OCI and earning a professional wage serving the interests of US global capital or ensuring that Japanese organized crime is not threatening US hegemony in the New Economy. Cosmopolitan cultural knowledge, including bilingual interpreting skills, defines Rei for her boss Michael. Finally, Rei's "ability to think like the bad guys" who threaten the "free" market of the global economy renders her a valuable neoliberal worker (Mizejewski 11).

In addition to essentialist cultural definitions of Rei as an ideal worker, she is reduced to an essential racialized gender identity that also circulates globally, but in this construction she is more of an object. The cover of *Girl in a Box* (fig. 4.1) represents Rei as a commodity fetish by depicting a clothing store window display that features a reflection of Rei in a PI-style trench coat next to the torso of a fashionable mannequin. The cosmopolitan detective is visible only in refracted relation to the idealized commercial image of femininity in the global fashion industry.

Suzy is similarly perceived as the ideal cosmopolitan laboring subject whose cultural knowledge helps US authorities manage crime and maintain public order. But if Rei's cosmopolitanism is figured in terms of belonging to both the United States and Japan, Suzy's is figured as impartial world citizenship. Suzy recalls nothing of Korea and has lived in New York City since she was five, but she does not identify with American culture and found it shockingly "foreign" when she went to Columbia (S. Kim 165). More to the point, Suzy makes the important distinction that "knowing about a culture is different from feeling it" (165). Tellingly, Kim

FIGURE 4.1. Cover of *Girl in a Box* features a fashionable mannequin and a reflection of Rei Shimura as the Cosmopolitan Op. Cover of *Girl in A Box*, by Sujata Massey.

also represents Suzy's cosmopolitan citizenship as explicitly objectified, establishing her status in the opening chapter of *The Interpreter* with the introduction of Suzy's first lover, Damian, whose interest in Suzy is described as xenophilia and later as an "addiction" to her Asian face (288). Damian's "intrepid search for beauty" operates at a professional level, since he is the foremost academic expert on East Asian art, and at a personal level, since he cycles through Asian women, first his wife Yuki Tamiko, a scholar-colleague of Japanese literature, then Suzy (46). By the time events of *The Interpreter* begin, however, Suzy's relationship with Damian is part of her past, and she understands that his fetishistic desire for Asian women was about his self-loathing and running from his whiteness, which render him unable to love anyone: "His purpose was searching [for] the other" to his "Ralph Lauren Land" Americanness (288). Suzy's lover in the present of the novel, Michael, is perhaps less learned in his fascination with Suzy, but he nonetheless "wants Suzy in the latest fashion" and adorns her with Tiffany earrings and Chanel perfume (28). As an international business-man, Michael regards her as his cosmopolitan mistress, telephoning Suzy only from European airports and hotels, and managing the details of their intermittent rendezvous at the Waldorf-Astoria through his professional assistant. Interpellated in the New Economy as ideal laboring subjects and as status objects of desire, Rei and Suzy are defined in large part by a market fundamentalism that values them only for how their knowledge or their image may work in support of neoliberal cosmopolitanism. All that lies in between their legibility as neoliberal cosmopolitan subjects and neoliberal cosmopolitan objects is the unknown, unrecognized, or even missing Asian American female subject.

At first glance, Rei and Suzy seem to be privileged and valued female subjects. Indeed, rather than represented as having only narrow and irrel-evant or "subnational" skills based on particular loyalties and identity politics, as ethnic minorities are customarily represented in cosmopolitan discourse, Rei and Suzy have expertise that enables them to traverse the cosmopolitan landscape, and their ability to interpret different cultural registers and codes, as signified by their translation skills, is central to their employment within the global economy (Koshy, "Minority Cosmopolitan-ism" 592). Upon closer consideration, however, their labile knowledge skills are misappropriated by corrupt social institutions or used superficially in a neoliberal cosmopolitanism that simply reverses the binary of European cosmopolitanism that denies the minority subject's worldliness and con-flates the cosmopolitan subject (typically white, Western, and male) with the global, missing their mutual imbrication, or "linkages between the home and the world" (595). Read in this way, the purloined letter or the text that is missing in *Girl in a Box* and *The Interpreter* is a more capacious representation of Asian American women's cosmopolitanism that recognizes both worldliness and particularity and revises the dualistic "logic of small and large" (595). In significant ways, the opposition between the minority and the cosmopolitan is precisely where Rei and Suzy are wedged as they labor in those most cosmopolitan locations of Tokyo and New York. Instead of highlighting alternative visions of cross-cultural exchange and transnational affiliation, an implicitly comparative perspective, and "the 'scale jumping' properties of the minority," Massey's and Kim's mobilizations of detective fiction disclose that the model of political subjectivity in neoliberal cosmopolitan citizenship recognizes only a portion of Rei's and Suzy's worldly but still marginalized difference (594). This portion is the gendered racial knowledge of the Asian American female subject that is useful for globalization and that labors to read and interpret the codes of the New Economy.[30]

THE CONTINENTAL OP

While Rei and Suzy are not technically private investigators in Dashiell Hammett's famous conception of the term "Continental Op," neither are they public figures in the sense that they openly investigate crimes or murders, as in the more recent model of the police procedural where female detectives working on teams have made very high-profile appearances, especially on television. Mostly, Rei and Suzy do their detective work on the margins, emphasizing the outsider status of the detective, and they do it largely on their own. Various forms of disguise and impersonation indicate that *Girl in a Box* and *The Interpreter* retain from detective fiction an abiding ontological interest in the detecting hero— that is, an interest in the nature of being, identity, and subjectivity— which overshadows the epistemological interests in solving the mystery of the crime, even if they fully recognize the central role of criminality in contemporary social life in the corruption of the neoliberal global economy. To be sure, Rei and Suzy are implicated both in the murderous crimes they are investigating and in the extralegal operations of the New Economy they are employed to monitor. So Massey and Kim do not provide Asian American female impostors of the masculinist private eye, or pretenders who set out to save the world (and the genre) with inauthentic swagger and fraudulent street smarts. Instead, they present Cosmopolitan Ops who are imperfect doubles or impersonations that, as Tina Chen influentially suggests, simultaneously pay homage to and challenge the authenticity of the Continental Op or the hardboiled private eye (7).

If Dashiell Hammett's short stories named the hardboiled detective as the Continental Operative of the Continental Detective Agency, it was John Daly's Race Williams who was the first hardboiled detective hero (Scaggs 55). He was a large, tough, and violent figure but also shrewd, a private investigator or "PI," an expert at covert surveillance (60). According to Sean McCann, Daly's hardboiled hero was "stranded between legal authority and the criminal underworld" (45). Unlike the contemporaneous golden age fictions of the interwar years, hardboiled narratives do not maintain the white, upper middle-class status quo through the detective as a representative of "respectability" (47). Rather than learning and refinement, "manners and brainwork, the hard-boiled story would foreground the detective's craft knowledge, his physical strength and skill" (46). Indeed, Daly's hardboiled hero, "speaks the vernacular of the working-class city," and is associated with the populism of that era:

> Navigating the furthest corners of the metropolis, he ranges across its social and geographic terrain, tying the disparate features of the urban landscape into a legible map. But, less obviously, he also does battle on behalf of the hard-working people of the metropolis, and he struggles to defend their interests against the illegitimate wealth, criminal violence and official indifference that otherwise seems to dominate their world. (McCann 47)

Hammett adapted the figure in a no-name private eye, the Continental Op, "a truly ordinary-seeming person who turns out to conceal extraordinary cleverness beneath his commonplace exterior" (McCann 49).

The enigmatic figure of the Continental Op, along with the explicitly Orientalist representations of Chinatown and Charlie Chan, present particular challenges for authors who wish to create Asian American sleuths, since the racialization of Asian Americans persistently includes inscrutability and unknowable Otherness, as discussed at the beginning of this chapter. Betsy Huang argues that Wayne Wang's 1982 noir parody *Chan Is Missing* and Ed Lin's 2007 mystery novel *This Is a Bust* both effectively use Dashiell Hammett's 1947 story "Dead Yellow Women" to contend with the challenge of revising the genre. Huang points out that while the Continental Op in Hammett's story contains vice within the borders of San Francisco's Chinatown, he fails to understand or solve the mystery of Chinatown, which extends well beyond figuring out who murdered two Chinese female employees of the wealthy Chinese

American Lillian Shan, and this unsolved mystery continues to disturb him. Huang's reading suggests that the work of the hardboiled detective, even without the large cast of racial stereotypes that inhabit Hammett's Chinatown, may always involve the detective's investigation into Others—racialized, gendered, national—whom he imagines and uses for the construction of his subjectivity and for self understanding. Here, the unrealized promise of the hardboiled detective lends itself to further investigation of social hierarchies and inequalities.

Reviewing changes in contemporary detective fiction by writers of color, Maureen Reddy argues that because the detective's voice is so central to the hardboiled, "to change the voice, to let the Other speak, is to transform the genre" (*Traces, Codes, and Clues* 9). Similarly, Linda Mizejewski writes that replacing the male body of the detective with that of the female detective necessarily disrupts the ideology of the hardboiled (15). In both of these formulations, an Asian American female detective would automatically and dramatically redraw the Continental Op. But the Cosmopolitan Op in *Girl in a Box* or *The Interpreter* is not an entirely new construction. Indeed, the novels highlight the "detective's efforts to imagine or borrow another's identity in order to solve a crime," so *Girl in a Box* and *The Interpreter* repurpose the appropriative dimensions of hardboiled subjectivity for Rei and Suzy (Merivale and Sweeney 17). More specifically, Rei and Suzy assume publically legible identities or the forms of identity into which they are interpellated as Others, and expose those identities as constructions, a process of subject formation for Asian Americans that Chen identifies in her study *Double Agency*. The destabilization of othered gendered racial identities in turn disrupts the hardboiled masculinity of the Continental Op that depends on those same constructions. In the following analysis, I show how Massey's and Kim's sleuths disguise identities and use covert identities quite effectively as they elaborate their complex relation to hardboiled subjectivity and to the New Economy.[31] Rei Shimura and Suzy Park are insubordinate to the authority of the Continental Op and also borrow from him as they remake the detective into the figure of the Asian American Cosmopolitan Op.

Because the hardboiled detective sees danger in modern industrial disorder, venturing into the mean streets typically involves taking on some sort of disguise, whether a borrowed name, an ideological facade, a physical alteration, or a full-blown assumption of a new identity. While Rei and Suzy disguise their gender identities, they do not try to adopt the hardboiled masculinity of the Continental Op or in some other way attempt to masculinize themselves. On the contrary, they assume hyper-feminine identities to disguise the investigative work they perform in a profession that has been historically and to a great certain extent remains defined by hypermasculinity in popular culture. The performance of hyperfeminine identities may be tiring given the relentless stereotyping of Asian women in popular culture through such sexually racialized figures as the China doll, the geisha, and the lotus blossom. In addition, adopting hyperfemininity closely resembles what McRobbie considers "post-feminist masquerade," or "a new form of gender power which re-orchestrates the heterosexual matrix in order to secure, once again, the existence of patriarchal law and masculine hegemony, but this time by means of a kind of ironic, quasi-feminist staking out of a distance in the act of taking on the garb of femininity" (*Aftermath of Feminism* 64). In the context of hardboiled subjectivity, however, the irony of using hyper-femininity as cover or disguise for hypermasculinized detective work draws attention to the conventionally gendered representational politics of the genre. Massey and Kim deploy hyperfemininity through female detectives who use it self-consciously, thereby exposing the appropriation of the feminized and racialized Other by the Continental Op and the genre's reliance on this form of hegemonic white masculinity.

Rei's disguise as a Japanese girl in a box is especially ironic because its image of ideal womanhood as protected and sheltered sharply contradicts the street-smart skills for which Rei is hired by OCI and which she uses in her detective work as a spy. As the title and primary conceit of Massey's novel, girl-in-a-box femininity is explicitly addressed as a culturally specific construction of gender identity, with detailed attention in the first few chapters to how Rei creates it and how difficult it is to perform. Rei undergoes a feminizing makeover in DC that includes ideology, as she must learn the middle-class manners and cultural capital that go with the girl-in-a-box persona. Rei also impersonates the visual and physical appearance of this modern Japanese hyperfemininity, though she does not need to disavow her biracial heritage since that is part of her assumed cosmopolitan Japanese identity or *kokusaijin*.

The intense process of Rei's "appearance modification" preceding her assignment in Tokyo involves another OCI translator, Mrs. Taki, who also takes on the role as the Defense Department's self-proclaimed expert on Japanese appearance (Massey, *Girl in a Box,* 20). There is a three-day shopping trip for the perfect designer suit, shoes, and bag to prepare for Rei's Mitsutan interview, but just as importantly a four-hour trip to Dora's salon, which specializes in Asian "beauty jobs" (21). Dora is "good at changing identity" Mrs. Taki tells Rei, because she used to live in Tokyo and did the makeup for the Takarazuka Revue, "the girl actresses who perform as boys" (22). In fact, there is little sense of a natural Japanese feminine identity in the novel. When Rei suggests that she doesn't need alteration because she won't be using a false identity and will retain her real name, Michael produces a magazine with a perfect cover girl, insisting that she needs "to resemble an ideal Japanese twenty-three-year-old woman" (21). Seeing as the image was obviously Photoshopped, Rei wryly observes that she would need "multiple surgeries to look like that" (21). After Rei is installed in her apartment and new job in Japan, the narrative continues to make reference to heterosexual femininity as a culturally specific construct whose codes Rei performs, emphasizing that Rei is quite anxious about performing them successfully.

After only a few days of work at Mitsutan, Rei complains, "[M]y toes were blistered and my lower back ached. I walked around a lot trying to concentrate on maintaining the correct posture: tummy sucked in and buttocks clenched" (Massey, *Girl in a Box*, 92). Rei also worries that her athletic muscle tone will give her away: "I realized after covertly inspecting the others, that I was different. Not fatter, exactly, but I had wider shoulders, and more developed upper arms and thighs. Weight-lifting and spinning had done me in" (71). In addition to the attention given to cultural differences in the embodied discipline of middle-class femininity, the construction and performance of Japanese femininity is emphasized by Rei's expertise in tasteful presentation and self-fashioning through the conspicuous consumption of power brand fashions, original low- and high-fashion bricolage or "styling," and vintage kimono or retro style, a trend called "ultrafeminine" in Japan, readers are told. Finally, however, Rei is a little too worldly for her girl-in-a-box impersonation, which is seriously undermined when she inadvertently reveals her navel ring to her male bosses. In fact, the navel ring alerts the corrupt department store management team to her disguise, and they use it in an attempt to spy on her. The girl-in-a-box disguise, which ultimately fails establishes that femininity is a construction and highlights the work required to create and maintain gender identity, even or especially exaggerated versions of it.

In *The Interpreter* Suzy does not don a disguise when she ventures into the mean streets, as much as others mistake her for Grace. Indeed, other characters often describe Suzy and Grace as identical or as doubles. At times Suzy uses their close association to gather information, but her most effective disguise is, like Rei's, a heterosexual and hyperfeminine one, since it is as Michael's "mistress," which is increasingly a publically legible identity. If fascination with celebrity couples and a resurgence of the concept of "the trophy wife" led Ying Chu to declare in 2009 that Asian women are the "new" trophy wives for cosmopolitan Western men such as Rupert Murdoch, the figure of the Asian woman as a hyperfeminine and sexualized status partner is limited in *The Interpreter* to the designation of ideal lover for global movers and shakers married to white women. In this novel as well as *Girl in a Box*, the protagonists in some ways resemble, when not undercover or in disguise, a discursive figure more like the "gold misses" or young Asian women that Hanna Rosin claims are "taking over the world" by declining marriage and traditional gender roles and instead directing their efforts toward or working on behalf of the global economy (231). Contending with the figure in popular culture of the ideal but socially threatening Asian female as global worker, Asian American authors also draw on the femme fatale who conventionally played opposite but in codependent relation to the Continental Op, critically revealing the social order that the gendered racial figure of the simultaneously productive and destructive Asian woman now underwrites.

Kim's narrative insists that Suzy willingly plays the role of mistress, both because she "knows how to be a kept woman" (29), and because it provides an emotionally self-protective relationship that works well for the "no involvement" rule she adopted after her relationship with Damian ended (15). Similar to the girl-in-a-box gender identity that Rei uses as a disguise, the mistress identity that Suzy assumes is understood in Kim's novel to be a self-conscious adoption of an assigned role or interpellation, and Suzy's mistress identity is also represented as crafted and performed, especially through her display of extravagant gifts—silk shirts, cashmere sweaters, and diamonds—from Michael. "Often she stands in front of the mirror, clad in whatever strikes her as carefully sewn and stitched money, lots of it. She hardly recognizes herself. A bona fide mistress, whose clothing shields her from herself" (28). While the mistress identity seems to have serious implications for Suzy's identity, in *The Interpreter* the hyperfeminine disguise once again functions as effective cover for neoliberal detective work, but Michael never suspects anything about Suzy's investigation, even as he subsidizes and unwittingly participates in it. Suzy enlists him at a crucial point to discover her own citizenship status. When Michael uses connections at INS to learn that there is no record of how she became a citizen, he tells her to let it go, which is exactly what he does. This important clue is, however, a key to solving the mystery of her parents' murder. With her impersonation of the hyperfeminine identity of the sexually racialized mistress, Suzy's investigative work is made possible yet largely goes undetected, at least by one hypermasculine character in the novel.

While the disguise of hyperfemininity is insubordinate to the hard-boiled masculinity of the Continental Op, *The Interpreter* and *Girl in a Box* also pay homage to the Continental Op through positioning their heroines covertly or nominally as professional detectives. In their self-presentations as amateur, novice, or inexperienced sleuths, they disavow their expertise and their connections to institutions of authority. Although institutions may credential Suzy and Rei, such associations also mitigate their ability to operate on the margins or independently and thus implicate the women even more in the neoliberal cosmopolitan criminality they investigate. Suzy and Rei both hide or otherwise misrepresent their professional service to a greater legal authority as contingent, new, or temporary. Technically an amateur detective, Suzy's disavowals are factual statements. Still, on several levels she hides her detective work or the fact of her efforts, from her lover, from her friends Jen and Caleb, and certainly from those she interrogates or pursues as part of her investigation.

In *Girl in a Box*, the special assignment in Tokyo is Rei's first professional job as a detective, and she continually reminds herself (and the reader) that she is just learning how OCI works and is "such an amateur" (99). Still, seven of Massey's ten books in the Rei Shimura series focus on the episodic adventures of this sleuth as she moves from one short-term job to another between different, typically urban locations in the United States and Japan. In the series, Rei starts out as an English teacher, but by the second book Rei is an antiques collector and buyer. She also follows her aunt's advice that she needs to know ikebana or flower arranging for marriageability, and becomes an arts and antiques writer/reviewer, a fashion and textiles curator, a family genealogist, an interior designer, an antiquities preservationist, and, in *Girl in a Box*, a salesgirl at an upscale department store. In the final three books, Rei is no longer an amateur sleuth, but she continues to present herself as nominally professional, hiding her expertise, which is obviously substantial. Although her denial of her interpretation skills may be read as an irritatingly gendered example of self-deprecation, it is also a method for honoring the voluntarily marginal status of the hardboiled detective, who not only takes pride in maintaining some measure of independence from social institutions but also understands his own limitations, both in terms of detection or knowledge and in terms of individual power in the world. In fact, the Continental Op is consistently figured as an ambivalent and flawed member of society rather than a fully formed, triumphant individual hero.

Perhaps the most obvious connection between the Continental Op and the Cosmopolitan Op as represented in *Girl in a Box* and *The Interpreter*, and one that retains foundational elements of hardboiled subjectivity, is the Asian American female detective's role as interpreter. In this role, the Cosmopolitan Op operates as a liminal figure who straddles geopolitical and cultural borders in the neoliberal global economy, not entirely unlike the Western adventuring hero turned hardboiled detective who straddled legal authority and the criminal underworld in the industrial city. In Kim's novel, the narrator describes interpretation as an "art" and the interpreter as "the most astute listener in the world. She listens between the lines, between the words. Nothing goes unnoticed" (99). Rei and Suzy are hired by US government entities specifically for the translation skills with which they expertly navigate the complex geography of the New Economy. But those same skills also pull the Cosmopolitan Ops into and reveal massive corruption. As discussed above, Rei uncovers US government involvement in the manipulation of international business and financial markets, and Suzy is drawn into undocumented immigration and the surveillance or management of international borders.

Interpretations of the New Economy in these novels lead more to alienation than to world citizenship or cosmopolitan understanding. This is particularly true for Suzy when her work in the criminal courts turns into an investigation of her parents' murder. As clues start adding up, Suzy questions her interpretive abilities, condemning herself for not figuring out why they moved so often when she was a child, why Grace would only accept a private scholarship to finance her education at Smith College, and why her parents "had disappeared while [she] wasn't even looking" (Kim, *The Interpreter*, 110). Even after Suzy discovers, through her own independent investigation, that Grace had functioned as an interpreter to help her parents turn in other immigrants, that Johnny/DJ had killed her parents, and that Grace had killed Johnny/DJ, Suzy disparages her interpretive abilities to read texts, including that final text in Grace's will: "A title to a Korean market—what's she supposed to do with that? Give it to Kim Yong Su as an apology? A piece of the American Dream? A family heirloom? What the hell's an interpreter if she can't even interpret her own sister?" (293). For this deeply perceptive sleuth, "Being bilingual, being multicultural should have brought two worlds into one heart, and yet for Suzy, it meant persistent hollowness"

(166). If Rei emerges from her investigations somewhat less psychically scathed, both novels' representations of Cosmopolitan Ops borrow from the hardboiled detective who knows, perhaps too much, about modern life and his place in it.

As Mizejewski has pointed out, the conventional glamorization of the female detective and the coupling of the female detective with a man as sexual or potential sexual partner are symbolic strategies for containing the threatening image of a woman who has taken over a traditional male role, especially in narratives that are not fundamentally about marriage or mating but about paid work. The first book series with professional female detectives featured heroines as "hard-working women with domestic and financial problems. They were loners, wise about taking care of themselves, skilled with a gun and ready to use it if necessary" (Mizejewski 19) These female detective figures, especially when women of color, were popularly considered threatening representations in the context of women's increased participation in the labor force, a fact that also led to the "uneven media history" for different versions of the subgenre, with speedy leaps for the mid-century male hero from print magazine and literary fiction to radio, film, and television, but slower migrations to visual culture for the female detective in popular novels (20).

The strategies of disguise and disavowal through which Massey's and Kim's female sleuths impersonate the Continental Op similarly constitute symbolic relationships with a masculinized figure. Rather than merely containing a gendered racial sleuth, however, the relationships are mobilized to both destabilize and retain traits of the hardboiled detective, which combine to open narrative space for a self-consciously feminized and culturally labile Asian American Cosmopolitan Op. Recalling how Dupin extends the minister's logic of duplicates and inconspicuous replacements, *Girl in a Box* and *The Interpreter* use the hardboiled's hypermasculinity against itself and also mobilize the subgenre to provide narrative investigations into neoliberal cosmopolitan citizenship. The novels disclose the ways in which neoliberal capitalism is appropriating Asian American women through denying them subject status outside of market fundamentalism, which ultimately undermines their assignments as ideal neoliberal subjects. By recasting the hardboiled narrative and the metaphysical detective story, *Girl in a Box* and *The Interpreter* elaborate upon "the failures of the legal and social order to protect decent people from elite predation and criminal abuse" to question neoliberal constructions of Asian American females as ideal or successful cosmopolitan citizens (McCann 56).

5 /   Food Writing and Transnational Belonging in Global Consumer Culture

> *What is so delicious as a comical-satirical-farcical-epical-tragical-*
> *romantical novel? The reader picks it up with the sort of high anticipation*
> *that she feels when ordering the lemon raspberry mousse cheesecake with*
> *chocolate sauce off the dessert menu.*
>
> —JANE SMILEY, "RECIPE FOR SUCCESS"

> *I have an entry in my journal that reads, "Oh my god, I'm writing a*
> *thriller!"*
>
> —RUTH OZEKI, "A CONVERSATION WITH RUTH OZEKI"

> *Whatever people may think of my book, I will make it public, bring it to*
> *light unflinchingly. That is the modern thing to do.*
>
> —JANE TAKAGI-LITTLE, MY YEAR OF MEATS

Ruth Ozeki's *My Year of Meats* (1998) is, as Jane Smiley suggests, a post-modern remix—a montage or pastiche. The up-to-the minute tone of the novel is also a result of Ozeki's expansive vision, for she folds into the narrative not only identifiable conventions from the different literary modes that Smiley references but also codes from different media, such as those of film noir. In this book, the print novel converges in the early 1990s with visual media such as television and film, and electronic media such as the fax. Looking backward to the epistolary novel and forward to reality TV, *My Year of Meats* is palpably self-conscious of connections between the literary and the commercial. Ozeki was herself surprised by the depth of the correspondence, as she recalls her realization during the writing process that the book was also a thriller—a type of crime fiction and part of a genre that scholars have long recognized as a bridge between the literary and the popular, as discussed in chapter 4. In fact, Jane Takagi-Little, one of the two primary female characters in *My Year of Meats*, investigates the unhealthy and even criminal global practices of the US meat industry as she is producing a television series for Japanese audiences based on the notion that "beef is best" (Ozeki 12). Ozeki's first novel is perhaps most evidently a type of food writing, but one that does not exactly deliver the anticipated gastronomical delight that Smiley's review ironically references. Instead, the reader is served a decidedly unsavory figurative platter, one with a variety of social ills, including a toxic food supply, epidemic levels of racial and gender violence, and a manipulative media industry, all operating on transnational levels that connect the United States and Japan.

In this final chapter, I extend the argument that Asian American women writers may mobilize popular genres to engage discourses of neoliberal belonging and to critically participate in the reformulation of US citizenship. Rather than innovate a single genre, *My Year of Meats* combines identifiable conventions of several popular genres and cultural forms, significantly enhancing crossover appeal while also rigorously resisting generic classification. Moreover, at least one of the genres that Ozeki deploys in *My Year of Meats*, food writing, is largely undermined in her narrative practice by fundamentally confounding the reader's expectation. Unlike in detective fiction, rule subversion and the violation of the reader's expectations for some kind of pleasurable consumption or "hyperreal eating" is not one of the generic conventions of food writing (Mannur 82–83). There must be some consumable at the close of a culinary narrative, even and especially in the most daring of food-adventuring narratives that focus on the challenge of consuming what some consider inedible.

Although Ozeki's refusal of the narrative payout may be understood as a resounding rejection of the tendency in food writing to reinscribe dominant ideologies of race, gender, class, and nation, and thus a declarative statement about the global injustices that the novel depicts, my reading explores a more complex role for food writing or culinary narrative in Ozeki's text. I consider the way in which *My Year of Meats* both accepts food writing as a global site of consequential cultural expression and social negotiation, principally in its own extensive use of culinary discourse, and addresses the deficiencies of food writing, thus commenting upon its own deficiencies and by extension those of all representational texts— literary, popular, and those that crossover—to fully convey the complexity of social belonging under global neoliberalism. Far from a defense of US neoliberalism, this register of contemporary social life is nevertheless a hopeful statement about agency and about the capacity of the Asian American female subject to elude the totalizing force of advanced-capitalist globalization.

The novel focuses intently on meat as a specific global commodity that has been mismanaged and more likely threatens rather than sustains life, and meat operates as a literary conceit or metaphor that extends the abuses of the US meat industry to a number of other industries, social phenomena, and, for some readers, America itself. Scholars largely agree that the US meat industry in *My Year of Meats* functions as a metonym for the globalization of US capital. In this novel, globalization is depicted as a process of restructuring characterized by monopoly capital accumulation, environmental degradation, neocolonialist biopolitics and necropolitics, and the uneven flow of people, goods, capital, and information or knowledge across national borders. More accurately, then, *My Year of Meats* addresses the social conditions created by globalization and expresses concern for them, making use of a decidedly critical globality.[1]

As much as meat illustrates the harmful processes and effects of globalization, *My Year of Meats* also questions representations of global culture emerging from the United States. I contend that the novel is equally if not more interested in the fictions that circulate transnationally in its world, in this case fictive narratives about meat (and food), most obviously but not exclusively through *My American Wife!,* a Japanese television series that is sponsored by the US beef industry and one that nearly dominates Jane Takagi-Little's life for a year. To wit, *My Year of Meats* highlights how culinary narratives appear in numerous cultural forms, are produced through a variety of global commercial media in neoliberal consumer cultures, and are the site of the negotiation of national and transnational belonging. *My Year of Meats* is itself a type of culinary narrative—a narrative of culinary tourism—that trades in the culinary cultural capital of global food tourism and self-consciously explores the practice of US neoliberal transnational citizenship through an examination of the production and consumption of popular food narratives. My reading thus emphasizes Ozeki's mobilization of food writing, and specifically the narratives of culinary tourism, in the novel's commentary on globalization, a popular discourse of transnational citizenship that centralizes the neoliberal mandate to participate in global consumer culture.

My Year of Meats appropriately includes twelve chapters, one for each of the months of 1991 that Jane Takagi-Little recounts in her story about a "life-changing" experience working on the production team of *My American Wife!* While Jane initially imagines that the fifty-two-segment cooking show will be a "day-in-the-life type of documentary" featuring American housewives who cook their favorite meat recipes, she quickly learns otherwise; more accurately, the show is a paid advertisement for the American meat industry in Japan, and its sole sponsor is the Beef Export and Trade Syndicate lobbying organization BEEF-EX (Ozeki, *My Year of Meats*, 10). As Jane recollects, the mandate for the show was "to foster among Japanese housewives a proper understanding of the wholesomeness of U.S. meats," particularly beef (10). The episodes that she has a hand in creating do not feature "healthy" meals but do feature plenty of embedded advertising, all targeting Japanese women who are encouraged to emulate the American women presented in the show. BEEF-EX clearly deploys the ideology of the "civilizing mission" that has justified so much Western capitalist expansion in the past, that has structured imperial travel narratives used to endorse colonialism, and that now underwrites neoliberal global economic development. To the extent that Ozeki's novel traces the marketing strategies of global agribusiness in the production of *My American Wife!* and is itself a narrative of culinary tourism, it too makes use of the civilizing mission's teleology.

A third-person narrative about Akiko Ueno, a fan of *My American Wife!* and the wife of Jane's boss in Japan, Joichi "John" Ueno, alternates with and complements Jane's first-person narration in every chapter, undercutting to some extent the geopolitical and racial hierarchy of the civilizing mission that *My American Wife!* relies upon. While Akiko often seems far removed from the narrative's focus on the production of *My American Wife!*, her role as consumer exerts important influence over the development of the television show, as well as the production of more critical media in 1991. Ozeki's professional website, *Ozekiland*, summarizes *My Year of Meats* as "the story of Jane and Akiko, two women on opposite sides of the planet, whose lives are connected by a TV cooking show," suggesting that Jane and Akiko are both protagonists in the novel. In some ways this is accurate, but the novel hews toward Jane in much of its storytelling, not only because hers is the first-person narrative voice of the novel but also because her experience is the focus of the prologue, she narrates the epilogue, and "J. T.-L." provides the "author's note" for the bibliography of resources that is included at the end of the book. Moreover, if Jane's role as a fabulist fiction writer is emphasized over her role as a documentarian (she describes herself as both), there is a way to read the entire text, including sections written from the perspective of Akiko, as Jane's creation. Regardless, the stories of two women, along with a variety of other materials, are interwoven and ultimately come together in the novel when Akiko becomes pregnant and reaches out to Jane for help in escaping her abusive husband.

While Akiko eventually does leave Ueno and immigrates to the United States to give birth (a plot development that several scholars find problematic because it too strongly suggests the United States as a site of liberation or even civilization for immigrant women), Jane's year of meats is life-changing primarily because she learns that she is a "DES daughter," exposed in utero to diethylstilbestrol; a man-made toxic version of estrogen, DES was prescribed to between four and six million women in the United States from 1948 to 1971 to prevent miscarriages and for a dubious mishmash of other reasons.[2] Diethylstilbestrol was also used by US farmers to fatten chickens, cows, and other livestock, and it is through this connection to the livestock industry and to global agribusiness that Jane learns during her year of meats about the source of her own struggles with fertility and about the other effects of DES.

Jane narrates how she becomes dissatisfied with the fantasy of America, the "spectacle of raw American abundance" that is featured in *My American Wife!* and presented to an audience of Japanese married women as a model (35). Jane connects the retrogressive racial ideology of the show to a book in her hometown library, Frye's *Grammar School Geography*, which she consulted as a twelve-year-old child after a painful PeeWee League softball game at which she was called "chink" (148). She read "Races of Men," an entry detailing the "race science" of 1902 that still operated in Quam, Minnesota (and many other places in the United States), in the 1970s. She recalls, "Even as a kid, I knew there was something very wrong with this picture of the world—after all, I had gone to the library as a twelve-year-old searching for amalgamation, not divisiveness" (150). On a visit home later in the year that she documents, Jane returns to the library and retrieves the book to take that narrative out of circulation, at least in her hometown. In this spirit, and encouraged by Akiko, Jane alters *My American Wife!*, defying her boss's directions to focus on middle-to upper-middle-class white women with two to three children and "All-American values" (13). The cooking show also becomes, then, Jane's platform for redressing the ideologies of Western white supremacy, heteropatriarchy, and capitalist overconsumption that continue to circulate so perniciously and globally in contemporary popular media, including narratives of culinary tourism. Still, Jane's efforts are constrained by her context, and in *My American Wife!* she largely adopts the 1990s model of liberal multiculturalism, which included, as Emily Cheng has pointed out, an ideological narrative of racial mixing that was part of a larger set of "optimistic" millennial discourses positing an inclusive and postracial America (195).

Jane's contending but not quite alternative multicultural discourse features the delicious home cooking of the Mexican immigrant family of Bert and Cathy Martinez in Texas; of the African American family of Mr. and Mrs. Helen Dawes in Memphis; of the lesbian, multiracial, and vegetarian family of Dyann and Lara in Massachusetts; and of the transnational and transracial adoptive family of Vern and Grace Beaudroux in Louisiana. Although clearly more representative of the diversity of the United States, Jane's vision for the show is a tokenizing, rainbow image of American repronormative families, with parents all neatly coupled, but Jane calculates that this is as much pushback as she can manage without losing her job. Jane decides to augment her efforts in *My American Wife!* by making an independent film from a far more critical angle, one that looks closely at what American families are eating and what American agribusiness is exporting.

In the section titled "Documentary Interlude," Jane recounts the filming of her muckraking investigation into the continued illegal use of DES in US beef production. This visual text focuses on the disfiguring hormonal effects of DES on Rosie Dunn, the five-year-old daughter of cattle ranchers Bunny and John Dunn who has fully developed breasts and has started menstruating due to exposure to illegal agricultural hormones on her parents' ranch in Colorado. Jane met the Dunns while filming a segment for *My American Wife!*, and former rodeo queen Bunny has stepped up to tell her daughter's story and to allow the child to be filmed. The novel ends with a breaking story in the mainstream media about DES and the purchase of Jane's documentary by all major US networks and public television stations in the United States, England, and Japan. So, although Jane produces fantasy culinary narratives in *My American Wife!* "about an exotic and vanishing America for consumption on the flip side of the planet," she describes in *My Year of Meats* an inspiring twelve months in which she learned "something real about America" and made her own more critical and profitable film as well (15). Looking back, Jane believes that she succeeded in her desire to effect change by getting a "small but critical piece of information about the corruption of meats in America out to the world" (360). In her year of meats Jane becomes an activist, using her access to global media capitalism and her filmmaking skills to create an exposé about a harmful commodity, US consumer culture, and the abuses of globalization. In her words, Jane becomes "half-documentarian, half-fabulist" of an era in which "you have to make things up to tell truths that alter outcomes" (360). *My Year of Meats* explores the powerful role of commercial media in neoliberal consumer culture and largely condemns it, but the repertoire of genres and narrative forms Ozeki uses to comment upon the contexts of global-ization and the consumer culture of the United States insists that liter-ary culture and commercial culture are irrevocably intertwined and that transnational belonging is mediated through food writing.

Food Writing: A National and Transnational Genre

Drawing on various literary forms, *My Year of Meats* is recognizable as a female bildungsroman and borrows from the Anglo-American tra-dition discussed in previous chapters, with pedagogical agendas for both protagonist and reader. It also incorporates an epistolary structure, with Jane's first-person culinary narrative presented in a diary format that includes faxes, letters, and excerpts from other documents. Most of the literary forms at play in *My Year of Meats* are closely associated with traditions of women's writing, as emphasized by the epigraphs from *The Pillow Book* that begin each chapter. This early eleventh-century master-piece of Japanese literature was written by Sei Shonagon, a contempo-rary of the two other most famous Japanese women writers, Murasaki Shibiku and Izumi Shibiku. Importantly, Shonagon's text, which the poet describes as "notebooks with odd facts," itself defies neat catego-rization and is composed of sixteen *waka* or Japanese prose poems that are organized into 164 lists, a diary-like second section that scrupulously details the author's life, and a third section that apparently balances the outer and inner worlds of subjective experience represented in the previ-ous sections (Miner, Odagiri, and Morell 227). Jane admires Shonagon, she explains, because Shonagon wrote bold, "presumptuous scatterings" in Chinese characters, which was largely the preserve of male writers at the time. Indeed, Shonagon inspires Jane's decisions "to become a docu-mentarian, to speak men's Japanese, to be different" (Ozeki, *My Year of Meats* 15).

While Shonagon is a part of Jane's cultural heritage, the parallel that Jane explicitly draws between herself and Shonagon extends from their mutual dissatisfaction with a gender division of labor that regulates access to the means of cultural production, a shared desire to document their own lives, and finally the similarly complex assemblages that they create in their hybrid texts. Jane refers to the private forms of writing that women have typically been confined to and still are often confined to by exclusion from US television production and commercial filmmak-ing when she declares in the epilogue that she will bring her "book" to light (Ozeki 361).³ Some have read in this passage a kind of confusion between or a conflation of Ozeki the author and Jane the character—an unintended consequence of the layering of narrative voice in the novel—since it is actually a documentary film that Jane produces. By contrast, I read Jane's use of the word "book" to describe her documentary film as a reference to Shonagon's "pillow book" and as a closing attempt to draw a parallel between her own work and Shonagon's poetry, or, more accurately, between their respective conditions of production. Jane begins the final entry of her diary, which comprises the epilogue, by characterizing Shonagon as "a fellow documentarian," reclassifying the canonical Japanese literary poem to bring it into closer association with her own work and to recognize its use value as a kind of chronicle of Shonagon's historical moment (355). In Jane's usage, "book" becomes a more open term for narrative that may take different forms. Scholars agree, actually, that Shonagon's original text likely took an unorthodox material form since its *kanji* or Chinese characters denote a sewn book or booklet, rather than a scroll (the standard at the time), and a pillow; they have speculated that the pillow book "may have been a memorandum book, a collection of secret jottings, or a notebook kept under a pillow or otherwise close at hand" (McCullough 156–57).⁴

While Jane draws a parallel between her own and Shonagon's cultural production in this passage, she also points out that Shonagon's Heian era required women to write surreptitiously out of feminine modesty or decorous belonging, but that the new millennial era demands that the "modern" female reveal her cultural narrative, or, as Jane puts it, "make it public," in whatever form it may take, whether a television show, a film, a novel, a diary, or some convergent medium that combines media. The importance of publicity in the neoliberal era of synergistic media is also illustrated in the stories of the other women in the novel, such as that of Bonnie Dunn, which became public when they were shared as episodic culinary narratives in *My American Wife!* Certainly, the stories of various other women are embedded in or are part of Jane's year of meats—providing the meat, as it were, of Ozeki's novel.

Popular food writing in the United States is clearly not new, extending back to the earliest published American cookbook by Amelia Simmons in 1796.⁵ Food writing has been, in fact, one of the few acceptable forms of writing for women historically. Moreover, although male celebrity chefs currently dominate the discursive landscape of popular culinary narrative, the contemporary phenomenon is rooted in the works of female authors, especially M. F. K. Fisher, Irma Rombauer, and Julia Child.

Child in particular played a central role in the development of American taste cultures in the late twentieth century, as well as in the migration of food writing to television and thus the recent explosion of food narratives that began with the Food Network in 1993 and that *My Year of Meats* acknowledges.[6]

In addition to Ozeki's persuasive indictment of globalization through the example of the US meat industry, scholarship on the novel has linked it to a US multiculturalism that produces "palatable difference" or popular narratives of inclusion that use food themes to incorporate racialized Others whose cultural identities fall outside or exceed dominant narratives. But little has been said about Ozeki's use of culinary narrative more specifically. Fortunately, since *My Year of Meats* was published in 1998, and in the context of rapidly expanding culinary discourse, the field of cultural studies has developed sophisticated critical tools with which to analyze food writing as a site of intense negotiation of cultural, social, and political belonging and as "an alternative register through which to theorize gender, sexuality, class, and race" (Mannur 19).[7] Indeed, the millennial fascination with food writing and culinary narratives is one important context that many readers will correctly recognize for the novel. At the time of this writing, more than a decade after the novel's publication, Penguin is marketing *My Year of Meats* as "[t]he perfect fiction companion to *The Omnivore's Dilemma* and *In Defense of Food*," which became *New York Times* nonfiction best sellers for Michael Pollan in 2006 and 2008, respectively. Described as "a sexy, poignant, funny tale about global meat and media production," the novel is situated as an exploration of the transnational landscape of consumer culture in Penguin's summary.

Penguin's summary points to the recent saturation of the global media landscape with culinary narratives, which is a distinct part of the heightened address, since the 1990s, of female consumers/workers that serves as a backdrop for this study. It also points to a globalizing media industry characterized by intense remediation.[8] Some may now think that Ozeki's novel was prophetic, but I suggest that Ozeki was able to use her decade of experience in documentary television and film production and her personal knowledge of media industry conditions in the 1990s to project that the restructuring of production in the interests of lowering costs and maximizing profits would change programming significantly, moving cable channels and networks alike toward the far less expensive "reality-based television."[9] The novel initially received enthusiastic praise from reviewers, some of whom were attentive to, if anxious about, the changes that *My Year of Meats* addresses. John Sayles, for example, provided a blurb for the back cover of one edition: "This is a very cool book, satirical but never mean, funny, peopled by fully inhabited characters who are both blind and self-aware. Ruth Ozeki's *My Year of Meats* reassures us that media and culture, though bound inextricably, will never become one." With an up-to-the-minute tone that foregrounds global changes in culture, citizenship and capitalism, and remains current today, the novel received accolades as well. In 1998, Pacific Rim Voices awarded *My Year of Meats* the Kiriyama Prize for encouraging greater understanding of and among the peoples and nations of the Pacific Rim and South Asia. According to Ozeki's website, Ozekiland, *My Year of Meats* "was an international success," and has been translated into eleven languages and published in fourteen countries. On Goodreads, the largest website for readers and book recommendations in the world, *My Year of Meats* has an overall score of 3.86 out of 5 (of 4,124 ratings). "Food" is the fourth most popular generic category in the "top shelves" ranking (out of one hundred different reader-chosen categories) for *My Year of Meats*, following the categories "To-Read," "Fiction," and "Currently Reading."

The Discourse of Globalization

The elaboration of globalization as a popular discourse of neoliberal transnational consumer citizenship in *My Year of Meats* identifies widespread processes and practices that traverse national borders, and this may partly account for the novel's international success. The novel's address of the increasingly complex global media landscape is, in this regard, no less important than its critique of the US meat industry. The novel clearly registers the economic restructuring of the US media industry, especially the television industry, which began in the late 1980s as part of neoliberal globalization. Furthermore, *My Year of Meats* highlights that, rather than being truly global and deterritorialized, the migrations associated with globalization, whether of capital, commodities, people, or culture, are actually between (usually two) nations with formerly established and unequal relationships, especially formal colonial relationships but also relationships defined through war and conflict, as in the relationship between the United States and Japan. As Inderpal Grewal argues, the "'global,' by the last decade of the twentieth century, was a powerful imaginary produced through knowledges moving along specific transnational connectivities, [which] constituted a web of connections that moved along historicized trajectories" (22). It is perhaps more accurate, then, to observe that national identifications and affiliations have been reaffirmed, strengthened in new ways, and even multiplied rather than displaced in globalization discourse.

At the same time, culture, family, and home are no longer exclusively associated with a single nation, as Néstor Canclini has influentially argued, so globalization discourse also depends upon nonterritorialized sites of belonging, primarily consumer culture itself, to produce community and subjectivity (5). In this context, US transnational citizenship is constituted through the knowledge of global commodities, consumer desires, and a focus on market-based choices. In short, if we understand globalization as a discourse that reformulates the location of belonging, the transnational citizen may likely demonstrate that belonging resides "in consumer culture." As forms of US neoliberal citizenship, and despite differences in scale, transnational consumer citizenship and postfeminist citizenship, as discussed in chapter 3, have clear correspondences—chiefly their definition of the citizen-subject as a choice-making consumer. Similar to the cosmopolitan citizen who is produced through economic institutions and affiliations that are supranational but who cannot claim freedom from belonging or "world citizenship," the consumer citizen is produced through transnational networks of consumers and connections to commodity markets or even producers via global brand identification and loyalty (Calhoun 442). Grewal has also pointed out that, in addition to reconstituting nationalisms through transnational networks of US consumer culture, the discourse of globalization has produced gendered affiliations, such as new versions of consumer feminism, and, I would add, consumer femininity, with overlap between the two (81).

In one of the few scholarly comments on the specific televisual production of transnational consumer citizens within *My Year of Meats*, Emily Cheng cites a memo Jane wrote to her research staff in which she spins the gendered, racialized, classed, and national ideologies that the American meat industry dictates for *My American Wife!* The memo is included in the opening pages of the novel, and in it Jane relays the idea that, thanks to Japan's "economic miracle" of US-mandated, export-led development, it is no longer enough to sell appliances or gadgets to Japanese housewives for the kitchen, as modeled by American housewives in the 1950s (E. Cheng 13). Instead, Japanese housewives now want to buy high-quality, nourishing food for their families to demonstrate their modern, middle-class femininity. Ozeki thematizes how contemporary womanhood is constructed through transnational culinary narratives that connect Japanese and American women. In the context of neoliberal globalization, *My Year of Meats* represents Japan as a market, rather than Japan as a threat (204). Trading in the cultural capital of such phenomena as perfected domesticity, the organic and slow food movements, celebrity chef restaurants, and global food tourism, all of which emerged in the 1990s in the United States and soon circulated transnationally, *My Year of Meats* discloses how culinary narratives signify transnational taste distinctions, thereby addressing transnational class formations that remain firmly invested in neoliberal American cultural values.

My Year of Meats accepts food writing as a site of consequential cultural expression and social negotiation, most obviously in its own extensive use of culinary discourse, but it also comments upon the deficiencies of food writing, at times even parodying the genre. In reading *My Year of Meats* as a type of fictional culinary narrative and specifically a narrative form of culinary tourism, I contend that Ozeki self-consciously explores how popular food narratives are produced and consumed in the practice of US transnational citizenship. In other words, culinary tourism provides a narrative frame through which to examine globalization as a discourse of transnational citizenship, a form of US belonging that is defined by participation in transnational consumer culture. I focus not on a comprehensive reading of the culinary adventure undertaken in the novel by Jane and the production crew of *My American Wife!* but instead on their visit to the Boudreaux family in Askew, Louisiana. An initial visit is described early in the novel, and the narrative later returns to the Boudreaux family to provide a frame that links the quest in culinary tourism to the quest for the neoliberal American Dream in globalization discourse and transnational consumer citizenship.

Culinary tourism is commonly understood as *"exploratory eating"* in which unfamiliar foods are seen as an encounter with Otherness (Molz 77–78, emphasis in original); and, as narrative culinary tourism is "the act of writing about one's deliberate and engaged efforts to travel to other places to document the culinary particularities of non-normative subjects" (Mannur 171). Culinary tourism is most often associated with privileged, white Westerners looking for new cultural or authentic experiences through which they typically exoticize Others in order to define themselves (Heldke xv), as thoroughly demonstrated in Elizabeth Gilbert's 2006 memoir *Eat, Pray, Love: One Woman's Search for Everything across Italy, India, and Indonesia.* Culinary tourism has been closely linked to imperial travel, "discovery," and now adventuring, as popularized by food adventuring television programs such as Anthony Bourdain's *No Reservations* (2005–2012) on the Travel Channel and his current, unabashedly titled endeavor *Parts Unknown* (2013–present) on CNN.

However, culinary tourism may also include less predictable narratives, with some even flipping the dynamic to redefine "which foods are deemed 'exotic,' un-American, and desirable" (Mannur 173). As Anita Mannur has suggestively observed in her analysis of the film *Harold and Kumar Go to White Castle* (2004), culinary tourism may include narratives about the racialized subject's impulse to "eat back" (173). Such a revised use of culinary tourism both allows for a critique of culinary narratives, especially in terms of the racial ideologies they customarily signify, and "casts Asian Americans as consumers and producers of American taste mechanisms" (177). *My Year of Meats* suggests that when an Asian American female becomes the culinary tour guide, the gendered dimensions of food adventuring narratives are also questioned, since, like the quests in imperial travel narratives and adventure novels, as well as the quest for the American Dream in immigrant narratives, the quest in culinary tourism has largely been conceived in the masculinist terms of individual control, appropriation, and profit. Finally, although the class and national ideologies of culinary tourism may be under recognizable revision as the food adventuring genre is pushed beyond its previous parameters, Ozeki's novel also suggests the limits of generic revision.

Layered narratives of transnational culinary tourism in *My Year of Meats* emphasize how food writing mediates ideologies of race, gender, class, and nation "across national affiliations" and within the context of a globalizing US neoliberal consumer culture (Mannur 29). From the textual pastiche that Ozeki creates for her novel, to the transnational advertising project of *My American Wife!*, to the culinary narratives of several of the families chosen for episodes, Ozeki provides plenty of opportunity for readers to consider how culinary tourism is connected to transnational consumer citizenship. When Jane and the crew travel to Askew, Louisiana, to film the Beaudroux family in April, they find in them perhaps the most identifiably transnational culinary tourists of their year-long food adventure. It is Jane's second chance to direct an episode. Her first was the troubleshooting episode about the immigrant Martinez family, which received high ratings because "it was different" and it "widened the audience's understanding of what it is to be American" (Ozeki, *My Year of Meats* 64). Jane builds on this when she sends her proposal for the Beaudroux episode to Tokyo, writing that she "would like to continue to introduce the quirky, rich diversity and strong sense of individualism that make the people of this country unique" (64). In this communiqué we can see Jane positioning the families in *My American Wife!* as exotics in relation to or against whom Japanese women may construct their identities. Although Jane elsewhere admits discomfort with the "confidence game" of finding families for episodes, and even describes the women as "casualties" of *My American Wife!*, she deliberately constructs her episodes as narratives of transnational culinary tourism, especially the Beaudroux family episode (176).

The Beaudroux Family Episode

The Beaudroux family consists of white parents Grace and Vern who fell in love based on their shared desire for a large adoptive family. Along with Jane's proposal to Tokyo, the chapter provides scripted set directions for the episode: an "Opening" scene that introduces the twelve children, two born to Grace and Vern and ten from transnational adoptions; a "Regional Corner" scene in which the family goes to the annual Askew Pig Festival, where Bobby Joe Creeley sings "Poke Salad Annie"; a "Meat" scene or "Cooking Corner" in which Vern gives Grace a break and makes Cajun-style baby back ribs for the family; a "Cherry Street" scene in which the local ritual of cruising is filmed as a backdrop for the narrative of Grace and Vern's courtship; and a "Family History Corner" scene in which each adopted child's story is shared. Audiences in the United States might consider these scenes quintessential snapshots of small-town life in Louisiana, but as the set directions indicate, Jane designs the Beaudroux family episode of *My American Wife!* as a culinary adventuring text for a Japanese audience, or part of transnational culinary tourism. The chapter shifts back and forth between the script and Jane's account of the trip to Askew, with a short section also devoted to Grace's perspective.

The initial Beaudroux chapter, which carries the Shonagon title of "Hateful Things," begins with the question of who is considered exotic and a steamy sex scene featuring Jane and her musician lover Sloan Rankin—a "cinematic night" in a "seedy motel" (Ozeki, *My Year of Meats* 53). By the end of the chapter, however, the location has shifted to the Beaudroux kitchen and the question has shifted to which foods are exotic. In fact, the exotic and now ubiquitous Japanese kudzu plant is an important metaphor in the chapter, and, like most culinary tourism, the adventure in Louisiana explores the reproduction of racial, gender, class, and national ideologies through food narratives, in this case a transnational narrative about kudzu. A "Documentary Interlude" sandwiched within the chapter provides a history of kudzu's introduction as an exotic plant at the Centennial Exposition in Philadelphia in 1876, where the "alien twiner" was billed as "the miracle plant" (76). The narrative goes on to describe how it was never understood as an edible plant, was misused, and became an invasive weed after World War II. The section ends with kudzu's current status: "Mostly, nowadays its only use is metaphoric, to describe the inroads of Japanese industry into the nonunionized South" (77). Indeed, when Jane and the Japanese television crew arrive in Louisiana, a demonized and exoticized culinary metaphor is waiting for them. But similar to the forms of culinary tourism that "eat back," the visit to the Beaudroux family redefines which foods are exotic, and through the transnational culinary tourism of *My American Wife!* kudzu is thoroughly domesticated. When crew members Suzuki and Oh observe the Beaudroux family tearing out and throwing kudzu away as a weed, they dig up the tubers of the plant and teach the family how to use it as a nutritious starch. Entrepreneurial chef that he is, Vern becomes obsessed with making it into a cash crop, and Grace delights in hearing how pleased her husband is with his kudzu-based crispy chicken batter, which he hopes will take a prize at the state fair.

Parallel to the domestication of kudzu, the Beaudroux family embraces the Japanese production team and Jane. This is no simple reversal in which Asians become American national subjects and white Americans become exotic Others, however. The question of who is defined as Other and who defines Otherness is posed in relation to a large, complex, and multiracial family formed through transnational connectivities, primarily between the United States and Korea, the birthplace of most of the ten adopted children. It is Joy, or Min Jung, an Amerasian born in Korea and adopted at three and a half from a Christian adoption magazine, who plays a major role in the redefinition of the exotic, in part because of her own contribution to their family story but more importantly because she becomes the central consciousness in their culinary narrative. As Grace, Vern, and Joy drive down Cherry street giving Jane a tour of Askew, Grace points out the main attraction of the "shameful" Civil War memorial with a "Rebel's Negro Manservant." In this moment, Joy rolls her eyes at her parents and their "primitive Southern Custom" of "cruising" in a deliberate attempt to reroute the racialized power dynamics and white gaze of the tour (Ozeki, *My Year of Meats* 67). Later, however, when the novel returns to the Beaudroux narrative, Joy laughs as Grace asks if she and Vern are exotic. This time Joy says that "Jane Takagi is exotic" because she has a Chinese character tattoo for the astrological sign of the tiger on her shoulder (332). In directly addressing the question of what is exotic in the Beaudroux culinary narrative, this chapter, appearing near the end of the book, reframes the terms of the broader investigation into transnational culinary tourism that is undertaken both in *My American Wife!* and in Ozeki's novel. If the definition of exotic shifts in certain ways for each episode of the television show, Joy ultimately demonstrates that the definition is unstable or open to negotiation depending on who holds the power to define it or who produces the narrative.

In addition to the object of fascination in culinary tourism, the role of the culinary tour guide is destabilized in the Beaudroux narrative. Although the white male patriarch would typically take up this position, and Vern is a professional chef and restaurateur, he remains primarily in the background. Jane continues to function as the behind-the-scenes tour guide, taking care of the logistics of negotiating proposals, creating itineraries for the production team, and thus programming for the audience in Japan. During filming, Grace ushers the audience into the Beaudroux story, playing a function similar to the other American wives who act as local experts or guides and reveal family recipes and even secrets. These female culinary tour guides, especially the women of color, are crucial to Jane's challenge to the dominant ideologies of the series, since they help defy the directive of filming only white, normative families. In the Beaudroux narrative, moreover, Joy takes a turn as culinary tour guide, so *My Year of Meats* casts a second Asian American and transnational female subject into a central role in the production and consumption of culinary narrative.

As mentioned above, the narrative of transnational culinary tourism relies heavily on the quest, a trope that is most identifiable in the United States in the American Dream, which is specifically a search for material rewards and possessions or for a level of participation in consumer culture that signifies belonging. Initially, *My Year of Meats* makes use of the pattern of the racialized subject's culinary quest for the iconic American food, with Jane seeking beef (or, actually, the image of it) for use in *My American Wife!* and for her own dream of becoming a successful director and filmmaker. Of course, the revelations about DES deconstruct and parody the iconicity of beef and the quest for it that structures the novel. Still, food adventuring remains intact, and the quest for the American Dream is registered primarily in the individual wives' culinary narratives.

The Beaudroux family's culinary narrative, and especially Grace's expression of it, simultaneously reveals the extent to which the American Dream is firmly entrenched in neoliberalism and operates through transnational consumer culture. As *My Year of Meats* explains, shared ambition drew Grace and Vern together, and their ambitions included a large family. While they both preferred country living and were not interested in corporate success, they were nonetheless aspiring Americans, and that took a decidedly heternormative form, as Jane's script of the "Family History Corner outlines":

> Grace and Vern got married, and during the next three years, their project began to materialize. Alison was born, then Vernon Junior followed two years after. Vern Senior had a talent for food, and Gracie had her talent for numbers. Together they bought a rundown mill outside town and turned it into one of the most famous Cajun restaurants in Louisiana. When Alison was seven and Vernon Junior just turned five, they bought the old plantation house, opened the gates, and started to fill it with children. (70)

Here is a classic American Dream narrative of upward mobility, replete with bootstrap diligence, meritocratic reward, and the acquisition of private property. In addition and far more problematically, "their project" refers specifically to the transracial and transnational adoption of ten children, which is strictly cased in the material terms of the American Dream. In ways that recall the profile of neoliberal maternal discourse discussed in chapter 2, Grace crudely imagines adopting "all the little Oriental babies from Korea and Vietnam who don't have anyone to care for them or buy them toys or educations . . . (69). This scene also describes how, as the restaurant became more successful, adoptions "became a yearly event. Once a year, at Christmas," suggesting further links between adoption and commerce (74).

The Beaudroux project of transracial and transnational adoption is made possible by and is mediated through the Cajun cuisine the family has made into a booming restaurant business. Ozeki surely draws on an association with the celebrity chef Emeril Lagasse and the many restaurants that are part of the "Emeril Empire" or the global brand of Emeril culinary products. Of course, Cajun cuisine is an ethnic cuisine that signifies the historical Othering of the francophone population that was deported from British Canada and moved to Louisiana in the eighteenth century. Beyond affiliation with transnational culinary networks, the Beaudroux family project is made possible by the international adoption route from Korea to the United States, one intimately connected to both Christian missionizing and US military projects.[10] On several levels, the Beaudroux culinary narrative reveals that the American Dream is deeply intertwined with transnational consumer culture and with the transnational connectivities that are historically embedded in the contemporary globalization of US capital.

On Happy Endings

The transnational culinary tourism of the Beaudroux family project is so inspiring to Akiko that it helps this devoted fan of *My American Wife!* begin her own quest. After Akiko learns that she is pregnant and a brutal beating by her husband lands her in the hospital, she plans her escape, determined to have her child in the United States. She reasons that, if the child is a girl, she can "become an American wife" like those depicted in Jane's episodes of *My American Wife!* (Ozeki, *My Year of Meats*, 318). Akiko takes two-thirds of the couples' savings and flies to the United States, spends a few days with Jane, and then takes the train to visit the Beaudroux family. Akiko is moved by the "amplitude of feeling and openness of Grace and Vern's life" (337). While they offer her a home, she declines and returns to the Northeast to visit Lara and Dyann, who are touched that their story also inspired Akiko to such courageous change. As noted, some readers find Akiko's sudden empowerment and arrival in the United States too contrived, or they consider the various plot resolutions in the final few pages of the novel an indication of Ozeki's investment in the liberal multiculturalism of the 1990s, the American Dream, or a kind of global feminism.

If the novel's tidy resolution is unsatisfying, it is worth considering why it ends as it does. Foremost, I read the resolution of the novel, and especially the happy ending for Akiko, as compensatory, since as a culinary narrative and certainly as culinary tourism, *My Year of Meats* does not deliver the expected pleasurable consumption. In fact, the public success of Jane's documentary about DES, with its clear indictment of the US meat industry's expansion globally, effectively undermines the culinary questing narrative that is the novel's primary formal inspiration. But the resolutions also do not deliver, and the narrative remains less than fully satisfying. This may be understood as a rejection of food writing's customarily retrograde ideologies, but Ozeki's extensive use of the genre in her novel combined with revisions to culinary tourism, specifically the ways in which *My American Wife!* is consumed oppositionally and redefines exotica or "eats back," suggest a more complex commentary on food writing as a site of consequential cultural expression and social negotiation, involving constraints and possibilities.

Another reason Akiko's resolution is too tidy to be satisfying or even to be taken at face value is that it is echoed in similar resolutions for nearly all the other women who were "casualties" of *My American Wife!* Such a neat resolution for so many characters, some of whom become increasingly complex as the novel progresses, is simply unbelievable, particularly at the end of a novel like *My Year of Meats*, which is so thoroughly a narratively layered work. Rather than accepting this series of pat endings, I suggest that Ozeki invites the reader to reject them by having the narrator disavow her own storytelling. Jane does her "best" to imagine a happy ending and offers one to the reader, but she also comments, "I don't think I can change my future simply by writing a happy ending. That's too easy and not so interesting" (361). This statement is made with direct reference to what she knows about DES and its implications for her individual future health. It also builds from other statements Jane has made in earlier entries about the unreliability of narrative, the difficulty of separating fact from fiction, and the necessity that authors of our current moment be "half documentarian, half fabulist" to alter outcomes (360). Jane continually questions the truth-value of any single narrative, particularly media texts that circulate in transnational consumer culture, and especially corporate-sponsored texts such as *My American Wife!* Jane's final entries and the ending of the novel may well parody the happy ending of the American Dream, liberal multiculturalism, culinary tourism, or even the neat resolutions of the more canonical literary forms Ozeki also draws upon, such as the bildungsroman, the epistolary novel, and crime fiction.

Similarly, and related to the refusal to deliver the consumable pleasure of culinary narrative, we might reject the concluding suggestion that Akiko finds safety and happiness in the United States based on the rest of the novel that precedes this turn of events, since *My Year of Meats* consistently represents the United States as a very unsafe and unhappy place indeed. Well beyond the inhumane treatment of animals in meat-processing plants and the production of unhealthy food, the United States is presented as a site of pervasive violence. Instead of liberation for immigrants, the novel describes yellow peril xenophobia; gun violence, such as the factual murder of Yoshihiro Hattori by Rodney Dwayne Peairs in 1992; the sexual assault of Jane by Gale Dunn; the everyday racism or microaggression of the "Where are you from?" sort that Jane encounters and chronicles in her diary; and the 1991 backdrop of Desert Storm or the Persian Gulf War. The indictment of DES as part of a corrupt global US meat industry with continuing but unacknowledged serious effects on women's fertility is only one piece of the abundant evidence for "how deeply violence is embedded" that the production team of *My American Wife!* gathers as they travel across America filming episodes (89). Violence dominates, in fact, the portrayal of the United States in this novel. After all, it represents the historical moment of resurgent anti-immigrant movements, including especially the new nativism that scapegoated immigrants for rapid deindustrialization and economic hardship. While I read the novel as being ideologically quite self-conscious, perhaps a more reliable testament to both Jane and Ozeki's abilities to contend critically with US nationalist discourses that surface in and impinge on *My Year of Meats* may be that the bulk of scholarly attention devoted to the novel has focused on its disturbing representation of the United States.

On the other hand, the ending may be more believable than most allow if we remember that Akiko is a sophisticated consumer of the American Dream or the questing narrative that circulates via global media texts such as *My American Wife!* and that interpellates transnational consumer citizens. Akiko enjoys the show and tries all the recipes as part of her wifely obligation to Ueno, but she does not always like the recipes or the meat that it promotes. More than anything, she is interested in the familial relationships she sees depicted each week. Instead of naïve, she may be a more complex transnational consumer citizen than any of the other characters in the novel. Akiko is a college-educated woman who has been schooled in several ways to be a media consumer. In addition to the popular training in middle-class domesticity that structures desires and encourages consumption, Akiko has worked in the media industry as a manga writer. She met Ueno through connections in the global media industry, she has access to information technology and substantial material resources (the five thousand dollars she converts is only a portion of the cash she brings to the United States), and, perhaps most important, she possesses neoliberal cultural capital. She reads English and appreciates "exotic" cuisines, international travel, and classical Japanese literature. As Jennie Molz observes, culinary tourism is foremost about "the traveler's performance of cosmopolitan competence" and acquiring additional cultural capital through food adventuring (91). Although Akiko's immigration to the United States may not hold for all readers as an example of culinary tourism, certainly *My American Wife!*

does, and Akiko thoughtfully negotiates its ideologies. Indeed, the novel suggests that Akiko struggles mightily with *My American Wife!*'s mediation of ideologies of race, gender, sexuality, and nation across national affiliations and within the context of globalization or the transnational networks of US neoliberal consumer culture. When her involvement with the show on behalf of Jane undermines Ueno's authority, it is met with a brutal assault that nearly costs Akiko her life, a threatening reality that women in abusive relationships keenly understand and continuously calculate to survive.

While food-themed novels are often understood as narrative strategies for maintaining or critiquing patriarchal national identities, associated as they are with domesticity, home, and tradition, or more recently with the consumption of palatable multicultural difference in the qualified inclusion of the racial-ethnic Other within the United States, I extend scholarship that emphasizes how food writing mediates the production of gendered racial citizen-subjects across national affiliations. In the ways she reproduces, revises, and even rejects the conventions of culinary tourism, Ozeki indicates that such narratives are important and productive sites for negotiating national and transnational consumer citizenship. *My Year of Meats* provides a felicitous example of how the novel is adapting to a complex media environment since its fictional culinary narrative converges with, incorporates, and remediates various popular formats of food writing, such as food television, cookbooks, the food adventuring memoir, and the filmic exposé, borrowing from what is now a vast repository of popular cultural fantasy and anxiety that circulates transnationally.

6 / Conclusion: Crossing Over and Going Public

There are lessons to be learned, in whatever media one chooses, that have valuable crossover potential.

—RUTH L. OZEKI, "THERE AND BACK AGAIN"

More directly than any of the other texts discussed in *Asian American Women's Popular Literature*, *My Year of Meats* explores the contemporary novel's relationship to other forms of commercial popular culture that participate in the production of neoliberal citizen-subjects, both through thematizing the collision and coexistence of various media forms and through the example of its own storytelling techniques. It chronicles how the novel participates in a sophisticated media landscape or uses popular media symbolically and formally in complex ways. Echoing John Sayles, David Palumbo-Liu finds reassurance about the novel form in *My Year of Meats*, reading Ozeki's book as an intervention into the information technologies and entertainment forms more closely associated with globalization. He points out that *My Year of Meats* raises questions "about the persisting role of a literary genre, or indeed, *all* cultural forms in an age of increasingly extensive and intensive media" and the ability of the "literary," as well as the "non-literary," to deliver "an ethically effective text" on its own ("Rational and Irrational Choices" 65, 64, emphasis in original). For Palumbo-Liu, however, Ozeki exploits "literature's modernist ability to lend new forms of information an affective and ethical content" (64). The novel that is *My Year of Meats* provides an explicit ethical critique of globalization as exemplified by the toxic US meat industry, and it is equally critical, although more implicitly, of the global media industry that deploys structural inequalities in the production and management of consumer-subjects. Still, in the story that *My Year of Meats* tells, it is through the documentary film, not the print novel, that Jane creates a sort of counternarrative that exposes the DES scandal to viewers around the world. While Jane's documentary is independently produced and makes its way to a global audience through publically supported distributors/outlets, the novel attests to how the documentary is actually made possible by the people who are brought together in the production and consumption of the corporate-sponsored and -produced reality television show *My American Wife!*

Instead of championing the novel as an ethical and aesthetic counterweight to popular media culture, a position that clings to an opposition between the literary and the commercial, or the affective imaginary and the heartless informational, Ozeki pokes fun at in order to reproach cultural binaries and hierarchies, especially the taste distinctions that adhere to them. As I read *My Year of Meats*, this is one of the primary benefits or even purposes of Ozeki's exploration of popular food writing and culinary discourse, in which the production, consumption, and reproduction of taste distinctions is most literal. Culinary discourse dramatizes the importance of consumption to cultural capital and, as we see with Akiko and the Beaudroux family, to transnational subjectivity and belonging. Rather than asking which is the best or most effective media form for the affective and ethical exploration of globalization, Ozeki's central question is concerned with the value of the contemporary novel in relation to other popular media forms and with how we may use all that is available to us in contemporary convergence culture to create subjectivity, belonging, and social change as we contend with the destructive and dehumanizing conditions of global capitalism. Ozeki's understanding of today's novel is perhaps best described in the quotation that appears at the beginning of this conclusion, which comes from an article she wrote about the global popularity of *My Year of Meats* and how her first career in filmmaking helped her write the novel: "If you want to tell a story and the means of production are out of reach, tell it differently, but tell it well. There are lessons to be learned, in whatever media one chooses, that have valuable crossover potential. Nothing is wasted. Content is King" ("There and Back Again" 42).

The question of the novel's use value is key to understanding the emergence in the United States in recent years of a popular literary culture that converges with commercial and political cultures. As I pointed out in chapter 1, the novel is increasingly prominent in popular culture because reading novels has become part of the social display of taste distinctions, which is necessary for subject formation, the re-creation of the self in consumer culture, and belonging, with particularly crucial consequences for women. What you are reading and especially with whom you read (Oprah, Nancy Pearl, Bill Clinton) convey important messages about your knowledge of and participation in the market-place, and thus your belonging in the United States. While it is often the case that novels become best sellers because of a tastemaker or curator's endorsement, which now functions much like a literary award such as the Pulitzer Prize, some novels become popular because they take up the function of the contemporary tastemaker, offering explicit guidance to readers for negotiating social life within neoliberalism. The contem-porary popular novel thus potentially participates on two levels in an ever-expanding US therapeutic culture, helping readers perform coded transactions and helping them develop marketplace expertise (J. Collins 189).

It is no surprise that adaptations to the big screen are frequently drawn from those popular works that both signify marketplace expertise and offer advice for successfully negotiating neoliberal consumer cul-ture. I suggest that three of the most celebrated texts in the category of Asian American women's literature—*The Woman Warrior*, *The Joy Luck Club*, and *The Namesake*—all help readers in precisely the ways they now expect literature to help them, which in part explains not only why these books were commercially popular but also why they were adapted (in various ways) for the big screen.[1] Indeed, filmic adaptations are one especially salient marker of Asian American women writers' influence in popular literary culture. To illustrate the point, I turn to the 2006 adap-tation of Jhumpa Lahiri's first novel, *The Namesake*, as another example of the crossover appeal of popular literature from the recent generation of Asian American women writers considered in this study. The book was spectacularly successful, both commercially and with a majority of reviewers, and it positioned Lahiri as the most celebrated South Asian American writer in the United States and perhaps globally.[2]

Rather than an extended reading of Lahiri's narrative as portrayed on film, I want to point out that it offers guidance specifically on the uses of literature, providing rather direct commentary with respect to contem-porary changes in literary culture. While the novel opens with Ashima Ganguli, the mother of the main character, giving birth, Nair's adaptation opens with another life-affirming, melodramatic scene, this one depict-ing the events in 1974 that would provide Gogol Ganguli (Kal Penn) with his decidedly literary name.[3] Gogol's father, the young Ashoke Ganguli (Irrfan Kahn), boards a train in Calcutta bound for Jamshedpur, settles in to read Nikolai Gogol's "The Overcoat," and is interrupted, first by a fellow traveler and then by a derailment. Here literature is most valuable not for helping readers make abstract revelations about the meaning of life (which they do make) but for literally saving a life, because the pages of the book by Nikolai Gogol fluttering in the wind attract the attention of rescue workers who save the gravely wounded Ashoke.

Nair's opening scene references the novel's literary concerns, but it also alerts the viewer to how the film is different from the novel, rearranging and reprioritizing elements of the narrative. More specifically, it recognizes the significance of the literary backstory in the narrative but highlights that the importance of reading literature will not revolve around the allegorical relationship Lahiri sets up, most obviously through the novel's title, between Gogol Ganguli and Nikolai Gogol, nor does it concern a relationship between Gogol and Akaky Akakyevich, the main character of "The Overcoat." Various readings of Lahiri's heavy-handed allegorical device have provided interesting possibilities. For example, Bakirathi Mani writes, "Gogol Ganguli mirrors Akakyevich, a man who assumes that his life can only function as a duplicate or copy, a reproduction rather than an original" (81). More applicable to the filmic adaptation, however, is Mani's observation that the analogy between Nikolai Gogol and his namesake is based on an arbitrary connection or catachresis. While the story is of course about naming, the film emphasizes that the allegorical overcoat is a clever literary ruse that ultimately amounts to a very light covering. Or, as Mani contends, it is too heavy: "[S]o crowded is his given name with various narratives of the past that there is hardly any room for Gogol himself" (81). Nair's version of the narrative focuses on how reading literature has changed and what it means in the present, and this highlights and magnifies particular elements of Lahiri's commentary on the contemporary use value of the novel and literature in general.

Lahiri clearly draws attention to the literary canon and canonical reading practices, such as the interpretation of allegory and the identification of allusion, and she invites her reader to participate in these practices. Nair's version emphasizes that the main character is thoroughly unconvinced of the value of canonical literature in his life and declines his father's invitation to understand how important books are and certainly to understand books *as* his father does. Instead of attachment, the young Gogol is ashamed of his association with the Russian writer, in part because the name emphasizes his cultural difference from his white peers in 1990s suburban New York. A key scene in the film shows the teenage Gogol in a high school literature class, where homophobic and racist schoolmates harass him after they learn that the Russian author was quite probably homosexual and died tragically. Indeed, scenes in the film alternate between Ashoke's reverence for literature, on the one hand, and Gogol's disdain and disidentification, on the other. For Ashoke, literature could transport him "without moving an inch," provide the "blessings" of his life, and secure a sense of belonging through the kinship he felt with Nikolai Gogol, who also "spent his adult life outside his homeland." Referring to the fact that the book was a gift from his grandfather but also speaking metaphorically, Ashoke tells his son, "[W]e all came out of Gogol's overcoat." Gogol, by contrast, considers the novella and his name relics of the past, and he changes his first name to Nikhil (which is actually his "good" given name from his family) as he is about to enter college. In the film, he continues to be bothered by his literary name up until the final scenes. When his new wife Moushumi (Zuleikha Robinson), a scholar of French literature, has an affair and they split up, Gogol leaves behind any possibility for a romantic involvement with literature, the plot suggests. A few scenes later, however, at the close of the film, and as part of an effort to hold on to his recently deceased father, the narrative quickly revives Gogol's interest in the book his father bequeathed, providing a sentimental resolution that is neither convincing nor redemptive.

One difference between Ashoke and his son is generationally related. Min Song's contention that Lahiri's novel captures some of the cultural meaning of "the children of 1965" is persuasive since "Gogol is not a member of a model minority," like his immigrant father, who is ambitious and hard-working (355). Emphasizing the point, Ashoke's death takes place while he is at work, away on a visiting professorship, whereas Gogol performs his job as an architect in perfunctory and uninspired ways. Gogol is not primarily defined by his work, nor does it guide his life. The role of generational difference creates distance between father and son as signified by their contrasting relationships to both literature and work. This distance constitutes a gap at the center of the narrative, suggesting that neither is wholly successful at negotiating relationships or contemporary belonging.

Between these two men, however, stands Ashima (Tabu), who enacts a third and different narrative about belonging. Although Ashima's position in relation to the male characters in the novel is problematic since she seems to function as a foil to the male protagonist's development (Bhalla 110), I bracket this reading for the moment and add that Ashima provides the most salient guidance for contemporary viewers with respect to belonging since her identifications are more expressly and directly explored. She regularly goes to the library and takes a part-time job there, and this context becomes an important source of identity and support for her. Relaying Ashima's different use of literature or books, an apparently incidental moment in the film puts the recently widowed Ashima at the library with her white colleague and friend Sally (Brooke Smith). In this very brief scene, Sally suggests that Ashima try a meditation exercise called "following your bliss," to help with her grief. "Follow your bliss" was a philosophy made popular by American mythologist and writer Joseph Campbell, and various versions of it swept the United States, particularly after Bill Moyers and Campbell collaborated on a 1988 PBS television special titled *The Power of Myth*. There are troubling power relationships and no doubt intentional ironies at play in this Orientalist-saturated moment, not least of which is Campbell's appropriation of the concept from the Upanishads, but through the exercise Ashima suddenly locates and clarifies her own subjective desires or, in the popular language of self-help culture, "finds herself," which is "without borders," as the translation of her name suggests.

In fact, rather than signaling a direct route to unambivalent assimilation in the United States, Ashima's realization is that she wants to live in both the United States and India, splitting time between her children and her passion for singing. Through this scene, popular literary culture, including the Lahiri novel that the film adapts, is presented to viewers as part of a therapeutic culture that helps Asian American women negotiate belonging through everyday sociality and cultural practices. The self that Ashima locates through guidance from and within the pages of popular literature clearly possesses considerable cultural and financial capital and is poised to use it, but if literary scholars may regret the use of literature to prompt readers in appropriate behavior for consumer culture, here literature does more than simply endorse commercial desires. Nair's film underscores that popular literary culture, including especially Asian American women's popular literature, plays the valuable role of helping readers (and viewers) negotiate belonging in a neoliberal era characterized by intense reformulation and the promise of ongoing instability.

In the past, the novel was a key participant in an ideological and material shift in England and the United States away from what was perceived to be a corrosive public preoccupation with capitalist accumulation and the importance of wealth toward middle-class values of demonstrable moral character, as exemplified by the private and virtuous figure of the "domestic woman." The contemporary novel is similarly a key participant in another major ideological and material shift, and an influential component of a far more complex popular culture, especially popular visual culture, in the late twentieth and early twenty-first centuries. This time the shift is in many ways returning to or reviving the unqualified virtues of the public sphere of commerce and competition, with the difference that neoliberalism has now blurred the boundaries between public and private, politics and culture, as part of its market fundamentalism.

The appropriately feminized neoliberal citizen-subject must function in an amorphous and ubiquitous marketplace, moving deftly across the contemporary capitalist landscape to manage family and fertility, gain marketplace expertise, work in the global economy, and participate in consumer culture. Rather than attribute the popularity of "Asian American women's literature" primarily to authors' successful assimilation to this model of the female citizen-subject and the dominant cultural values of neoliberal consumer culture, analysis of the archive in *Asian American Women's Popular Literature: Feminizing Genres and Neoliberal Belonging* suggests that changes in the function of literature and debates surrounding contemporary citizenship have elicited participation, encouraged the construction of markets, trained a public, increased visibility, and enabled legibility for the concerns of these writers, who are responding to the constraints of neoliberalism. The popular literature or crossover fiction written by Asian American female authors that I examine engages this terrain and provides guidance in negotiating it, while also disclosing the limitations of neoliberal models of belonging for Asian American women as gendered racial subjects. *Asian American Women's Popular Literature* does not argue that the concern for belonging is the exclusive, inevitable, primary, or cohesive concern of Asian American women's writing. Taken together, the novels analyzed in this study demonstrate that while the power of liberal political citizenship claims may have diminished, new citizenship claims are developing along overlapping and multiple axes. Foremost, these texts illuminate that citizenship practices and the political subjectivity that enables them are now imagined and produced in a variety of ways by active participants in the contemporary neoliberal marketplace.

NOTES

1 / Asian American Women's Popular Literature

1. For additional background on Hearst's involvement in the Symbionese Liberation Army in this and the following paragraph, see Shana Alexander's *Anyone's Daughter* and Penny Vlagopoulos's "The Beginning of History and Politics."

2. For a different understanding of the heightened role of publicity in social life, see Noelle McAfee's *Democracy and the Political Unconscious*, which offers a psychoanalytic and semiotic analysis of the pathologies of the post-9/11 era and the human need for participation in the public sphere. For discussion of visibility for Asian Americans, see Laura Kang, "Si(gh)ting Asian/American Women"; Shilpa Davé, LeiLani Nishime, and Tasha Oren, *East Main Street*; Karen Shimakawa, *National Abjection*; and Celine Parreñas Shimizu, *Hypersexuality of Race*. Some note that Asian American women may be hypervisible in certain ways (as workers, racialized sexual objects) while invisible in other ways (as mothers, sexual agents). As Lynn Fujiwara observes, for example, "Asian immigrant and refugee women as subjects within the contemporary American politic represent an invisibility as women, mothers, and caretakers that contradicts a visibility as global migrants, workers, and an exploitable labor pool" (xvii).

3. Vlagopoulos contends that *American Woman* is preoccupied, both stylistically and in content, with "how we tell stories," insisting "that we look beyond geographical and temporal borders" (130).

4. Morris Young contends that cultural citizenship is expressed, contested, and revised through literary texts, specifically what he terms "literacy narratives" (6).

5. All subsequent references to Aihwa Ong in this book are to *Neoliberalism as Exception*, unless otherwise indicated.

6. Author Heinz Insu Fenkl has recently suggested, "When an initially marginal literature finally establishes itself . . . works in that category tend to demonstrate a heightened self-consciousness of their subtexts" and "begin to cross the boundaries

of genre and form. This is especially true these days with the increasing prevalence of mixed-media and web-based works."

7. See Manisha Das Gupta's *Unruly Immigrants* for discussion of the organization of inequalities through citizenship (55). See Helen Heran Jun's introduction to *Race for Citizenship* for a discussion of the constraints of juridical citizenship on struggles for inclusion and citizenship discourses. See Fujiwara for the relationships among political, social, and economic citizenship (23–26).

8. Recent scholarly monographs on Asian Americans and popular culture include Hye Seung Chung, *Hollywood Asian*; Jane Iwamura, *Virtual Orientalism*; Nhi T. Lieu, *The American Dream in Vietnamese*; Krystyn R. Moon, *Yellowface*; Nitasha Tamar Sharma, *Hip Hop Desis*; Celine Parreñas Shimizu, *The Hypersexuality of Race*; and Thuy Linh Nugyen Tu, *The Beautiful Generation*.

9. For book buying and reading statistics, see the Romance Writers of America website; Charlotte Abbott, "The New Book Buying Realities"; and Mary Ann Gwinn, "Who Buys Books: 40 Year Old Women and Others." Fiction buyers in every category are predominantly women. In 2010, 62 percent of women in the United States bought books, while only 44 percent of men did.

10. For a brief discussion of the media as a technology of citizenship, see Nikolas Rose's "Governing 'Advanced' Liberal Democracies" (58). See also Laurie Ouellette's "Take Responsibility for Yourself."

11. We might also look to how political citizenship as the most conventional signifier of national belonging is increasingly represented in popular culture (e.g., *Commander in Chief, The West Wing*) or presented as entertainment, for example in, *Sarah Palin's Alaska* and *The War Room*.

12. Communication scholars have referred to the mediation of every aspect of social life and the power of new media in particular as "mediatization." In this view, the media has "annexed" the power of traditional authorities such as government, politics, religion, family, or education to become the most important storyteller in and about society (Livingstone 7). Theorists of participatory culture, such as Henry Jenkins, address citizenship in digitized culture, which requires an individual to be visible on public sites. See also Larry Gross on the politics of media visibility for sexual minorities. For excellent discussion of how new media has become part of self-regulation and the technological regulation of the household in the domestic sphere, see also James Hay.

13. Brenda Weber observes that 90 percent of reality TV addresses women (131).

14. For a helpful description of biopower and biopolitics, see Rose's *The Politics of Life Itself* (52–54).

15. The Association for Asian American Studies issued a critical response to the Pew Report on 16 July 2012, citing its failure to capture the diversity of Asian Americans, among other shortcomings. In *The End of Men*, Hanna Rosin also makes a claim about Asian women as ideal workers in the global economy, but it remarks the deferral of marriage and increased rates of divorce as indications of the preference for employment and careers, playing directly into recent yellow peril anxieties with her chapter entitled "The Gold Misses: Asian Women Take Over the World."

16. This section of the Pew report echoes the "Oriental Style" of contemporary Hollywood that Jane Chi Hyun Park critiques in *Yellow Future* for the association of Asians with the futurity that high-technology promises. See also Lisa Nakamura's "Comfort Women of the Digital Industries."

17. The 1998 Lois Ann Yamanaka controversy could also be included here. Interestingly, the most intense controversies in Asian American literary studies have centered on the cultural politics of gender and sexuality in popular texts, from *The Woman Warrior* to *The Joy Luck Club* to *Jasmine* to *Miss Saigon* to *Blu's Hanging*. Or, perhaps it is more accurate to say that these have been the controversies that literary critics have most written about.

18. One might expect a study of contemporary Asian American women's literature such as this to open with a passage from *The Woman Warrior,* since it is often understood as not only the originary text of contemporary Asian American women's literature, and even of Asian American literature more broadly, but also as the originary moment of unease with the field's ideological rigidity.

19. Connected to even earlier popular works, such as *Mrs. Spring Fragrance* (1912), by Sui Sin Far (Edith Maude Eaton); Jade Snow Wong's *Fifth Chinese Daughter* (1950), and Monica Sone's *Nisei Daughter* (1953), *The Woman Warrior* has perhaps been the subject of more scholarly discussion than any other single work in Asian American literature. See Wendy Ho's *In Her Mother's House* for a discussion of antecedents for *The Woman Warrior* (42–43); Elaine Kim, in "Myth, Memory, and Desire," details the popularity of the text, as does Shirley Geok-lin Lim in *Approaches to Teaching Kingston's "The Woman Warrior"* (3–17). *The Woman Warrior* remains the sole Asian American literary text in the important Modern Language Association's Approaches to Teaching series. In *Tell This Silence*, Patti Duncan places *The Woman Warrior* in what she calls "the historical period of reclamation" of Asian American cultural and nationalist politics (131).

20. The charges in this "pen war" have involved, among others, "selling out" to popular desires for exotic, Orientalist representations; undermining Asian American cultural politics and panethnic identity; mimicking liberal feminist critiques of patriarchy; and reconstructing inauthentic Chinese culture (K.-K. Cheung, "The Woman Warrior" 238). See Yoonmee Chang's *Writing the Ghetto* for a discussion of Frank Chin's term the "Chinatown book," or for the "ethnographic imperative" (22) and the role of cultural ethnography in the ghettoization of Asian American literature and the privatization of economic injustice (58–61). Chang asserts that Kingston resists the imperative explicitly (66–67).

21. For critical commentary on the debates, see S. G.-L. Lim, *Approaches to Teaching Kingston's "The Woman Warrior"*; K.-K. Cheung, "Reviewing Asian American Literature" and "*The Woman Warrior*"; Duncan, *Tell This Silence*; Kang, *Compositional Subjects*; Lowe, *Immigrant Acts*; P. Chu, *Assimilating Asians*; and D. Kim, *Writing Manhood in Black and Yellow*. See also Josephine Park, who observes in *Apparitions of Asia* that *The Woman Warrior* is closer to a mother-daughter epic memoir than a bildungsroman, as most read it (126).

22. In *Reading Asian American Literature*, Sau-ling Cynthia Wong gives *The Woman Warrior* a key role in the emergence of Asian American literary studies and popular critical recognition of Asian American writing.

23. Christopher Shinn notes in "Homocidal Tendencies" that popular thriller writer Gus Lee has expressed indebtedness to Amy Tan, whose *The Joy Luck Club* spent eight months on the *New York Times* best-seller list, for opening the doors of popular literature to Asian American authors (127). Shinn also suggests that popular fiction's doors were opened wider when established writers of literary fiction, including Chang-rae

Lee, Lisa See, and Amitav Gosh, ventured into the "riskier" realm of popular or "pulp" fiction (111). "Women's genres" may be characterized by women as the intended audience, a relationship as central subject matter, and a female as protagonist constrained by a patriarchal social structure.

24. The publication of numerous multigenre anthologies of Asian American women's writing, such as *Making Waves* (1989), *The Forbidden Stitch* (1989), and *Our Feet Walk the Sky* (1993), also contributed to public visibility of contemporary Asian American women's literature. For a discussion of the cultural politics of multigenre anthologies, see Cynthia Franklin's *Writing Women's Communities*.

25. David Harvey traces neoliberalism's roots to the market principles of neoclassical economics of the late nineteenth century and nineteenth-century liberalism (19–24), noting that the first neoliberal state was Pinochet's Chile in 1973 (7).

26. On the parameters of neoliberalism, see Harvey's introduction to *A Brief History of Neoliberalism* (1–4); on reasons for the neoliberal turn, see pages 5–38; and on contradictions in neoliberalism, see pages 64–70. For cultural values or political rationalities of neoliberalism, see also Ong's *Neoliberalism as Exception* (10–12).

27. Historian Lizabeth Cohen writes in *A Consumers' Republic* that over the course of the twentieth century, "citizen and consumer were ever-shifting categories that . . . always reflected the permeability of the political and economic spheres" and the organization of inequalities that create both inclusion and exclusion in the United States (8). In this view, neoliberalism may be seen as a broadening of earlier forms of consumer culture, one in which the political order now justifies itself by claiming to serve the interests of consumers (15).

28. As Ong outlines, neoliberalism is a "technology of governing," a form of governmentality "that relies on market knowledge and calculations for a politics of subjection and subject-making" (*Neoliberalism as Exception* 12).

29. Ong follows Rose in this descriptive summary of the enterprising subject of neoliberal rationality (*Neoliberalism as Exception* 14).

30. As Rose describes Foucault's notion of biopower, technologies of subjection are biopolitics or biopolitical strategies through which governments more directly regulate populations and address rates of reproduction, illness, and public health, while technologies of subjectivity are those mechanisms that seek to produce the subjective conditions of self-discipline needed for governance in free and "civilized" society ("Governing" 44).

31. Jan Pakulski describes cultural rights as "a new breed of claims for unhindered representation, recognition without marginalization, acceptance and intergration without normalizing distortion" (quoted in Stevenson, *Cultural Citizenship: Cosmopolitan Questions* 7).

32. For an excellent summary of cultural citizenship and its relation to transnational changes in citizenship, see Inderpal Grewal's *Transnational America* (7–14).

33. See Miller's *Cultural Citizenship* for a discussion of the United States as the least socially mobile advanced Western economy (5–7).

34. For a summary of Habermas and critiques, see Warner's introduction to *Publics and Counterpublics*.

35. See also Nick Stevenson, who writes that cultural citizenship involves struggle, pointing to the social value of knowledge; it refers to "the possibility of communication and dialogue" within a cultural or information society in which "the power to

name, construct meaning and exert control over the flow of information" is central to structural divisions and struggles for justice within a global arena (*Cultural Citizenship* 2–5). For Young, cultural citizenship is constructed, contested, and revised through literary texts and their reception.

36. There are several versions of the thesis that celebrations of cultural sameness and difference have become commodified as "style" or "lifestyle," in a flattening of racial and ethnic identity. They most often call for some kind of "rejection" of commercial culture, although the extent to which this is possible is entirely unclear.

37. According to Robert Reich, in the 1960s, 12 percent of all married women with young children in the United States worked outside the home for wages, while by the late 1990s, 55 percent of women did. This flow of women into the workforce fueled the growth of consumer capitalism and maintained the standard of living of the middle class in the United States.

38. For discussion of "responsible citizenship" and welfare reform, see Fujiwara 38–43.

39. The USA Patriot Act of 2001 is one among many. See Fujiwara's conclusion to *Mothers without Citizenship* on the continuing significance of racialized citizenship (179–97).

40. Family reunification policies have a long history but were significantly developed after federal immigration control was institutionalized in 1891 (Luibhéid 8). In the 1965 act, 20 percent of slots went to workers with skills in demand by US employers, and 6 percent to refugees. Hemispheric quotas remained, and while no country could receive more than twenty thousand slots, Western Hemisphere countries were exempted from the cap (22). Seven preference categories were created: four for family reunification, not counting spouses of citizens who were not subject to quota limits or preferences; two for professionals and workers; and one for refugees (Lowe 182). For a discussion of immigration laws prohibiting Chinese women's immigration, see also Bill Hing.

41. Numerous scholars have examined presumptions about the expansion of access to immigration in the 1965 act. I cite Lowe for recognizing its increased regulations (9) and Eithne Luibhéid for its reproduction of the normative family (3).

42. Neoliberal globalization has produced "sovereignty, citizenship, public cultures, and forms of labor that are striated across multiples 'zones' that are not nations, but which articulate with nations and with other, transnational forces," according to Laura Briggs, Gladys McCormick, and J. T. Way (635).

43. See Siu on accepting citizenship to mean participation and membership in a variety of political communities, its separation from the nation-state, and diaspora (8). See Nira Yuval-Davis's "Multi-layered Citizen" (122).

44. Yuval-Davis estimates in *Gender and Nation* that 80 percent of refugees are women and children, though most Western nations' immigrant populations are not significantly refugee.

45. Lowe argues that the necessity of participating in hegemonic cultural practices allows for the disruption of hegemonic power (97).

46. The work of Asian Women United of California, a nonprofit organization founded in 1976 in San Francisco, is foundational, producing books and films on Asian American women that bring attention both to stereotypes and to Asian American women's cultural production.

47. Viet Nguyen's argument extends Fredric Jameson's groundbreaking scholarship on the political unconscious.

48. For analyses of the gender politics of the works of Maxine Hong Kingston, Amy Tan, and Fae Myenne Ng in the contexts of feminist, Eurocentric, and cultural nationalist discourses, see Wendy Ho, *In Her Mother's House*. See more recent contributions in Erin Khuê Ninh, *Ingratitude* and Silvia Schultermandl, *Transnational Matrilineage*.

49. Ho confronted conventional literary criticism that dismisses pleasurable responses to contemporary popular texts authored by Asian American women, pointing to elitist assumptions about "the culture of the unsophisticated reading masses or . . . sentimental, melodramatic narratives favored by nonintellectual or apolitical women" (55).

50. As Davé, Nishime, and Oren point out, recent scholarship has also brought the field of Asian American studies, or the "celebrated margins," "into productive dialogue with both new and well established disciplines" of the mainstream, including film studies, media studies, and popular culture studies (2–3).

51. See essays in Davé, Nishime, and Oren. See also Pamela Butler and Jigna Desai on chick lit, and Shinn on pulp fiction.

52. J. Jack Halberstam's understanding of failure as a "counterintuitive mode of knowing and doing that refuses the normalizing models of success that often have the effect of disciplining us into heterosexist capitalist structures of knowledge, feelings, and ideas about the world and ourselves" has particular resonance for the cultural critique in Asian American studies of the model minority myth and its variations, as well as this study's desire to duly acknowledge both the "good" and the "bad" neoliberal subjects in popular Asian American literature authored by women (Pham 330).

53. James Truslow Adams originally coined the term "American Dream" during the Great Depression to describe how people seek in the United States "a land in which life should be better and richer and fuller for everyone," though the redefinition of the American Dream within neoliberalism has become far more overtly about individual success at all costs, even to the social good (Reich).

54. Conventionally, "citizenship often evokes the role of formal politics and governmentality, while belonging alludes to social and cultural realms of everyday life" (Siu 10). See also, Fujiwara 23–26.

2 / Asian American Mother-Daughter Narrative

1. The white, middle-class nuclear family remains tethered to the male breadwinner and female homemaker model, even if it little resembles most families in the contemporary United States. See the "Race and Racism" entry in the *Encyclopedia of Motherhood* for discussion of the model (O'Reilly 1047–53). See also Chapter 2 in Stephanie Coontz's *The Way We Never Were*.

2. Katherine Franke coined the term "repronormative" to name "the social forces that incentivize motherhood," with citizenship being one of those social forces (181).

3. My argument departs from Berlant's in *The Female Complaint: The Unfinished Business of Sentimentality in American Culture*, which asserts that the intimate public sphere of "women's culture" is one of privatized citizenship that produces a normative ideology of femininity in which women "will manage personal life and lubricate emotional worlds" but not politically challenge the terms of social life (6).

4. All subsequent references in this study to Berlant are from *The Queen of America Goes to Washington City: Essays on Sex and Citizenship*, unless indicated.

5. "Matrilineal discourse" is Helena Grice's term; she identifies narrative codes of "the fiction of matrilineal discourse" and provides a summary of Asian American women writers' interventions in the form (35–51). See S.-L. Wong for a critical assessment of "Asian American matrilineal discourse" as racial accommodation ("Sugar Sisterhood" 177). See Marianne Hirsch's *The Mother/Daughter Plot* for discussion of "maternal discourse," which she locates in postmodernist plots that revise or reject the Freudian family romance (15–16).

6. In *Motherhood and Representation*, E. Ann Kaplan ties mother discourses to economic/social/technological change, more specifically. See chapter 2, "The Historical Sphere," 17–26, and chapter 9, "Sex, Work, and Mother/Fatherhood," 180–219.

7. Authors whose works could be described as mother-daughter writing include, among others, Theresa Hak Kyung Cha, Fiona Cheong, Hua Chuang, Ronyoung Kim, Cynthia Kadohata, Joy Kogawa, Sky Lee, Lydia Minatoya, Fae Myenne Ng, Ruth Ozeki, Rahna Reiko Rizzuto, Bapsi Sidhwa, Julie Shigekuni, Cathy Song, R. A. Sasaki, Mitsuye Yamada, Hisaye Yamamoto, Lois Ann Yamanaka, and Wakako Yamauchi.

8. In 2009, 64 to 65 percent of book purchases were by women, and romance, which is consumed primarily by women, was the largest category of book sales (Gwinn). In addition, book clubs, whose membership is predominantly made up of women, are extremely popular, with Oprah Winfrey leading millions as a national curator or librarian. See Jim Collins's *Bring on the Books for Everybody: How Literary Culture Became Popular Culture*, and Kathleen Fitzpatrick's *Anxiety of Obsolescence: The American Novel in the Age of Television,* on the contemporary vibrance of reading in the United States.

9. Popular feminist texts in the neoliberal era that address the maternal include Nancy Friday's *My Mother/My Self* (1977), Alice Walker's *In Search of Our Mother's Gardens* (1983), and Ann Crittenden's *The Price of Motherhood* (2001); inspirational tales and difficult journeys include Josefina Lopez's *Real Women Have Curves* (1987), Bharati Mukherjee's *Jasmine* (1999), and Jodi Picoult's *My Sister's Keeper* (2004); and acclaimed works about traumatic or untenable circumstances for mothering and daughtering include Toni Morrison's *Beloved* (1987), Dorothy Allison's *Bastard Out of Carolina* (1992), and Kim Edwards's *The Memory Keeper's Daughter* (2005). Heather Hewitt defines "mommy lit" as "all forms of writing that explore the private and public dimensions of motherhood" and are marketed to mothers, whether or not they are written from the perspective of or produced by mothers (135). There is also a decidedly critical corner of NMD that "talks back to the experts" on mothering, to normative models of mothering, and to "the mamasphere," as Beth Haines points out. See, for example, Cherríe Moraga's *Waiting in the Wings: Portrait of a Queer Motherhood*, and the significant body of work on feminist mothering by Andrea O'Reilly.

10. Indicating the size of the industry of NMD and its span across the media landscape, Cori Howard estimated in 2012 that there are 4 million mom blogs in North America (Jones), and her online classes on writing memoirs, which are marketed as "less expensive than therapy," cost approximately Can$400. Mommyblogs have been critiqued for their whiteness and erasure of difference, but this supports rather than refutes assertions that "motherhood blogs are an important component of feminist

discourse" (Haines 271). See also "Mothers of Intention" and May Friedman and Shana Calixte's *Mothering and Blogging*.

11. The new momism emerged in public discourse in the midst of the women's movement of the 1970s, exploded in the media in the 1980s to "redomesticate the women of America through motherhood," and triumphed in the marketplace by the late 1990s, when "conspicuous consumption . . . conquered childhood, motherhood, and the nursery" (Douglas and Michaels 9, 300).

12. See Jennifer Pozner's *Reality Bites Back* on the creation of the "Mommy Wars" in the late 1980s by the media and publishing industries (104–6). The term was used in the Chua controversy and remains in general use, especially when a mother figure becomes the object of public derision.

13. As Naoko Sugiyama asserts, "Dualistic images of mothers as self-effacing, all embracing, nurturing and affectionate, and/or all powerful, devouring, and domineering still prevail not only in anti-feminist literature and the mass media, but feminist discourse as well" (76).

14. Neoliberalism remakes feminist discourse, including or perhaps especially those forms that seem empathetic, self-conscious, or critically aware, such as multicultural, cosmopolitan, or anti-imperialist feminisms. See also Malini Johar Schueller's "Cross-cultural Identification."

15. The critical knowledge needed for citizens' political subjectivity is contracted and exchanged for passivity, overdependence, and innocence in relation to the state, which Berlant calls "infantile citizenship" (*Queen of America* 20–21). While Berlant is careful not to blame feminism, she does implicate certain versions of feminism in linking women and children to the nation, particularly in her discussion of pornography.

16. See Miller's *Cultural Citizenship* for discussion of the United States as the least socially mobile advanced Western economy (5–7).

17. See also Chandan Reddy's *Freedom with Violence: Race, Sexuality, and the US State* (182–219).

18. In *Reading the Literatures of Asian America*, S.-L. Wong describes *The Woman Warrior* as the first "crossover hit" and largely attributes to it the establishment of Asian American literature (214).

19. The association is so widely accepted that Asian authors from outside the United States are sometimes translated and then similarly marketed in the United States, as in the recent example of Kyung-Sook Shin's *Please Look After Mom*.

20. The reaction may indicate a discomfort with the disavowal of racial essentialism in ethnic entrepreneurialism that V. Nguyen discusses (*Race and Resistance* 85).

21. I thank one of my readers at Temple for emphasizing this important point. There is also an unremarked (and likely unintentional) alliance with a far less embattled motherhood than Chua's title suggests, since the author of "The Battle Hymn of the Republic," pacifist Julie Ward Howe, was also the author of the "Mother's Day Proclamation," which protested the war making of nation-states worldwide soon after the US Civil War and became the forgotten basis of today's commercial version of mother's day (Schmidt 348).

22. There are other popular or commercial texts about parenting or motherhood written by Asian American women that hew toward less normative models or that question mainstream American models. See, for example, Mei-Ling Hopgood's *How Eskimos Keep Their Babies Warm and Other Adventures in Parenting*.

23. I borrow and modify Clare Jean Kim's theorization of the "racial triangulation of Asian Americans" (106–8).

24. The quotation is from the book jacket of *Battle Hymn of the Tiger Mother*. Chua's logic is the logic of "reproductive futurism," as Lee Edelman has recently theorized in *No Future: Queer Theory and the Death Drive* (2–4).

25. A review in *AsianWeek*, for example, compared Cao to Amy Tan (H. Lee). While Cao's novel drew more mainstream acclaim and subsequent scholarly treatment than Kim's, in some ways it has been treated more specifically as Vietnamese American literature; it was included in the 1998 anthology *Watermark: Vietnamese American Poetry and Prose*, edited by Barbara Tran, Monique T. D. Truong, and Luu Truong Khoi, whereas an excerpt of *A Cab Called Reliable* was included in Rajini Srikanth and Esther Iwanaga's 2001 panethnic anthology *Bold Words: A Century of Asian American Writing*.

26. With the exception of commentary on the works of Kingston and Tan, scholarship on mother-daughter writing qua mother-daughter writing has been sparse in all of the three phases of forty years of Asian American literary studies that Stephen Hohn Sohn, Paul Lai, and Donald Goellnicht identify. The scholarship of Ho, Grice, and P. Chu has recently been joined by related studies by Schultermandl and Ninh.

27. Lowe's critique of aesthetic realism in her landmark study, *Immigrant Acts: On Asian American Cultural Politics*, has been influential. See also Shelley Sunn Wong's summary of the use of realist forms in Asian American literature in "Unnaming the Same: Theresa Hak Kyung Cha's *Dictée*."

28. See especially P. Chu, *Assimilating Asians*. Reading the contestation of normative femininity and gendered national subjectivity in authors' modifications to the female bildungsroman, or against the grain of overriding narrative conventions, has been an important critical strategy and insight of feminist literary studies.

29. "Recognizing both the difference and the continuity between realist and non-realist works helps reveal," Jinqi Ling asserts, "not only the ideological and rhetorical complexities of representation . . . but also ongoing relevance [of Asian American literature] as active cultural agent to contemporary cultural formations in Asian American history" (23). See also P. Chu, *Assimilating Asians*, 16.

30. For discussion of Cao's desire to write a mother-daughter story and *Monkey Bridge's* genealogical relation to Kingston and Tan, see Hane Lee's "Waiting to Be Told: A Mother-daughter Story Takes on Epic Proportions."

31. See Jacques Derrida on declarations of genre on the material book itself in "The Law of Genre." The pastiche is reminiscent of Cha's *Dictée*, since it quite profoundly challenges official history and shares a deep concern for retrieving the diasporic mother.

32. For discussion of the Althusserian bad subject and the Asian American body politic, see V. Nguyen's conclusion to *Race and Resistance,* 143–71.

33. "Liberal multiculturalism" is the term Joe Kincheloe and Shirley Steinberg use to refer to a populist form of US education about diversity that relies upon abstract individualism, sameness, and free will. In this model, whiteness is the unexamined norm for unity while studies of racism, sexism, ethnocentrism, and homophobia are divisive. See also Lowe for a discussion in relation to establishment of a canon of Asian American literature (42, 84–96).

34. Maxine's struggle against the internalization of "American-feminine" as figured through assault of an Asian American classmate in Kingston's *The Woman Warrior* is a well-known intertext (172). See A. Cheng's chapter on Kingston's memoir in *The Melancholy of Race* (70–102).

35. The origins of intensive mothering lie in the World War II era (Hays 49).

36. The concept of "ethnic entrepreneurialism" is from V. Nguyen, who describes it in *Race and Resistance* as a narrative strategy and negotiation of different cultural registers in which authors construct personas who are sold on the American Dream and sell themselves as bona fide Americans; ambivalence and authorial irony may result in "failed" ethnic entrepreneurs, as in the cases of Carlos Bulosan and John Okada (109).

37. The separation of the family is, as several scholars have duly noted, a norm for transnational labor under neoliberal globalization. See Rhacel Salazar Parreñas, 80–115.

38. "Voice" and "speech" have been privileged in mainstream feminist literary scholarship, as it is in Hirsch's study of the mother/daughter plot, which traces "the slow emergence of maternal speech from silence" (16). For a problematizing treatment of this issue in Asian American women's writing, see Duncan's *Tell This Silence*.

39. Although reading *Monkey Bridge* as a commentary on American belonging risks, as Cao has said, reproducing Viet Nam as a "domestic theater" for glorifying America's own power, my analysis suggests that Cao foregrounds an investigation into why consuming and producing cultural narratives such as these is so important in US belonging (quoted in Janette 65). Renny Christopher writes in *The Viet Nam War/The American War* that for Euro-American readers, Vietnamese exile writers may hold up an uncomfortable mirror, "making [them] look at themselves at the same time that they are looking at the exotic 'other'" (30).

40. For discussion of responsible citizenship in welfare reform politics, see Fujiwara 37, 183–88.

41. The most influential expert on parenting and babies in the United States has been Dr. Benjamin Spock, according to Sharon Hays.

42. Self-help is "a $2.48 billion-a-year industry of tapes, DVDs, videos, books, and 'seminars' on making oneself anew" (Miller, *Makeover Nation* 3).

43. Marita Sturken points out that an aesthetic of absence now commonly informs the design of contemporary memorials in the United States and is suggestive of the kinds of affective and ideological work they perform.

44. Thanh (and Cao) allude to Nguyen Du's classic, *The Tale of Kieu*. As V. Nguyen explains, this is a poem in which a female who becomes a prostitute to save her father functions as an allegory for the nation of Viet Nam, which remains chaste despite the compromising circumstances of colonization (*Race and Resistance* 120–22).

45. While I treat the adoption trope in these narratives largely as a variation of a stock plot convention in mother-daughter writing, analysis of the adoption trope in relation to the respective histories and contemporary politics of transnational adoption in South Korea and Viet nam would be productive and necessary for a fully contextualized consideration. In chapter 5, I briefly reference some of this history in relation to South Korea. See also Grice's *Negotiating Identities* on recuperation of the

mother and rewriting of the mother-daughter relationship outside Western psychological models of the dyad, both Freudian and feminist.

46. Coontz's analysis of the "traditional family" also makes clear that nostalgia is a longing for a fictive past.

47. See P. Chu on the "mother-daughter romance" in Tan's *The Joy Luck Club* (143).

3 / Romancing the Self

1. See Rosalind Gill and Elena Herdieckerhoff for how romance as a discourse has recently been rewritten (493); Chrys Ingraham for discussion of how weddings provide security and comfort, (9); and Elizabeth Freeman for how weddings stage relationships and social belonging (44).

2. Revealing the extent to which its tenets have become naturalized, neoliberalism often rejects outright the rights of individual citizens to democratically choose collective social policies and protections, as in the case of disallowing labor organizing, but this is popularly understood as ensuring a "free" market rather than protecting the freedom of citizens to organize themselves or social relations outside market fundamentalism. See Harvey on neoliberalism's hostility to all social solidarity (75–76).

3. Scholars who connect chick lit to the tradition of Anglo-American women's writing contend that any assessment of chick lit should be made in relation to the popular literature written by and/or for women that is now considered classic but which initially had been excluded from serious consideration by aesthetic theories of enduring value that place a premium on conventional notions of quality, such as psychological interiority, complex character development, figurative language, and innovation to literary genres rather than the affinity, empathy, affect, entertainment, education, and engagement that are hallmarks of women's fiction. See Juliette Wells for a list of literary "elements" (64) and Cecilia Farr for canonical qualities of "literature." See also Nan Enstad on how middle-class reading practices are inadequate for understanding the value and reception of one of the first novel forms produced for working women—dime novels—since they overlook melodramatic adventure and dramatic reward (36–46).

4. Following Grewal, and as an alternative to postfeminism, Pamela Butler and Jigna Desai have suggested "neoliberal feminisms," which refers to multiple contemporary feminist discourses (8).

5. Distinguishing it from backlash, Angela McRobbie argues in "Post-feminism and Popular Culture" that postfeminist discourse claims that women are now "free to choose" whatever paths they desire, and thus feminism is "no longer needed," so in certain ways postfeminist texts assume the "success" of feminism (256). See also discussion of backlash in McRobbie's *The Aftermath of Feminism* (14–15). Yvonne Tasker and Diane Negra recognize the complexity of postfeminist culture's relationship to feminism in their collection *Interrogating Postfeminism* (8).

6. Anne Cronin defines consumer citizenship as the ability to translate cultural rights into economic and political privilege (106), but, as discussed in chapter 1, for Asian American women, cultural rights are not a given and must be established at substantial cost.

7. For discussion of sexual subjectification and agency in chick lit, see Gill and Herdieckerhoff's "Rewriting the Romance," 499.

8. Jane Arthurs writes that in HBO's serialization of *Sex and the City*, the world of work disappears from view, "although the women's autonomy from men is underwritten by their economic independence" (84).

9. For an excellent discussion of the connections between nineteenth-century tales of working women and contemporary chick lit, see Kirsten Fest's "Angels in the House."

10. See Elizabeth Hale's discussion of "underling lit" or "assistant lit" in "Long Suffering Professional Females." See also Gill and Herdieckerhoff's "Rewriting the Romance" and Jennifer Scanlon's "Making Shopping Safe for the Rest of Us."

11. Arlene Dávila points out in *Latinos, Inc.* that commercial culture is constitutive of every feature of our lives, and thus "branding" becomes important in identities, perceived entitlements, and belonging (9–11).

12. As noted in chapter 2, in *Motherhood and Representation* E. Ann Kaplan influentially argued that popular culture registers major changes in social formation through a focus on the imaginary or mythic mother, and I add that popular culture also now responds by focusing on reinvention of the self, more broadly.

13. Many trace the emergence of chick lit in Britain to Helen Fielding's *Bridget Jones's Diary* (1996) and in the United States to Candace Bushnell's *Sex and the City* (1996). Alternative genealogies begin in the United States with Terry McMillan's *Waiting to Exhale* (1992) or with Chris Mazza and Jeffrey Deshell's anthology of fiction which first used the term in the collection *Chick-Lit: Postfeminist Fiction* (1995). Some, such as Rachel Donadio, note that chick lit has "traveled" to Indonesia, Poland, India, and Scandinavian countries, while others, such as Anna Isozaki, contend that various neoliberal consumer cultures, including Japan, have independently spawned chick lit. Certainly, neither readership nor authorship is confined to the United States or Britain, as sales figures and marketing campaigns make clear. See also Scanlon for the global reach of chick lit.

14. "Peaking in 2005 at about $140 million (US) in sales," Jeffrey Yang writes, chick lit ballooned for several years "at the staggering (for the book industry) pace of 7 percent per year" ("Asian Pop"). See Gill and Herdieckerhoff for discussion of how chick lit was from the start heavily marketed to female commuters and became "the archetypal women's read for their journeys to and from work" (488). Rather than endless complaints about chick lit, one might have expected to hear it applauded, given recent anxieties about falling reading and literacy rates and "the death of the book" (Memmott). See also Fitzpatrick's *Anxiety of Obsolescence,* for a discussion of anxieties about reading in America.

15. See Christine Seifert's "Bite me!" on *Twilight* fandom, and April Alliston and Susan Celia Greenfield's "Mommy Porn" on the popularity of *Fifty Shades*. In 2009, 67 percent of adult women in the United States bought at least one print book (Abbott, "New Book Buying Realities"). The largest share of book sales went to romance fiction, at 13.2 percent or $1.36 billion, and within that category chick lit made up about 2 percent of sales ("Romance Literature Statistics").

16. L. Park contends that "upward social or economic mobility of children of immigrants is, in fact, the hard-won struggle or economic mobility of children who follow Asian . . . based ideals as passed down by their immigrant parents and communities" (17).

17. Such critique at times descends into complaints about women's narcissism. For this reason I resist referring to *China Dolls* and *Goddess for Hire* as "subversions" of

chick lit, which implies too dismissive a stance toward the genre in its mainstream versions. I agree with Krista Lysack, who, in *Come Buy, Come Buy*, analyzes the different context of British women's literature of the Victorian era, arguing that the focus on consumer practices "makes visible the ways in which the subject may respond to and even resist her condition under capitalism" (7).

18. I am not setting up a hierarchy of oppression among immigrant, working-class, and professional working women but rather pointing out that the novels assert that barriers to entry and success are also substantial for high-status occupations.

19. Butler and Desai contend that although Maya at first most enjoys her job as an evil-avenging goddess for the gifts and donations she receives from worshippers, the material rewards become less important, and "the sign of her growth and self-knowledge at the end of the novel is her dedication to saving the world from malevolence" (20).

20. See Scanlon for a discussion of the Shopoholic series as cautionary tale.

21. In a phenomenon that is related to but seems to go beyond the Asian fetish problem thematized in *China Dolls* and popularly known as "yellow fever," Ying Chu wrote in 2009 in *Marie-Claire* that Asian women had become the new trophy wives for powerful white Western men. Catherine Hakim has coined a term, "erotic capital," that is similar to Susan Koshy's "sexual capital," though it is not understood exclusively with respect to Asian American women, as Hakim elaborates in *Erotic Capital: The Power of Attraction in the Boardroom and the Bedroom*.

22. I disagree with Berlant's characterization of chick lit in *The Female Complaint*; she considers it part of a historically consistent, commodified mass genre of "women's culture" in the United States that thwarts women's desires for social change and political agency by producing feelings of belonging based on identification, recognition, and reflection of a shared sense of disappointment in their personal, romantic lives and in their social marginalization (ix).

23. At the same time, Stephen Duncombe acknowledges in *Dream: Re-Imagining Progressive Politics in an Age of Fantasy* that the fascination with celebrity and desire for recognition through escape into celebrity culture can be understood as an escape from democracy (123).

24. Several critics have argued that the status of heterosexual romantic relationships in chick lit is quite unstable, even if the narrative conventions of romance and the affective power of romantic desire and fantasy often provide its structure. See Stephanie Harzewski's "The Limits of Defamiliarization," Jane Gerhard's "*Sex and the City*," and Katherine Hyunmi Lee's "Hello Lover."

4 / Neoliberal Detective Work

1. See Amanda Seaman's *Bodies of Evidence* for a discussion of the "bubble" economy in Japan in the 1990s, its relation to the "boom" in women's detective fiction, and its correspondence to similar booms in the United States and the United Kingdom (11–14).

2. See Kelly Gallagher and Charlotte Abbott for statistics about who buys and reads fiction in the United States. Detective/mystery and romance make up over half of all fiction purchased in the United States, and it is purchased most often by women.

3. *The Interpreter* has been translated into Korean, Japanese, French, and Dutch, and Kim was awarded the Pen Beyond Margins Award and the Gustavus Myers

Outstanding Book Award for it. Massey's series has been translated into fifteen languages, and she has won the Agatha Award and the Macavity Award and been nominated for many more (Massey, "Re: Translations of *Girl in a Box*").

4. Excerpts from Ruth Jordan's fall 2006 review of *Girl in a Box* in *Crimespree* are reprinted on Massey's website http://www.sujatamassey.com.

5. In "The Game's Afoot," Patricia Merivale and Susan Sweeney identify six characteristic themes of the metaphysical detective story that combine various iterations of conventions or tropes and include the defeated sleuth; the world, city, or text as labyrinth; the purloined letter or text within the text; the ambiguity or meaninglessness of clues; the missing person or the lost, stolen, or exchanged identity; and a lack of closure (8).

6. For the "long view" of the history of the genre, most broadly referred to as "crime fiction," see John Scaggs's introduction to *Crime Fiction.* See also Martin Priestman's *Detective Fiction and Literature.* For discussion of romance in the hardboiled detective novel, see Sean McCann's "The Hard-Boiled Novel."

7. See "Around the World in 80 D.I.'s" for a map of international sleuths.

8. See McCann's "The Hard-Boiled Novel" for a brief overview of American hardboiled detective fiction, and Christopher Breu's *Hard-Boiled Masculinities* for an alternative genealogy that reverses the hardboiled novel to film noir narrative chronology.

9. The early twentieth century was an era of intense racial strife and national debates about belonging, with escalating KKK violence and Supreme Court rulings on immigration, whiteness, and naturalization that continued to restrict citizenship, particularly for Asians, as Maureen Reddy points out in "Race and American Crime Fiction" (137–39). See also Redddy's first chapter titled "Cracking Codes" in *Traces, Codes, and Clues* for discussion of whiteness and yellow-peril discourse in the genre, especially Hammett's fiction (6–40). On hardboiled fiction as a "white genre" with a "parasitic" relationship to blackness, see Liam Kennedy. See also Sara Crosby's "Early American Crime Writing."

10. In "Race, Region, Rule," Charles Rzepka considers rule subversion a hallmark of detective fiction since Poe.

11. See also Linda Mizejewski for how gender stereotypes in the genre are tied to the history of professional law enforcement in the United States (18–20).

12. For analysis of how hegemonic masculinity reformulates itself and maintains privilege in the contemporary period through appropriating the identity politics and cultural practices of marginalized or subcultural groups, see Hamilton Carroll's excellent study of popular culture and white masculinity in *Affirmative Reaction*. There is broad recognition that detective fiction is characterized by anxiety about the Other, but also that recent expressions now break to varying degrees from the gumshoe who safeguards the interests of mainstream America to explore the experience of Otherness. See M. Reddy, *Traces, Codes, and Clues*; G. and A. MacDonald, "Ethnic Detectives"; and Cranny-Francis, *Feminist Fiction*.

13. In *Traces, Codes, and Clues*, M. Reddy identifies the basic features of the feminist countertradition in crime fiction as "violation of linear progress, an ultimate absence of authority as conventionally defined in crime fiction, and use of a dialogic form" (49). I disagree with Reddy's assertion that revisions by writers of color and feminists place their works outside the hardboiled category (15).

14. Charles Alexander's article served as a rather prescient description of long-term economic changes that apply in many ways to the current global economic downturn.

15. The "New Economy" as synonym and shorthand for neoliberal political economy is ubiquitous in popular, industry, and academic discourse alike, even some thirty years on, when global neoliberalism is not so new. A recent example is found in Steve Stout's book *The Tanning of America: How Hip-Hop Created a Culture That Rewrote the Rules of the New Economy*. Results for a book search using "The New Economy" on Amazon.com yields seventy-eight thousand items.

16. V. Nguyen provides a brief summary of objections to cosmopolitanism in "Remembering War, Dreaming Peace."

17. Pnina Werbner describes the broader category of alternative, non-Western cosmopolitanism as "openness to difference, whether of other ethnic groups, cultures, religions or nations," while "vernacular cosmopolitanism," following Homi Bhabha, "joins contradictory notions of local specificity and universal enlightenment," as seen in scholarship focusing on "indigenous, demotic or popular forms of intercultural life worlds" ("Paradoxes" 112).

18. Scholars have theorized a proliferation of new cosmopolitanisms, with some decidedly not elite, as in Paul Gilroy's "vulgar cosmopolitanism," which is characterized by an everyday, vernacular style and a refusal of state-centeredness in contemporary British popular culture (*Postcolonial Melancholia* 67). See also Kwame Anthony Appiah's *Cosmopolitanism: Ethics in a World of Strangers*. For statements on ethical criticism, see for example, Marjorie Garber, Beatrice Hanssen, and Rebecca Walkowitz, *Turn to Ethics*; Adam Zachary Newton, "Versions of Ethics"; and Martha Nussbaum, *For Love of Country*.

19. Craig Calhoun's reservations about cosmopolitanism, understood as "a [virtuous] claim to be already global and to have the highest ethical aspirations for what globalization can offer," include whether it is as different from nationalism as it is typically assumed to be, whether it is actually supplanting nationalism in global politics, and whether it is an ethical complement or merely a substitution for politics (428).

20. Gilroy has also sounded a warning about "armored cosmopolitanism" or how elitism translates in practice into imperialistic military and economic interventions under neoliberalism (*Postcolonial Melancholia* 60).

21. As Massey was born in England to an Indian father and German mother, she is the only author in this study who does not write about, at least on some level, her personal cultural heritage. While she was educated in the United States, her interest in Japan was inspired during two years in the late 1990s when she and her American husband lived there while he was serving in the US military.

22. One branch of criticism contends that the hardboiled, either as novel or film, is not uniquely American. Jennifer Fay and Justus Neiland argue in *Film Noir*, for example, that film noir is deeply cosmopolitan, dramatizing local crimes and crises in the context of global cultural phenomena, such as modernization, decolonization, and migration.

23. In the post-9/11 context of the US "War on Terror," with its paternalistic rhetoric of saving Muslim women, this approach has potentially important implications for understanding how the popular genre of detective fiction may productively engage neoliberal citizenship discourses that position the United States simultaneously as a victim of terrorism, an arbiter of gender justice, and a global imperial power.

24. Massey's *Shimura Trouble* (2008) explores Rei's family history in Hawaii and specifically land stolen during World War II.

25. For a summary of the influential readings by Jacques Lacan, Jacques Derrida, and Barbara Johnson of "The Purloined Letter," see John T. Irwin's "Mysteries We Reread."

26. In "The Purloined Letter," Poe turned away from the murder mysteries that the Dupin character solved in Poe's earlier tales "The Murders in the Rue Morgue" (1841) and "The Mystery of Marie Rogêt" (1842–43). The corpse became a requirement, however, in the detective novel by the golden age (interwar) period, when plot was elevated in the whodunit puzzle story or mystery. As many scholars point out, one of the infamous "Twenty Rules for Writing Detective Stories" (1928) by S. S. Van Dine (Willard Huntington Wright) is that a corpse must motivate detective fiction, since "[n]o lesser crime than murder will suffice" to justify so much of the reader's time spent investigating it (Scaggs 43). Further, the corpse is often "the repository of clues" in Agatha Christie's work and in much detective and mystery fiction following it (44).

27. See Andy Kroll, "Follow the Dark Money."

28. For discussion of the cultural informant, see Betsy Huang, *Contesting Genres* (56).

29. See, for example, Kang's influential article "Si(gh)ting Asian/American Women," as well as her *Compositional Subjects*.

30. In contrast to how Rei and Suzy are valued, for Koshy, minority cosmopolitans should be valued for "translocal affiliations that are grounded in the experience of minority subjects and are marked by a critical awareness of the constraints of primary attachments such as family, religion, race, and nation and by an ethical or imaginative receptivity, orientation, or aspiration to an interconnected or shared world" ("Minority Cosmopolitanism" 594).

31. While this focus may recall the famous mathematical or puzzle analyses of "The Purloined Letter," I do not follow those interests as much as I follow Chen's understanding of double agency as a thematic of subject formation that is often represented in Asian American literature.

5 / Food Writing and Transnational Belonging

1. See Eleanor Ty's introduction in *Unfastened: Globality and Asian North American Narratives* for discussion of "globality" as a social condition, in contrast to "globalization" as a set of processes (xiii). Ty describes critical globality as a concern for health and environment across national borders, the globalization of markets, and the production of goods.

2. For background and details on DES, see Julie Sze, "Boundaries and Border Wars" (791–92). See Monica Chiu's "Postnational Globalization" for a critique of Jane's liberal multiculturalism. See also Black, "Fertile Cosmofeminism," for a compelling discussion of the novel's representation of feminism and transnational feminist cross-border solidarity.

3. The obstacles for women in Hollywood have become even worse since 1998, as Martha Lauzen's annual report "The Celluloid Ceiling" tracks, and it is emblematic of discrimination in commercial media industry broadly speaking, as the recent documentary *Miss Representation* asserts.

4. Unlike others who have written about the novel, I consider Jane to be the narrator who mediates and compiles all of the components of *My Year of Meats*. I base this on Jane's identification with Shonagon; on the epigraphs from Shonagon that are used to open each chapter; on a knowledge of and a close association with Akiko Ueno and personalities that would enable Jane to reconstruct their narratives from an omniscient point of view; on her direct address throughout the text of the mutually dependent nature of fiction and truth in contemporary life, as in her comment that "sometimes you have to make things up to tell truths that alter outcomes"; and on Jane's closing promise that she will unflinchingly bring not her documentary film but her "book" to light and "make it public" (Ozeki, *My Year of Meats* 361). Finally, a prologue, an epilogue, an author's note, a bibliography, and the footnotes are all written from Jane's point of view and frame the entire text.

5. See *Feeding America: The Historic American Cookbook Project* for information and images of Simmons's *American Cookery, or the Art of Dressing Viands, Fish, Poultry, and Vegetables, and the Best Modes of Making Pastes, Puffs, Pies, Tarts, Puddings, Custards, and Preserves, and All Kinds of Cakes, from the Imperial Plum to Plain Cake: Adapted to This Country, and All Grades of Life*.

6. See recent studies on Julia Child by Kathleen Collins and Dana Polan. See also Thoma, "What Julia Knew."

7. Echoing certain aspects of V. Nguyen's thesis in *Race and Representation*, Anita Mannur writes in *Culinary Fictions: Food in South Asian Diasporic Culture* that the bias in ethnic literary studies has had to do with food writing's status as popular and therefore not political (21); I would add that it is also related to its historically feminized status in the United States.

8. See Jay David Bolter and Richard Grusin's discussion in *Remediation: Understanding New Media* (35).

9. See Chad Raphael's "Political Economic Origins" for a summary of the economic restructuring of the American television industry in the 1980s.

10. See Sucheng Chan's discussion of this history in *Asian Americans: An Interpretive History*, especially Chapter 1, "International Context of Asian Emigration," and Chapter 2, "Immigration and Livelihood, 1840s–1930s." See also Hing (27–36).

6 / Conclusion

1. Disney's *Mulan* is not an adaption of *The Woman Warrior* itself but rather an animated version of the Chinese legend of Fa Mulan (or Hua Mulan). Maxine Hong Kingston first popularized the legend of Fa Mulan in the United States, which led to Disney's "adapation," according to Wikipedia. It is not entirely analogous to Wayne Wang's *The Joy Luck Club* or Mira Nair's *The Namesake*.

2. For a more thorough discussion of Lahiri's success, see Lavina Dhingra and Floyd Cheung, "Naming Jhumpa Lahiri"; Tamara Bhalla, "Being (and Feeling) Gogol"; and Min Hyoung Song, "Children of 1965."

3. Indeed, the narrative is in many ways focused on the allegorical power of the child and reproductive futurism, as Song provocatively argues in "Children of 1965," and it could be contextualized within neoliberal maternal discourse.

Bibliography

Abbott, Charlotte. "The New Book Buying Realities." *Follow the Reader.* NetGalley, 16 Oct. 2010. http://followthereader.wordpress.com/2009/05/14/bowker-reveals-new-book-buying-realities/. 1 April 2012.

Alexander, Charles P. "The New Economy." *Time.* 121.22 (30 May 1983): 62–70.

Alexander, Shana. *Anyone's Daughter: The Times and Trials of Patty Hearst.* New York: Viking, 1979.

Allison, Dorothy. *Bastard Out of Carolina.* New York: Plume, 1992.

Alliston, April, and Susan Celia Greenfield. "'Mommy Porn' Novel has Retro Message." *CNN Opinion.* CNN.com, 29 Mar. 2012. http://www.cnn.com/2012/03/29/opinion/alliston-greenfield-50-shades. 19 Aug. 2012.

Anagnost, Ann. "Maternal Labor In a Transnational Circuit." *Consuming Motherhood.* Eds. Janelle S. Taylor, Linda L. Layne, and Danielle F. Wozniak. New Brunswick: Rutgers University Press, 2004. 139–67.

Appiah, Kwame Anthony. *Cosmopolitanism: Ethics in a World of Strangers.* New York: W. W. Norton & Company, 2006.

"Around the World in 80 D.I.'s." *Your Library.* City of Edinburgh Council, 22 Sept. 2011. http://yourlibrary.edinburgh.gov.uk/blogs/2012/03/around-world-80-dis. 10 June 2012.

Arthurs, Jane. "*Sex and the City* and Consumer Culture: Remediating Postfeminist Drama." *Feminist Media Studies* 3.1 (2003): 83–98.

Asian Women United of California, ed. *Making Waves: An Anthology of Writings By and About Asian American Women.* Boston: Beacon Press 1989.

"Association for Asian American Studies Response to the Pew Center Report: 'Rise of Asian Americans." *Association for Asian American Studies.* 16 July 2012. http://aaastudies.org/content/index.php/77-home/117-whats-new. 15 July 2012.

Banet-Weiser, Sarah. *Kids Rule: Nickelodeon and Consumer Citizenship.* Durham, NC: Duke University Press, 2007.

Berlant, Lauren. *The Female Complaint: The Unfinished Business of Sentimentality in American Culture.* Durham, NC: Duke University Press, 2007.

———. *The Queen of America Goes to Washington City: Essays on Sex and Citizenship*. Durham, NC: Duke University Press, 1997.

Bhalla, Tamara. "Being (and Feeling) Gogol: Reading and Recognition in Jhumpa Lahiri's *The Namesake*." *MELUS* 37.1 (Spring 2012): 105–29.

Bilston, Sarah. "The Death of Chick Lit: How the Recession Is Transforming the Genre." *DoubleX*. The Slate Group, 11 Aug. 2009. http://www.doublex.com/section/arts/death-chick-lit?page=0,0. 16 Oct. 2010.

Black, Shameem. "Fertile Cosmofeminism: Ruth L. Ozeki and Transnational Reproduction." *Meridians: Feminism, Race, Transnationalism* 5.1 (2004): 226–56.

Bolter, Jay David, and Richard Grusin. *Remediation: Understanding New Media*. Cambridge, MA: MIT Press, 1999.

Bow, Leslie. *Betrayal and Other Acts of Subversion: Feminism, Sexual Politics, and Asian American Women's Literature*. Princeton: Princeton University Press, 2001.

Brennan, Teresa. *Globalization and Its Terrors*. New York: Routledge, 2003.

Breu, Christopher. *Hard-Boiled Masculinities*. Minneapolis: University of Minnesota Press, 2005.

Briggs, Laura, Gladys McCormick, and J. T. Way. "Transnationalism: A Category of Analysis." *American Quarterly* 60.3 (Sept. 2008): 625–48.

Brown, Wendy. *Edgework: Critical Essays on Knowledge and Politics*. Princeton: Princeton University Press, 2006.

Bushnell, Candace. *Sex and the City*. New York: Atlantic Monthly Press, 1996.

———. *Trading Up*. New York: Hyperion, 2003.

Butler, Pamela, and Jigna Desai. "Manolos, Marriage, and Mantras: Chick-lit Criticism and Transnational Feminism." *Meridians: Feminism, Race, Transnationalism* 8.2 (2008): 1–31.

Calhoun, Craig. "Cosmopolitanism and Nationalism." *Nations and Nationalisms* 14.3 (2008): 427–48.

Canclini, Néstor García. *Citizens and Consumers*. Trans. George Yúdice. Minneapolis: University of Minnesota Press, 2001.

Cao, Lan. *Monkey Bridge*. New York: Penguin, 1997.

Carroll, Hamilton. *Affirmative Reaction: New Formations of White Masculinity*. Durham, NC: Duke University Press, 2011.

Cha, Theresa. *Dictée*. 1982. Berkeley: Third Woman Press, 1995.

Chan, Sucheng. *Asian Americans: An Interpretive History*. New York: Twayne, 1991.

Chan Is Missing. Dir. Wayne Wang. Koch-Lorber Films, 1982.

Chang, Yoonmee. *Writing the Ghetto: Class, Authorship, and the Asian American Ethnic Enclave*. New Brunswick: Rutgers University Press, 2010.

Chen, Tina. *Double Agency: Acts of Impersonation in Asian American Literature and Culture*. Stanford: Stanford University Press, 2005.

Cheng, Anne Anlin. *The Melancholy of Race: Psychoanalysis, Assimilation, and Hidden Grief*. New York: Oxford University Press, 2000.

Cheng, Emily. "Meat and the Millennium: Transnational Politics of Race and Gender in Ruth Ozeki's *My Year of Meats*." *Journal of Asian American Studies* 12.2 (June 2009): 191–220.

Cheung, Hye Seung. *Hollywood Asian: Philip Ahn and the Politics of Cross-Ethnic Performance*. Philadelphia: Temple University Press, 2006.

Cheung, King-Kok. "Reviewing Asian American Literature." *An Inter-Ethnic*

Companion to Asian American Literature. Ed. King-Kok Cheung. Cambridge: Cambridge University Press, 1996. 1–38.

——. "*The Woman Warrior* versus the Chinaman Pacific: Must a Chinese American Critic Choose Between Feminism and Heroism?" *Conflicts in Feminism*. Eds. Marianne Hirsch and Evelyn Fox Keller. New York: Routledge, 1990. 234–51.

Chiu, Monica. "Postnational Globalization and (En)Gendered Meat Production in Ruth L. Ozeki's *My Year of Meats*." *LIT* 12.1: 99–128.

Choi, Susan. *American Woman*. New York: Harper Collins, 2003.

Christopher, Renny. *The Viet Nam War / The American War: Images and Representations in Euro-American and Vietnamese Exile Narratives*. Amherst: University of Massachusetts Press, 1995.

Chu, Patricia P. *Assimilating Asians: Gendered Strategies of Authorship in Asian America*. Durham, NC: Duke University Press, 2000.

Chu, Ying. "The New Trophy Wives: Asian Women." *Marie-Claire*. Hearst Communications, 5 Aug. 2009. http://www.marieclaire.com/sex-love/advice/asian-trophy-wife. 5 May 2012.

Chua, Amy. *Battle Hymn of the Tiger Mother*. New York: Penguin, 2011.

——. "Why Chinese Mothers Are Superior." *Wall Street Journal*. Dow Jones and Company, 8 Jan. 2011. http://online.wsj.com/article/SB10001424052748704111150457 6059713528698754.html. 9 Jan. 2011.

Chuh, Kandace. *Imagine Otherwise: On Asian Americanist Critique*. Durham, NC: Duke University Press, 2003.

Chung, Hye Seung. *Hollywood Asian: Philip Ahn and the Politics of Cross Ethnic Performance*. Philadelphia: Temple University Press, 2006.

Clifford, James. "Traveling Cultures." *Cultural Studies*. Eds. Lawrence Grossberg, Cary Nelson, and Paula Treichler. London: Routledge, 1992. 96–116.

Cohen, Lizabeth. *A Consumers' Republic: The Politics of Mass Consumption in Postwar America*. New York: Alfred Knopf, 2003.

Collins, Jim. *Bring on the Books for Everybody: How Literary Culture Became Popular Culture*. Durham, NC: Duke University Press, 2010.

Collins, Kathleen. *Watching What We Eat: The Evolution of Television Cooking Shows*. New York: Continuum, 2009.

Coontz, Stephanie. *The Way We Never Were: American Families and the Nostalgia Trap*. New York: Basic Books, 2000.

Cranny-Francis, Anne. *Feminist Fiction: Feminist Uses of Generic Fiction*. New York: St. Martin's Press, 1990.

Crittenden, Ann. *The Price of Motherhood*. New York: Picado, 2001.

Cronin, Anne M. *Advertising and Consumer Citizenship: Gender, Images and Rights*. New York: Routledge, 2001.

Crosby, Sara. "Early American Crime Writing." *The Cambridge Companion to American Crime Fiction*. Ed. Catherine Ross Nickerson. Cambridge: Cambridge University Press, 2010. 5–16.

Cruikshank, Barbara. "Revolutions Within: Self-Government and Self-Esteem." *Foucault and Political Reason: Liberalism, Neoliberalism and Rationalities of Government*. Eds. Andrew Barry, Thomas Osborne, and Nikolas Rose. Chicago: University of Chicago Press, 1996. 231–52.

Das Gupta, Manisha. *Unruly Immigrants: Rights, Activism, and Transnational*

South Asian Politics in the United States. Durham, NC: Duke University Press, 2006.

Davé, Shilpa, LeiLani Nishime, and Tasha G. Oren, eds. *East Main Street: Asian American Popular Culture.* New York: New York University Press, 2005.

Dávila, Arlene. *Latinos, Inc.: The Making and Marketing of a People.* Berkeley: University of California Press, 2001.

Davis, Emily. "Investigating Truth, History, and Human Rights in Michael Ondaatje's *Anil's Ghost.*" *Detective Fiction in a Postcolonial and Transnational World.* Eds. Nels Pearson and Marc Singer. London: Ashgate, 2009. 15–30.

Derrida, Jacques. "The Law of Genre." *On Narrative.* Ed. W. J. T. Mitchell. Chicago: University of Chicago Press, 1981. 51–77.

The Devil Wears Prada. Dir. David Frankel. Fox, 2006.

Dhingra, Lavina, and Floyd Cheung. "Naming Jhumpa Lahiri: Bengali, Asian American, Postcolonial, Universal?" *Naming Jhumpa Lahiri: Canons and Controversies.* Eds. Lavina Dhingra and Floyd Cheung. Lanham, MD: Rowman & Littlefield, 2012. vii–xxii.

Donadio, Rachel. "Chick Lit Translates into Global Zeitgeist." *The International Herald Tribune* 18 March 2006: F8.

Douglas, Susan J., and Meredith W. Michaels. *The Mommy Myth: The Idealization of Motherhood and How It Has Undermined Women.* New York: The Free Press, 2004.

Duggan, Lisa. *The Twilight of Equality: Neoliberalism, Cultural Politics, and the Attack on Democracy.* Boston: Beacon Press, 2004.

Duncan, Patti. *Tell This Silence: Asian American Women Writers and the Politics of Speech.* Iowa City: University of Iowa Press, 2004.

Duncombe, Stephen. *Dream: Re-Imagining Progressive Politics in an Age of Fantasy.* New York: The New Press, 2007.

Edelman, Lee. *No Future: Queer Theory and the Death Drive.* Durham, NC: Duke University Press, 2004.

"Editor's Forum." *Journal of Asian American Studies* 15.3 (Oct. 2012): 327–46.

Edwards, Kim. *The Memory Keeper's Daughter.* New York: Viking, 2005.

Eng, David L. *The Feeling of Kinship: Queer Liberalism and the Racialization of Intimacy.* Durham, NC: Duke University Press, 2010.

Enstad, Nan. *Ladies of Labor, Girls of Adventure: Working Women, Popular Culture, and Labor Politics at the Turn of the Century.* New York: Columbia University Press, 1999.

Far, Sui Sin (Edith Maude Eaton). *Mrs. Spring Fragrance and Other Writings.* Ed. Amy Ling and Annette White-Parks. Urbana: University of Illinois Press, 1995.

Farr, Cecilia Konchar. "It Was Chick Lit All Along: The Gendering of a Genre." *You've Come A Long Way Baby: Women, Politics, and Popular Culture.* Ed. Lilly J. Goren. Lexington: University Press of Kentucky, 2009. 201–14.

Fay, Jennifer, and Justus Neiland. *Film Noir: Hardboiled Modernity and the Cultures of Globalization.* New York: Routledge, 2009.

Featherstone, Mike. *Consumer Culture and Postmodernism.* New York: Sage, 1991.

Feeding America: The Historic American Cookbook Project. Michigan State University, 30 Sept. 2001. http://digital.lib.msu.edu/projects/cookbooks/. 2 July 2012.

Feiner, Susan. "A Portrait of *Homo Economicus* as a Young Man." *The New Economic*

Criticism: Studies at the Intersection of Literature and Economics. Eds. Martha Woodmansee and Mark Osteen. New York: Routledge, 1999. 193–209.

Fenkl, Heinz Insu. "The Future of Korean American Literature." *Heinz Insu Fenkl.* 25 Oct. 2003. http://heinzinsufenkl.net/future.html. 11 Oct. 2011.

Ferriss, Suzanne, and Mallory Young. "Introduction." *Chick Lit: The New Woman's Fiction.* Eds. Mallory Young and Suzanne Ferriss. New York: Routledge, 2006. 1–13.

Fest, Kirsten. "Angels in the House or Girl Power: Working Women in Nineteenth-Century Novels and Contemporary Chick Lit." *Women's Studies* 38 (2009): 43–62.

Fielding, Helen. *Bridget Jones's Diary.* London: Picador, 1996.

Fish, Cheryl J. "The Toxic Body Politic: Ethnicity, Gender, and Corrective Eco-Justice in Ruth Ozeki's *My Year of Meats* and Judith Helfand and Daniel Gold's *Blue Vinyl.*" *MELUS* 34.2 (Summer 2009): 43–62.

Fitzpatrick, Kathleen. *The Anxiety of Obsolescence: The American Novel in the Age of Television.* Nashville: Vanderbilt University Press, 2006.

Franke, Katherine. "Theorizing Yes: An Essay on Feminism, Law, and Desire." *Columbia Law Review* 101 (2001): 181–208.

Franklin, Cynthia. *Writing Women's Communities: The Politics and Poetics of Contemporary Multi-Genre Anthologies.* Madison: University of Wisconsin Press, 1997.

Fredriksen, Jeanne. "Deranged Marriage in Kali-fornia." *India Currents* 18.4 (July 2004): 40.

Freeman, Elizabeth. *The Wedding Complex: Forms of Belonging in Modern American Culture.* Durham, NC: Duke University Press, 2002.

Friday, Nancy. *My Mother/My Self: The Daughter's Search for Identity.* New York: Delta, 1977.

Friedman, May, and Shana L. Calixte, eds. *Mothering and Blogging: The Radical Act of the MommyBlog.* Toronto: Demeter Press, 2009.

Fujiwara, Lynn. *Mothers without Citizenship: Asian Immigrant Families and the Consequences of Welfare Reform.* Minneapolis: University of Minnesota Press, 2008.

Gallagher, Kelly. "The Customer's Always Right: Who Is Today's Book Consumer?" *SlideShare.* 8 May 2009. http://www.slideshare.net/bisg/4-making-information-pay-2009-gallagher-kelly-bowker-1406744. 6 Mar. 2012.

Garber, Marjorie, Beatrice Hanssen, and Rebecca Walkowitz, eds. *The Turn to Ethics.* New York: Routledge, 2000.

Gerhard, Jane. "*Sex and the City*: Carrie Bradshaw's Queer Postfeminism." *Feminist Media Studies* 5.1 (Mar. 2005): 37–49.

Gilbert, Elizabeth. *Eat, Pray, Love: One Woman's Search for Everything across Italy, India, and Indonesia.* New York: Viking, 2006.

Gill, Rosalind. "Postfeminist Media Culture: Elements of a Sensibility." *European Journal of Cultural Studies* 10.2 (2007): 147–66.

Gill, Rosalind, and Elena Herdieckerhoff. "Rewriting the Romance: New Femininities in Chick Lit." *Feminist Media Studies* 6.4 (Dec. 2006): 487–517.

Gilroy, Paul. *Postcolonial Melancholia.* New York: Columbia University Press, 2005.

Grewal, Inderpal. *Transnational America: Feminisms, Diasporas, Neoliberalisms.* Durham, NC: Duke University Press, 2005.

Grice, Helena. *Negotiating Identities: An Introduction to Asian American Women's Writing.* Manchester: Manchester University Press, 2002.

Gross, Larry. *Up From Invisibility: Lesbians, Gay Men, and the Media in America*. New York: Columbia University Press, 2001.

Gwinn, Mary Ann. "Who Buys Books: 40 Year Old Women and Others." *The Seattle Times*. The Seattle Times Company Network, 5 Sept. 2010. http://seattletimes.com/html/books/2012801171_litlife06.html. 6 May 2011.

Haines, Beth A. "Book Reviews." *Feminist Formations* 23.1 (Spring 2011): 264–73.

Hakim, Catherine. *Erotic Capital: The Power of Attraction in the Boardroom and the Bedroom*. New York: Basic Books, 2011.

Halberstam, Judith. *In a Queer Time and Place: Transgender Bodies, Sexual Subcultures*. New York: New York University Press, 2005.

Hale, Elizabeth. "Long Suffering Professional Females: The Case of Nanny Lit." *Chick Lit: The New Woman's Fiction*. Eds. Mallory Young and Suzanne Ferriss. New York: Routledge. 103–18.

Hariman, Robert, ed. *Popular Trials: Rhetoric, Mass Media, and the Law*. Tuscaloosa: University of Alabama Press, 1990.

Harold and Kumar Go to White Castle. Dir. Danny Leiner. New Line Cinema, 2005.

Harris, Lynn. *Death By Chick Lit*. New York: Berkley Trade, 2007.

Harris-Lacewell, Melissa. "Bad Black Mothers." *The Nation*. 24 Nov. 2009. http://www.thenation.com/blog/bad-black-mothers. 25 Nov. 2009.

Harvey, David. *A Brief History of Neoliberalism*. Oxford: Oxford University Press, 2005.

Harzewski, Stephanie. "The Limits of Defamiliarization: *Sex and the City* as Late Heterosexuality." *The Scholar and Feminist Online* 3.1. (Fall 2004): n. pag. http://sfonline.barnard.edu/hbo/harzewski_01.htm. 20 June 2007.

———. "Tradition and Displacement in the New Novel of Manners." *Chick Lit: The New Woman's Fiction*. Eds. Mallory Young and Suzanne Ferriss. New York: Routledge, 2005. 29–46.

Hattori, Tomo. "Model Minority Discourse and Asian American Jouis-Sense." *Differences: A Journal of Feminist Cultural Studies* 11.2 (1999): 228–47.

Hay, James. "Unaided Virtues: The (Neo)-Liberalization of the Domestic Sphere." *Television and New Media* 1.1 (2000): 53–73.

Hays, Sharon. *The Cultural Contradictions of Mothering*. New Haven: Yale University Press, 1998.

Heldke, Lisa Maree. *Exotic Appetites: Ruminations of a Food Adventurer*. New York: Routledge, 2003.

Heller, Dana. "Before: 'Things Just Keep Getting Better . . .'" Ed. Dana Heller. *The Great American Makeover: Television, History, Nation*. New York: Palgrave Macmillan, 2006. 1–10.

Hendershot, Heather. "Belabored Reality: Making It Work on *The Simple Life* and *Project Runway*." *Reality TV: Remaking Television Culture*. 2nd. ed. Eds. Susan Murray and Laurie Ouellette. New York: New York University Press, 2009. 243–59.

Hewitt, Heather. "You Are Not Alone: The Personal, the Political, and the 'New' Mommy Lit." *Chick Lit: The New Woman's Fiction*. Eds. Mallory Young and Suzanne Ferriss. New York: Routledge, 2006. 119–39.

Hing, Bill Ong. *Making and Remaking Asian America through Immigration Policy, 1850–1890*. Stanford: Stanford University Press, 1993.

Hirsch, Marianne. *The Mother/Daughter Plot: Narrative, Psychoanalysis, Feminism.* Bloomington: Indiana University Press, 1989.

Ho, Wendy. *In Her Mother's House: The Politics of Asian American Mother-Daughter Writing.* Walnut Creek, CA: AltaMira Press, 1999.

Hollows, Joanne, and Rachel Moseley, eds. *Feminism in Popular Culture.* Oxford: Berg, 2006.

Holmlund, Chris. "Postfeminism from A to G." *Cinema Journal* 44.2 (2005): 116–21.

Hong, Terry. "Building Character." *AsianWeek.* 29 Aug. 2003. http://www.asianweek. com/2003/08/29/building-character-susan-choi-re-emerges-with-her-second-novel-american-woman/. 16 July 2011.

Hopgood, Mei-Ling. *How Eskimos Keep Their Babies Warm and Other Adventures in Parenting.* Chapel Hill, NC: Algonquin Books, 2012.

Howard, Cori. *The Momoir Project.* N.p., 23 Apr. 2008. http://www.themomoirproject. com/. 19 Oct. 2012.

———. *Between Interruptions: Thirty Women Tell the Truth about Motherhood.* Toronto: Key Porter Books, 2007.

Huang, Yunte. *Charlie Chan: The Untold Story of the Honorable Detective and His Rendezvous with American History.* New York: Norton, 2010.

Huang, Betsy. *Contesting Genres in Contemporary Asian American Fiction.* New York: Palgrave Macmillan, 2010.

Ingraham, Chrys. *White Weddings: Romancing Heterosexuality in Popular Culture.* New York: Routledge, 1999.

Irwin, John T. "Mysteries We Reread, Mysteries of Rereading: Poe, Borges, and the Analytic Detective Story." *Detecting Texts: The Metaphysical Detective Story from Poe to Postmodernism.* Eds. Patricia Merivale and Susan Elizabeth Sweeney. Philadelphia: University of Pennsylvania Press, 1999. 27–54.

Isozaki, Anna. "Letter to the Editor: Chick Lit in Japan." *New York Times Sunday Book Review.* 9 Apr. 2006. http://www.nytimes.com/2006/04/09/books/review/09mail. html?_r=0. 12 Oct. 2011.

Iwamura, Jane. *Virtual Orientalism: Asian Religions and American Pop Culture.* New York: Oxford University Press, 2011.

Jain, Anupama. *How to Be South Asian in America.* Philadelphia: Temple University Press, 2011.

James, E. L. *Fifty Shades of Grey.* New York: Vintage, 2012.

Janette, Michele. "Guerilla Irony in Lan Cao's *Monkey Bridge.*" *Comparative Literature* 62.1 (2001): 50–77.

Jenkins, Henry. *Convergence Culture: Where Old and New Media Collide.* New York: New York University Press, 2006.

Jones, Beth-Anne. "Cori Howard of the Momoir Project." *4Mothers1blog,* 13 July 2012. http://4mothers1blog.com/2012/07/13/guest-blogger-cori-howard-of-the-momoir-project/. 15 Oct. 2012.

Jordan, Ruth. Review of *Girl in a Box. Crimespree* 14 (Fall 2006): 11. http://www. crimespreemag.com/BookReviews14.pdf. 15 Oct. 2012.

Joseph, Ralina L. "'Tyra Banks Is Fat': Reading (Post-)Race and (Post-)Feminism in the New Millenium." *Critical Studies in Media Communication* 26.3 (Dec. 2009): 237–54.

The Joy Luck Club. Dir. Wayne Wang. Buena Vista Films, 1993.

Jun, Helen Heran. *Race for Citizenship: Black Orientalism and Asian Uplift from*

Pre-Emancipation to Neoliberal America. New York: New York University Press, 2011.

Kakutani, Michiko. "*Monkey Bridge*: American Dream with Vietnemese Twist." *New York Times*. 17 Aug. 1997. http://www.nytimes.com/books/97/08/17/daily/monkey-book-review.html. 9 Oct. 2012.

Kang, Laura Hyun Yi. *Compositional Subjects: Enfiguring Asian/American Women*. Durham, NC: Duke University Press, 2002.

———. "Si(gh)ting Asian/American Women as Transnational Labor." *Positions* 5.2 (Fall 1997): 403–37.

Kaplan, Caren. "Resisting Autobiography: Out-Law Genres and Transnational Feminist Subjects." *De/Colonizing the Subject: The Politics of Gender in Women's Autobiography*. Eds. Sidonie Smith and Julia Watson. Minneapolis: University of Minnesota Press, 1992. 115–38.

Kaplan, E. Ann. *Motherhood and Representation: The Mother in Popular Culture and Melodrama*. New York: Routledge, 1992.

Kennedy, Liam. "Black *Noir*: Race and Urban Space in Walter Mosley's Detective Fiction." *Criminal Proceedings: The Contemporary American Crime Novel*. Ed. Peter B. Messent. Berkeley: Pluto Press, 1997. 42–61.

The Kids Are All Right. Dir. Lisa Cholodenko. Focus Features, 2010.

Kim, Clare Jean. "The Racial Triangulation of Asian Americans." *Politics & Society* 27.1 (1999): 105–38.

Kim, Daniel. *Writing Manhood in Black and Yellow: Ralph Ellison, Frank Chin, and the Literary Politics of Identity*. Stanford: Stanford University Press, 2005.

Kim, Elaine. "Myth, Memory, and Desire: Homeland and History in Contemporary Korean American Writing and Visual Art." *Holding Their Own: Perspectives on Multi-Ethnic Literatures of the United States*. Eds. Dorothea Fischer-Hornung and Heike Raphael-Hernandez. Tubingen: Stauffenburg, 2000. 79–91.

Kim, Patti. *A Cab Called Reliable*. New York: St. Martin's Press, 1997.

Kim, Soo Yeon. "Lost in Translation: The Multicultural Interpreter as Metaphysical Detective in Suki Kim's *The Interpreter*." *Detective Fiction in a Postcolonial and Transnational World*. Eds. Nels Pearson and Marc Singer. London: Ashgate, 2009. 195–207.

Kim, Suki. *The Interpreter*. New York: Picador, 2003.

Kincheloe, Joe, and Shirley Steinberg. *Changing Multiculturalism*. London: Open University Press, 1997.

Kingston, Maxine Hong. *The Woman Warrior: Memoir of a Girlhood Among Ghosts*. New York: Vintage, 1975.

Kinsman, Margaret. "Feminist Crime Fiction." *The Cambridge Companion to American Crime Fiction*. Ed. Catherine Ross Nickerson. Cambridge: Cambridge University Press, 2010. 148–62.

Koshy, Susan. "The Fiction of Asian American Literature." *Yale Journal of Criticism* 9. 2 (1996): 315–46.

———. "Minority Cosmopolitanism." *PMLA* 126.3 (May 2011): 592–609.

———. *Sexual Naturalization: Asian Americans and Miscegenation*. Stanford: Stanford University Press, 2004.

Kroll, Andy. "Follow the Dark Money." *MotherJones* (July/Aug. 2012): n.pag. http://

www.motherjones.com/politics/2012/06/history-money-american-elections. 19 June 2012.

Ladino, Jennifer. "New Frontiers in Ecofeminism: Women, Nature, and Globalization in Ruth L. Ozeki's *My Year of Meats.*" *New Directions in Ecofeminist Literary Criticism.* Ed. Andrea Campbell. Newcastle, UK: Cambridge Scholars Publishing, 2008. 124–47.

Lahiri, Jhumpa. *The Namesake.* Boston: Houghton Mifflin, 2003.

Lamm, Kimberly. "Getting Close to the Screen of Exile: Visualizing and Resisting the National Mother Tongue in Theresa Hak Kyung Cha's *Dictee.*" *Transnational, National and Personal Voices.* Eds. Begoña Simal and Elisabetta Marino. Berlin: Lit Verlag, 2004. 43–66.

Lauzen, Martha. "The Celluloid Ceiling: Behind the Scenes Employment of Women on the Top 250 Films of 2011." *Center for the Study of Women and Television and Film.* 19 Jan. 2012. http://womenintvfilm.sdsu.edu/files/2011_Celluloid_Ceiling_Exec_Summ.pdf. 28 May 2012.

Lebanthal, Alexandra. *The Recessionistas.* New York: Grand Central Publishing, 2010.

Lee, Chang-rae. *Native Speaker.* New York: Riverhead, 1995.

Lee, Hane. "Waiting to Be Told: A Mother-Daughter Story Takes on Epic Proportions." *AsianWeek* 19.5 (3 Dec. 1997): 21.

Lee, Katherine Hyunmi. "'Hello Lover': Commodification, Intimacy, and Second Wave Feminism on *Sex and the City.*" *Americana: The Journal of American Popular Culture 1900–Present* 6.2 (Fall 2007): 1–8. http://www.americanpopularculture. com/journal/articles/fall_2007/lee.htm. 3 Dec. 2011.

Lee, Rachel. *The Americas of Asian American Literature: Gendered Fictions of Nation and Transnation.* Princeton: Princeton University Press, 1999.

Lee, Robert G. *Orientals: Asian Americans in Popular Culture.* Philadelphia: Temple University Press, 1992.

Leonard, Suzanne. "'I Hate My Job, I Hate Everyone Here': Adultery, Boredom, and the 'Working Girl' in Twenty-First Century American Cinema." *Interrogating Postfeminism: Gender and the Politics of Popular Culture.* Eds. Yvonne Tasker and Diane Negra. Durham, NC: Duke University Press, 2007. 101–03.

Lesher, Linda Parent, ed. *The Best Novels of the Nineties: A Reader's Guide.* Jefferson, NC: McFarland, 2000.

Lieu, Nhi T. *The American Dream in Vietnamese.* Minneapolis: University of Minnesota Press, 2011.

Lim, Shirley Geok-lin, ed. *Approaches to Teaching Kingston's "The Woman Warrior."* New York: Modern Language Association, 1991.

Lim, Shirley Geok-lin, Tsutakawa Mayumi, and Margarita Donnelly, eds. *Forbidden Stitch: An Asian American Women's Anthology.* Corvallis, OR: Calyx, 1989.

Lim, Shirley Jennifer. *A Feeling of Belonging: Asian American Women's Public Culture, 1930–1960.* New York: New York University Press, 2006.

Lin, Ed. *This Is a Bust.* New York: Kaya Press, 2007.

Ling, Jinqi. *Narrating Nationalisms: Ideology and Form in Asian American Literature.* New York: Oxford University Press, 1998.

Liu, Betty Ming. "Parents Like Amy Chua Are the Reason Why Asian Americans Like Me Are in Therapy." *Betty Ming Liu.* 8 Jan. 2011. http://bettymingliu.com/2011/01/

parents-like-amy-chua-are-the-reason-why-asian-americans-like-me-are-in-therapy/comment-page-2/. 21 Jan. 2011.

Livingstone, Sonia. "On the Mediation of Everything." *Journal of Communication* 58 (2009): 1–18.

Long, Lisa M. "Culinary Tourism: A Folkloristic Perspective on Eating and Otherness." *Culinary Tourism*. Ed. Lisa M. Long. Lexington, Kentucky: The University Press of Kentucky, 2004. 20–50.

Lopez, Josefina. *Real Women Have Curves*. Brand New!!! Edition. New York: Dramatic Publishing, 1987.

Lowe, Lisa. *Immigrant Acts: On Asian American Cultural Politics*. Durham, NC: Duke University Press, 1996.

Luibhéid, Eithne. *Entry Denied: Controlling Sexuality at the Border*. Minneapolis: University of Minnesota Press, 2002.

Lury, Celia. *Consumer Culture*. New Brunswick, NJ: Rutgers University Press, 1996.

Lynch, Grace Hwang. "*Battle Hymn of the Tiger Mother*—Book Review." *Open Salon*. N.p. 13 Jan. 2011. http://open.salon.com/blog/hapamama/2011/01/13/battle_hymn_of_the_tiger_mother_-_book_review. 27 Apr. 2011.

Lysack, Krista. *Come Buy, Come Buy: Shopping and the Culture of Consumption in Victorian Women's Writing*. Athens: Ohio University Press, 2008.

Malmgren, Carl D. *Anatomy of Murder: Mystery, Detective, and Crime Fiction*. Bowling Green, OH: Bowling Green State University Popular Press, 2001.

Mani, Bakirathi. "Cinema/Photo/Novel: Intertextual Readings of *The Namesake*." *Naming Jhumpa Lahiri: Canons and Controversies*. Eds. Lavina Dhingra and Floyd Cheung. Lanham, MD: Rowman & Littlefield, 2012. 75–96.

Mannur, Anita. *Culinary Fictions: Food in South Asian Diasporic Culture*. Philadelphia: Temple University Press, 2010.

Marcus, Laura. "Detection and Literary Fiction." *The Cambridge Companion to Crime Fiction*. Ed. Martin Priestman. New York: Cambridge University Press, 2003. 245–67.

Massey, Sujata. *Girl in a Box*. New York: Harper Collins, 2007.

———. "Re: Translations of *Girl in a Box*." Message to the author. 18 Dec. 2011. E-mail.

Matzke, Christine, and Susanne Mühleisen, eds. *Postcolonial Postmortems: Crime Fiction from a Transcultural Perspective*. Amsterdam: Rodopi, 2006.

Mazza, Cris, and Jeffrey DeShell, eds. *Chick-Lit: Postfeminist Fiction*. Normal, IL: FC2, 1995.

Macdonald, Gina, and Andrew Macdonald. "Ethnic Detectives in Popular Fiction: New Directions for an American Genre." *Diversity and Detective Fiction*. Ed. Kathleen Gregory Klein. Bowling Green: Bowling Green State University Popular Press, 1999. 60–113.

McAfee, Noelle. *Democracy and the Political Unconscious*. New York: Columbia University Press, 2008.

McCann, Sean. "The Hard-Boiled Novel." *The Cambridge Companion to American Crime Fiction*. Ed. Catherine Ross Nickerson. Cambridge: Cambridge University Press, 2010. 29–56.

McCullough, Helen Craig, ed. *Classical Japanese Prose: An Anthology*. Stanford: Stanford University Press, 1990.

McEwan, Ian. "Hello, Would You Like a Free Book?" *The Guardian*. 19 Sept. 2005. http://www.guardian.co.uk/books/2005/sep/20/fiction.features11. 9 July 2012.

McGee, Micki. *Self-Help, Inc.: Makeover Culture in American Life.* New York: Oxford University Press, 2005.

McLaughlin, Emma, and Nicola Krauss. *The Nanny Diaries.* New York: St. Martin's Press, 2002.

McMillan, Terry. *Waiting to Exhale.* New York: Viking, 1992.

McRobbie, Angela. *The Aftermath of Feminism: Gender, Culture, and Social Change.* Los Angeles: Sage, 2009.

———. "Post-feminism and Popular Culture." *Feminist Media Studies* 4:3 (2004): 255–64.

Memmott, Carol. "Chick Lit Matures: Genre Confronts its Wrinkles." *USA Today.* Gannett, 21 June 2006. http://usatoday30.usatoday.com/life/books/news/2006-06-20-chick-lit_x.htm. 8 Nov. 2011.

Merivale, Patricia. "Gumshoe Gothics: Poe's 'The Man of the Crowd' and His Followers." *Detecting Texts: The Metaphysical Detective Story from Poe to Postmodernism.* Eds. Patricia Merivale and Susan Elizabeth Sweeney. Philadelphia: University of Pennsylvania Press, 1999. 101–16.

Merivale, Patricia, and Susan Elizabeth Sweeney. "The Game's Afoot: On the Trail of the Metaphysical Detective Story." *Detecting Texts: The Metaphysical Detective Story from Poe to Postmodernism.* Eds. Patricia Merivale and Susan Elizabeth Sweeney. Philadelphia: University of Pennsylvania Press, 1999. 1–24.

Middleton Meyer, Kim. "'Tan'talizing Others: Multicultural Anxiety and the New Orientalism." *High Pop: Making Culture into Popular Entertainment.* Ed. Jim Collins. Oxford: Blackwell, 2002. 90–113.

Miller, Toby. *Cultural Citizenship: Cosmopolitanism, Consumerism, and Television in a Neoliberal Age.* Philadelphia: Temple University Press, 2007.

———. "Cultural Citizenship." *Handbook of Citizenship Studies.* Eds. Engin F. Isin and Bryan S. Turner. London: Sage Publications, 2002. 231–43.

———. *Makeover Nation: The United States of Reinvention.* Columbus: The Ohio State University Press, 2008.

Miner, Earl, Hiroko Odagiri, and Robert E. Morell, eds. "Sei Shonagon." *The Princeton Companion to Classical Japanese Literature.* Princeton: Princeton University Press, 1985. 227–28.

Miss Representation. Dir. Jennifer Siebel Newsom. Girls' Club Entertainment, 2011.

Mizejewski, Linda. *Hardboiled and High Heeled: The Woman Detective in Popular Culture.* New York: Routledge, 2004.

Modleski, Tania. *Loving with a Vengeance: Mass-Produced Fantasies for Women.* 2nd ed. London: Routledge, 2008.

Molz, Jennie Germann. "Eating Difference: The Cosmopolitan Mobilities of Culinary Tourism." *Space and Culture* 10.1 (2007): 77–93. 8 Aug. 2011.

Moon, Krystyn R. *Yellowface: Creating the Chinese in American Popular Music and Performance. 1850s–1920s.* New Brunswick, NJ: Rutgers University Press, 2004.

Moraga, Cherríe. *Waiting in the Wings: Portrait of a Queer Motherhood.* Ann Arbor, MI: Firebrand Books, 1998.

Morrison, Toni. *Beloved.* New York: Alfred Knopf, 1987.

"Mothers of Intention: Five Bloggers on Race and Erasure in the Mommy Blogosphere." *Bitch* 52 (Fall 2011): 42–46.

Mukherjee, Bharati. *Jasmine*. New York: Grove Press, 1989.

"My Year of Meats: A Novel." *Goodreads*. Jan. 2007. http://www.goodreads.com/book/show/12349.My_Year_of_Meats. 3 May 2012.

Nakamura, Lisa. "The Comfort Women of the Digital Industries: Asian Women in David Fincher's *The Social Network*." *In Media Res*. MediaCommons, 17 Jan. 2011. http://mediacommons.futureofthebook.org/imr/2011/01/17/comfort-women-digital-industries-asian-women-david-finchers-social-network. 21 June 2012.

The Namesake. Dir. Mira Nair. Fox Searchlight, 2006.

Negra, Diane. *What a Girl Wants: Fantasizing the Reclamation of Self in Postfeminism*. New York: Routledge, 2009.

Newman, Amie. "Falling Behind: Single Mothers and Women of Color in the Recession." *RH Reality Check*. 9 Aug. 2010. http://rhrealitycheck.org/article/2010/08/09/falling-behind-single- mothers-women-color-recession/. 10 Oct. 2010.

Newton, Adam Zachary. "Versions of Ethics: Or the SARL of Criticism: Sonority, Arrogation, Letting-Be." *American Literary History* 13.3 (2001): 603–37.

Nguyen, Mimi Thi, and Thuy Linh Nguyen Tu, eds. *Alien Encounters: Popular Culture in Asian America*. Durham, NC: Duke University Press, 2007.

Nguyen, Viet Thanh. "Remembering War, Dreaming Peace: On Cosmopolitanism, Compassion, Literature." *Japanese Journal of American Studies* 20 (2009): 149–74.

———. *Race and Resistance: Literature and Politics in Asian America*. New York: Oxford University Press, 2002.

Ninh, Erin Khuê. *Ingratitude: Debt-Bound Daughters in Asian American Literature*. New York: New York University Press, 2011.

No Reservations. Narr. Anthony Bourdain. Travel Channel. 2005.

Nussbaum, Martha, ed. *For Love of Country*. Boston: Beacon Press, 1996.

Ommundsen, Wenche. "Sex and the Global City: Chick Lit with a Difference." *Contemporary Women's Writing* 5.2 (July 2011): 107–24.

Ong, Aihwa. *Buddha Is Hiding: Refugees, Citizenship, the New America*. Berkeley: University of California Press, 2003.

———. *Neoliberalism as Exception: Mutations in Citizenship and Sovereignty*. Durham, NC: Duke University Press, 2006.

O'Reilly, Andrea, ed. *Encyclopedia of Motherhood*. Thousand Oaks, CA: Sage Publications, 2010.

Ouellette, Laurie. ""Take Responsibility for Yourself': Judge Judy and the Neoliberal Citizen." *Reality TV: Remaking Television Culture*. 2nd ed. New York: New York University Press, 2009. 223–42.

Ozeki, Ruth. "Biography." *Ozekiland*. N.d. http://www.ruthozeki.com/about/biography. 28 May 2012.

———. *My Year of Meats*. New York: Viking Penguin, 1998.

———. "There and Back Again." *The Independent*. Oct. 1998: 40–42.

Palmer, Lindsay. "Gender as the Next Top Model of Global Consumer Citizenship." *Genders* 51 (Spring 2010): n. pag. http://www.genders.org/g51/g51_palmer.html. 16 June 2010.

Palumbo-Liu, David. *Asian/American: Historical Crossings of a Racial Frontier*. Stanford: Stanford University Press, 1999.

———. "Rational and Irrational Choices: Form, Affect, and Effect." *Minor Transnationalism*.

Eds. Françoise Lionnet and Shu-Mei Shih. Durham: Duke University Press, 2005. 41–72.

Park, Jane Chi Hyun. *Yellow Future: Oriental Style in Hollywood Cinema*. Minneapolis: University of Minnesota Press, 2010.

Park, Josephine. *Apparitions of Asia: Modernist Form and Asian American Poetics*. New York: Oxford University Press, 2008.

Park, Lisa Sun-Hee. *Consuming Citizenship: Children of Asian Immigrant Entrepreneurs*. Stanford: Stanford University Press, 2005.

Parreñas, Rhacel Salazar. *Servants of Globalization: Women, Migration, and Domestic Work*. Stanford: Stanford University Press, 2001.

Parreñas, Rhacel Salazar, and Winnie Tam. "The Derivative Status of Asian American Women." *The Force of Domesticity: Filipina Migrants and Globalization*. New York: New York University Press, 2008. 110–33.

Parts Unknown. Prod. Chris Collins, Lydia Tenaglia, and Sandra Zweig. Narr. Anthony Bourdain. CNN. 2013.

Pearson, Nels, and Marc Singer. "Open Cases: Detection, (Post)Modernity, and the State." *Detective Fiction in a Postcolonial and Transnational World*. Eds. Nels Pearson and Marc Singer. London: Ashgate, 2009. 1–13.

Pelaud, Isabelle Thuy. *This Is All I Choose to Tell: History and Hybridity in Vietnamese American Literature*. Philadelphia: Temple University Press, 2011.

Peterson, Latoya. "The *Wall Street Journal* Explains Why Chinese Mothers Are Superior." *Racialicious*. 10 Jan. 2011. http://www.racialicious.com/2011/01/10/the-wall-street-journal-explains-why-chinese-mothers-are-superior/. 12 Jan. 2011.

Pham, Minh-Ha T. "A Success Worse than Failure." *Journal of Asian American Studies* 15.3 (Oct. 2012): 330–34.

Picoult, Jodi. *My Sister's Keeper*. New York: Washington Square Press, 2004.

Polan, Dana. *The French Chef*. Durham, NC: Duke University Press, 2011.

Pollan, Michael. *In Defense of Food: An Eater's Manifesto*. New York: Penguin, 2008.

———. *The Omnivore's Dilemma: A Natural History of Four Meals*. New York: Penguin, 2006.

Powell, Julie. *Julie and Julia: 365 Days, 524 Recipes, 1 Tiny Apartment Kitchen*. New York: Little, Brown & Company, 2005.

Pozner, Jennifer L. *Reality Bites Back: The Troubling Truth about Guilty Pleasure TV*. Berkeley: Seal Press, 2010.

Prashad, Vijay. *The Karma of Brown Folk*. Minneapolis: University of Minnesota Press, 2000.

Precious. Dir. Lee Daniels. Lionsgate, 2009.

Priestman, Martin. *Detective Fiction and Literature: The Figure on the Carpet*. Basingstoke, UK: Macmillan, 1990.

———. "Introduction." *The Cambridge Companion to Crime Fiction*. New York: Cambridge University Press, 2003. 1–6.

Raphael, Chad. "The Political Economic Origins of Reali-TV." *Reality TV: Remaking Television Culture*. Eds. Susan Murray and Laurie Ouellette. 2nd ed. New York: New York University Press, 2009. 123–40.

Reddy, Chandan. *Freedom With Violence: Race, Sexuality, and the US State*. Durham, NC: Duke University Press, 2011.

Reddy, Maureen T. "Race and American Crime Fiction." *The Cambridge Companion* to *American Crime Fiction*. Ed. Catherine Ross Nickerson. Cambridge: Cambridge University Press, 2010. 135–47.

———. *Traces, Codes, and Clues: Reading Race in Crime Fiction*. New Brunswick: Rutgers University Press, 2003.

———. "Women Detectives." In *The Cambridge Companion to Crime Fiction*, edited by Martin Priestman, 191–207. New York: Cambridge University Press, 2003.

Reich, Robert. "Why Inequality Is the Real Cause of Our Ongoing Terrible Economy." *Nation of Change*. The Nation Magazine, 4 Sept. 2011. http://www.nationofchange.org/why-equality-real-cause-our-ongoing-terrible-economy-1315150330. 4 Sept. 2011.

"Romance Literature Statistics: Industry Statistics." *Romance Writers of America*. Romance Writers of America, Jan. 2011. http://www.rwa.org/p/cm/ld/fid=580. 13 Dec. 2011.

Rosaldo, Renato. "Cultural Citizenship, Inequality, and Multiculturalism." *Latino Cultural Citizenship: Claiming Identity, Space, Rights*. Eds. William V. Flores and Rena Benmajor. Boston: Beacon Press, 1997. 27–38.

Rose, Nikolas. "Governing 'Advanced' Liberal Democracies." *Foucault and Political Reason: Liberalism, Neo-liberalism, and Rationalities of Government*. Eds. Andrew Barry, Thomas Osborne, and Nikolas Rose. Chicago: University of Chicago Press, 1996. 37–64.

———. *The Politics of Life Itself: Biomedicine, Power, and Subjectivity in the Twenty-First Century*. Princeton: Princeton University Press, 2007.

Rosin, Hanna. *The End of Men: And the Rise of Women*. New York: Penguin, 2012.

Rzepka, Charles J. "Race, Region, Rule: Genre and the Case of Charlie Chan." *PMLA* 122.5 (Oct. 2007): 1463–81.

Sanders, Joshunda, and Diane Barnes-Brown. "Eat, Pray, Spend: Priv-Lit and the New Enlightened American Dream." *Bitch* 47 (Summer 2010): 29–33.

Sassen, Saskia. *The Global City: New York, London, Tokyo*. Princeton: Princeton University Press, 2001.

———. *Globalization and Its Discontents: Essays on the Mobility of People and Money*. New York: New Press, 1998.

———. *Territory, Authority, Rights*. Princeton: Princeton University Press, 2006.

Scaggs, John. *Crime Fiction*. London: Routledge, 2005.

Scanlon, Jennifer. "Making Shopping Safe for the Rest of Us: Sophie Kinsella's Shopaholic Series and Its Readers." *Americana: The Journal of American Popular Culture 1900–Present* 4.2 (Fall 2005): 1–14. http://www.americanpopularculture.com/journal/articles/fall_2005/scanlon.htm. 3 Jan. 2009.

Scarry, Elaine. *The Body in Pain: The Making and Unmaking of the World*. Oxford: Oxford University Press, 1987.

Schueller, Malini Johar. "Cross-cultural Identification, Neoliberal Feminism, and Afghan Women." *Genders* 53 (Spring 2011): n. pag. http://www.genders.org/g53/g53_schueller.html. 16 September 2011.

Schmidt, Eric Leigh. *Consumer Rites: The Buying and Selling of American Holidays*. Princeton: Princeton University Press, 1997.

Schönberg, Claude-Michel and Alain Boublil. *Miss Saigon*. New York: Hal Leonard Corporation, 1991.

Schultermandl, Silvia. *Transnational Matrilineage: Mother-Daughter Conflicts in Asian American Literature*. Berlin: Lit Verlag, 2010.

Seaman, Amanda. *Bodies of Evidence: Women, Society, and Detective Fiction in 1990s Japan*. Honolulu: University of Hawai'i Press, 2004.

Secretly Pregnant. Prod. Cheryl Horner Sirulnick. Narr. Kate Middleton. Discovery Fit & Health. New York. 2011.

Seifert, Christine. "Bite me! (Or Don't)." *Bitch* 42 (Winter 2009): 23–25.

Sharma, Nitasha Tamar. *Hip Hop Desis: South Asian Americans, Blackness, and a Global Race Consciousness*. Durham, NC: Duke University Press, 2010.

Sharma, Sarah. "Baring Life and Lifestyle in the Non-Place." *Cultural Studies* 23.1 (2009): 129–48.

Shimakawa, Karen. *National Abjection: The Asian American Body on Stage*. Durham, NC: Duke University Press, 2002.

Shimizu, Celine Parreñas. *The Hypersexuality of Race: Performing Asian/American Women on Scene and Screen*. Durham, NC: Duke University Press, 2007.

Shin, Kyung-Sook. *Please Look After Mom: A Novel*. Trans. Chi-Young Kim. New York: Alfred A. Knopf, 2011.

Shinn, Christopher A. "Homocidal Tendencies: Violence and Global Economy in Asian American Pulp Fiction." *Alien Encounters: Popular Culture in Asian America*. Eds. Mimi Thi Nguyen and Thuy Linh Ngyen Tu. Durham, NC: Duke University Press, 2007.

Singh, Sonia. *Goddess for Hire*. New York: Harper Collins, 2004.

Siu, Lok C. D. *Memories of Future Home: Diasporic Citizenship of Chinese in Panama*. Stanford: Stanford University Press, 2003.

16 and Pregnant. Prod. Morgan J. Freeman. MTV. 2009.

Slater, Don. *Consumer Culture and Modernity*. Cambridge, UK: Polity, 1999.

Smiley, Jane. "Recipe for Success." *Chicago Tribune*. Tribune Newspapers, 12 July 1998. http://articles.chicagotribune.com/1998-07-12/entertainment/9807120067_1_beef-industry-sei-shonagon-japanese-tv. 5 Sept. 2012.

Smith, Caroline J. *Cosmopolitan Culture and Consumerism in Chick Lit*. New York: Routledge, 2009.

Smith, Christopher Holmes. "Bling Was a Bubble." *International Journal of Communication* 3 (2009): 274–76.

So, Christine. *Economic Citizens: A Narrative of Asian American Visibility*. Philadelphia: Temple University Press, 2007.

Sohn, Stephen Hong, Paul Lai, and Donald Goellnicht, eds. "Introduction: Theorizing Asian American Fiction." *Modern Fiction Studies* 56.1 (2010): 1–18.

Sone, Monica. *Nisei Daughter*. 1953. Seattle: University of Washington Press, 1979.

Song, Min Hyoung. "The Children of 1965: Allegory, Postmodernism, and Jhumpa Lahiri's *The Namesake*." *Twentieth-Century Literature* 53.3 (2007): 345–70.

Spigel, Lynn. "After: The Reveal." *The Great American Makeover: Television, History, Nation*. Ed. Dana Heller. New York: Palgrave Macmillan, 2006. 231–38.

Srikanth, Rajini. *The World Next Door: South Asian American Literature and the Idea of America*. Philadelphia: Temple University Press, 2006.

Srikanth, Rajini, and Esther Y. Iwanaga, eds. *Bold Words: A Century of Asian American Writing*. Brunswick, NJ: Rutgers University Press, 2001.

Stevenson, Nick. *Cultural Citizenship: Cosmopolitan Questions*. Berkshire: Open University Press/McGraw-Hill, 2003.

Stewart, Susan. *On Longing: Narratives of the Miniature, the Gigantic, the Souvenir, the Collection*. Durham, NC: Duke University Press, 1993.

Stout, Steve. *The Tanning of America: How Hip-Hop Created a Culture That Rewrote the Rules of the New Economy.* New York: Penguin, 2012.

Strohmeyer, Sarah. *The Penny Pinchers Club.* New York: Dutton, 2010.

Sturken, Marita. *Tourists of History: Memory, Kitsch, and Consumerism from Oklahoma City to Ground Zero.* Durham, NC: Duke University Press, 2007.

Sugiyama, Naoko. "Postmodern Motherhood and Ethnicity: Maternal Discourse in Late Twentieth-Century American Literature." *Japanese Journal of American Studies* 11 (2000): 71–90.

Sze, Julie. "Boundaries and Border Wars: DES, Technology, and Environmental Justice." *American Quarterly* 58.3 (Sept. 2006): 791–814.

Tan, Amy. *The Joy Luck Club.* New York: G. P. Putnam, 1989.

Tapia, Ruby C. *American Pietas: Visions of Race, Death, and the Maternal.* Minneapolis: University of Minnesota Press, 2011.

Tasker, Yvonne, and Diane Negra, eds. *Interrogating Postfeminism: Gender and the Politics of Popular Culture.* Durham, NC: Duke University Press, 2007.

Taylor, Paul, ed. "The Rise of Asian Americans." *Pew Research Center.* 19 June 2012. http://www.pewsocialtrends.org/2012/06/19/the-rise-of-asian-americans/. 22 June 2012.

Thoma, Pamela. "What Julia Knew: Cooking, Writing, and Other Forms of Domestic Labor in Recession-Era Chick Flick Makeovers." *Gendering the Recession.* Eds. Diane Negra and Yvonne Tasker. Durham, NC: Duke University Press, forthcoming 2013.

Thompson, Mary. "Third Wave Feminism and the Politics of Motherhood." *Genders* 43 (Fall 2006): n.pag. http://www.genders.org/g43/g43_marythompson.html. 29 July 2008.

Traister, Rebecca. "Women's Studies." *Salon.* Salon.com, n.pag. 1 Nov. 2005. http://www.salon.com/2005/11/01/chick_lit_3.html. 25 Mar 2010.

Tran, Barbara, Monique T. D. Truong, and Luu Truong Khoi, eds. *Watermark: Vietnamese American Poetry and Prose.* Ann Arbor, MI: Asian American Writers' Workshop, 1998.

Tu, Thuy Linh Nguyen. *The Beautiful Generation: Asian Americans and the Cultural Economy of Fashion.* Durham, NC: Duke University Press, 2010.

The Twilight Saga: Breaking Dawn. Dir. Bill Condon. Summit Entertainment, 2011.

Ty, Eleanor. *Unfastened: Globality and Asian North American Narratives.* Minneapolis: University of Minnesota Press, 2010.

Udo, Annabelle. "China Dolls." *Asianweek* 4.12 (9 Nov. 2007): 12.

Van Slooten, Jessica Lyn. "Fashionably Indebted: Conspicuous Consumption, Fashion, and Romance in Sophie Kinsella's Shopaholic Trilogy." *Chick Lit: The New Woman's Fiction.* Eds. Mallory Young and Suzanne Ferriss. New York: Routledge, 219–38.

Van Zoonen, Liesbet. *Entertaining the Citizen: When Politics and Popular Culture Converge.* New York: Rowman & Littlefield, 2005.

Vlagopoulos, Penny. "The Beginning of History and Politics: Susan Choi's *American Woman* and the Shadow of US Imperialism." *Studies in American Fiction* 37.1 (Spring 2010): 127–51.

Walker, Alice. *In Search of Our Mother's Gardens: Womanist Prose.* New York: Harcourt, 1983.

Walters, Suzanna Danuta. *Lives Together/Worlds Apart: Mothers and Daughters in Popular Culture.* Berkeley, CA: University of California Press, 1994.

Warner, Michael. *Publics and Counterpublics*. New York: Zone Books, 2005.

Weber, Brenda. *Makeover TV: Selfhood, Citizenship, and Celebrity*. Durham, NC: Duke University Press, 2009.

Wells, Juliette. "Mothers of Chick Lit? Women Writers, Readers, and Literary History." *Chick Lit: The New Woman's Fiction*. Eds. Mallory Young and Suzanne Ferriss. New York: Routledge. 47–70.

Werbner, Pnina. "Paradoxes of Postcolonial Vernacular Cosmopolitanism in South Asia and the Diaspora." *The Ashgate Research Companion to Cosmopolitanism*. Ashgate, 2 June 2011. http://www.scribd.com/doc/90507555/Werbner-Pnina-2011-Paradoxes-of-Vernacular-Cosmopolitanism-in-South-Asia-and-the-Diaspora. 30 Oct. 2011.

Women of South Asian Descent Collective, eds. *Our Feet Walk the Sky: Women of the South Asian Diaspora*. San Francisco: Aunt Lute Books, 1993.

Wong, Jade Snow. *Fifth Chinese Daughter*. New York: Harper and Row, 1945.

Wong, Sau-ling Cynthia. "Denationalization Reconsidered: Asian American Cultural Criticism at a Theoretical Crossroads." *Amerasia Journal* 21.1–2 (1995): 1–27.

——. "Necessity and Extravagance in Maxine Hong Kingston's *The Woman Warrior*: Art and the Ethnic Experience." *MELUS* 15.1 (Spring 1988): 3–26.

——. *Reading the Literatures of Asian America: From Necessity to Extravagance*. Princeton: Princeton University Press, 1993.

——. "'Sugar Sisterhood': Situating the Amy Tan Phenomenon." *The Ethnic Canon: Histories, Institutions, and Interventions*. Ed. David Palumbo-Liu. Minneapolis: University of Minnesota Press, 1995. 174–210.

Wong, Shelley Sunn. "Unnaming the Same: Theresa Hak Kyung Cha's *Dictée*." *Writing Self, Writing Nation: A Collection of Essays on Dictée by Theresa Hak Kyun Cha*. Eds. Elaine Kim and Norma Alarcon. Berkeley: Third Woman Press, 1994. 103–40.

Yamamoto, Traise. *Masking Selves, Making Subjects: Japanese American Women, Identity, and the Body*. Berkeley: University of California, 1999.

Yamanaka, Lois-Ann. *Blu's Hanging*. New York: Avon, 1997.

Yang, Jeffrey. "Asian Pop/Bridget Jung's Diary." *SFGATE*. Hearst Communications, 13 Feb. 2007. http://www.sfgate.com/entertainment/article/ASIAN-POP-Bridget-Jung-s-Diary-2617939.php. 13 Feb. 2008.

——. "Mother Superior?" *San Francisco Chronicle*. Hearst Communications, 13 Jan. 2011. http://www.sfgate.com/entertainment/article/Mother-superior-2383957.php. 21 Jan. 2011.

Young, Morris. *Minor Re/Visions: Asian American Literacy Narratives as a Rhetoric of Citizenship*. Carbondale: Southern Illinois University Press, 2004.

Yu, Michelle, and Blossom Kan. *China Dolls*. New York: St. Martin's Press, 2007.

Yuval-Davis, Nira. *Gender and Nation*. London: Sage Publications, 1997.

——. "The 'Multi-Layered Citizen' Citizenship in the Age of 'Globalization.'" *International Feminist Journal of Politics* 1.1 (1999): 119–36.

Zeisler, Andi. *Feminism and Popular Culture*. Berkeley: Seal Press, 2008.

Zukin, Sharon. *Point of Purchase: How Shopping Changed American Culture*. New York: Routledge, 1994.

INDEX

autobiography, 14–15, 29, 42

backlash, 11, 21, 25, 42, 119; antifeminist, 83, 191n5
"bad subjects" and "good subjects," 29, 30, 75, 186n52
Banet-Weiser, Sarah, 9, 18, 82, 86, 89
Battle Hymn of the Tiger Mother (Chua), 11–12, 38–39, 40, 46–48 passim, 77, 188n21
Berlant, Lauren, 21–22, 41, 43–44, 125, 188n15; *The Female Complaint*, 35, 186n3, 193n22
Biggers, Earl Derr, 117
bildungsromane, 2, 50–55 passim, 62, 91, 92, 158, 170, 189n28
Bilston, Sarah, 79
binaries, 28, 29, 32, 134, 142, 174; in Asian-American studies, 14; cultural, 174; gender-related, 118, 119; in mother-daughter relations, 43; Orientalist, 112, 130; racial, 49
biopolitics, 35, 45, 184n30
biopower, 19, 184n30
Black, Shameem, 123, 124
black Americans. *See* African Americans
"black chick lit," 89, 92
blogs and blogging, 42, 93, 187–88n10
Bolter, Jay David, 7, 93
book clubs, 8, 187n8
book publishers and publishing. *See* publishers and publishing
bookselling and book buying, 7, 8, 118, 182n9, 187n8, 192nn14–15, 193n2
book series. *See* series books
bootstrap ideology, 19, 80, 168
Bourdain, Anthony, 164
bourgeois motherhood, 35, 39, 40, 45, 47, 52–53, 58–68 passim
Bow, Leslie, 29
branding, 88–90, 98, 101, 104, 192n11. *See also* rebranding
brand names, 95, 98, 100, 147, 162, 168
Brennan, Teresa, 45
Breu, Christopher, 119
Bridget Jones's Diary (Fielding), 92, 94, 192n13
Briggs, Laura, 185n42
Bring on the Books for Everybody (Collins), 8–9
Britain. *See* United Kingdom

Brown, Wendy, 88
Bushnell, Candace: *Sex and the City*, 89, 92, 93, 192n13; *Trading Up*, 92, 94
Butler, Pamela, 83, 85, 89, 193n19

A Cab Called Reliable (Kim), 5, 35, 45, 49–66 passim
Calhoun, Craig, 124, 125, 162, 195n19
Campbell, Joseph, 178
Canclini, Néstor, 162
canon, 3, 7, 9, 13–14, 28, 33, 176; chick lit use of, 92–94 passim; Japanese, 158–59
Cao, Lan: *Monkey Bridge*; 4–5, 35, 45, 49–55 passim, 65–75 passim, 190n39
Carroll, Hamilton, 119
Chandler, Raymond, 128
Chang, Yoonmee, 30, 34, 103, 183n20
Chan Is Missing (Wang), 144
Charlie Chan (fictional character), 111–12, 116–17, 130, 144
Chen, Tina, 143–44, 145
Cheng, Anne, 53
Cheng, Emily, 156, 162
Cheung, King-Kok, 183n20
chick lit, 5, 35–36, 79–110 passim, 114, 191n3, 192nn13–14; Berlant view, 193n22; heterosexual romantic relationships in, 193n24; subgenres, 92, 94
Child, Julia, 159–60
Chin, Frank, 14
China Dolls (Yu and Kan), 5, 79–81 passim, 87, 92, 94–110, 192–93n17
Chinatown (archetype), 112, 117, 129–30, 144–45
"Chinatown Regionalism" (Rzepka), 113
Chinese American literature, 13, 14, 46. See also *China Dolls* (Yu and Kan); *The Woman Warrior* (Kingston)
Chinese Americans, 46–47; in fiction, 145–46. *See also* Charlie Chan (fictional character); *China Dolls* (Yu and Kan)
Chinese mothers (and fathers), 12, 38, 46–47, 49
"chink" (word), 135, 156
Choi, Susan: *American Woman*, 1–3, 86, 112, 181n3
Christopher, Renny, 190n39
Chu, Patricia, 2–3, 30, 33, 35, 50–55 passim
Chu, Ying, 148, 193n21

About the Author

Pamela Thoma is Associate Professor of Critical Culture, Gender, and Race Studies and a member of the Graduate Faculty in American Studies at Washington State University.